CAMBRIDGE TEXTS IN THE
HISTORY OF POLITICAL THOUGHT

RICHARD HOOKER
Of the Laws of
Ecclesiastical Polity

CAMBRIDGE TEXTS IN THE
HISTORY OF POLITICAL THOUGHT

Series editors

RAYMOND GEUSS *Columbia University*
QUENTIN SKINNER *Christ's College, Cambridge*
RICHARD TUCK *Jesus College, Cambridge*

The series is intended to make available to students the most important texts required for an understanding of the history of political thought. The scholarship of the present generation has greatly expanded our sense of the range of authors indispensable for such an understanding, and the series will reflect those developments. It will also include a number of less well-known works, in particular those needed to establish the intellectual contexts that in turn help to make sense of the major texts. The principal aim, however, will be to produce new versions of the major texts themselves, based on the most up-to-date scholarship. The preference will always be for complete texts, and a special feature of the series will be to complement individual texts, within the compass of a single volume, with subsidiary contextual material. Each volume will contain an introduction on the historical identity and contemporary significance of the text concerned.

The first titles to be published in the series include:

ARISTOTLE *The Politics*, edited by Stephen Everson
BENTHAM *A Fragment on Government*, introduction by Ross Harrison
CONSTANT *Political Writings*, edited by Biancamaria Fontana
HOOKER *Of the Laws of Ecclesiastical Polity*, edited by A. S. McGrade
LEIBNIZ *Political Writings*, edited by Patrick Riley
LOCKE *Two Treatises of Government*, edited by Peter Laslett
MACHIAVELLI *The Prince*, edited by Quentin Skinner and Russell Price
J. S. MILL *On Liberty*, with *The Subjection of Women* and
Chapters on Socialism, edited by Stefan Collini
MONTESQUIEU *The Spirit of the Laws*, edited by Anne M. Cohler *et al.*
MORE *Utopia*, edited by George M. Logan and Robert M. Adams

RICHARD HOOKER

Of the Laws of Ecclesiastical Polity

Preface · Book I · Book VIII

EDITED BY

ARTHUR STEPHEN McGRADE

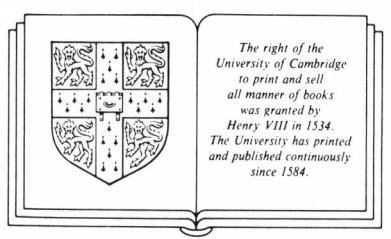

The right of the
University of Cambridge
to print and sell
all manner of books
was granted by
Henry VIII in 1534.
The University has printed
and published continuously
since 1584.

CAMBRIDGE UNIVERSITY PRESS

CAMBRIDGE

NEW YORK PORT CHESTER

MELBOURNE SYDNEY

Published by the Press Syndicate of the University of Cambridge
The Pitt Building, Trumpington Street, Cambridge CB2 1RP
32 East 57th Street, New York, NY 10022, USA
10 Stamford Road, Oakleigh, Melbourne 3166, Australia

Reprinted by permission of the publishers from
The Works of Richard Hooker. The Folger Library Edition,
W. Speed Hill, General Editor, Cambridge MA; Harvard University Press,
© 1977, 1981 by the President and Fellows of Harvard University.

© in the introduction and ancillary editorial matter
Cambridge University Press 1989

First published 1989

Printed in Great Britain at the Bath Press, Avon

British Library cataloguing in publication data

Hooker, Richard, *1553 or 4–1600*
Of the laws of ecclesiastical polity:
preface, book I, book VIII.
1. England. Christian Church.
Administration, history
I. Title II. McGrade, Arthur Stephen
262′.00942

Library of Congress cataloguing in publication data

Hooker, Richard, 1553 or 4–1600.
[Ecclesiastical polity. Selections]
Of the laws of ecclesiastical polity:
preface, book I. book VIII
Richard Hooker: edited by Arthur Stephen McGrade.
p.   cm.
– (Cambridge texts in the history of political thought)
Bibliography.
Includes index.
ISBN 0–521–37011–6. – ISBN 0–521–37908–3 (pbk.)
1. Church polity – Early works to 1800.
2. Ecclesiastical law – Early works to 1800.
3. Church of England – Doctrines – Early works to 1800.
4. Anglican Communion – Doctrines – Early works to 1800.
5. Church and state – Great Britain – Early works to 1800.
I. McGrade, Arthur Stephen.
II. Title. III. Series.
BV649.H825 1989
262.9′83 – dc 19   88–39274 CIP

ISBN 0 521 37011 6 hard covers
ISBN 0 521 37908 3 paperback

Contents

Of the Laws of Ecclesiastical Polity

Contents

Contents

Preface

This volume is designed to offer the most direct access possible to the argument and sources of a classic of English political and religious thought which has recently become a subject of critical controversy. There are difficulties. Hooker's sentences are long and his chapter-length paragraphs very long. His sources, tersely cited as a rule, are unfamiliar. The solutions to these problems chosen by the great nineteenth-century editor of his works, John Keble, were to segment Hooker's text – by heavy punctuation of sentences and the division of chapters into numbered sections – and vastly augment his notes. These measures had their point, but they are sometimes intrusive. In this edition, spelling has been modernized, but Hooker's punctuation and paragraph indivisions have been left alone for the Preface and Book I (which were published in his lifetime), and only a few changes have been made in the posthumously published Book VIII (the surviving manuscripts of which have paragraph divisions, one indication among others that our version of the book is not a finished one). The lack of paragraphs in the earlier parts of the work may seem a hardship at first, but if the reader will think of immersion rather than quick processing as the right approach to Hooker's prose, the result will be rewarding. In the notes, foreign titles and quotations have been translated, but in order to keep the notes down to something like their original bulk, virtually all further information beyond what Hooker himself offers has been put into a Guide to Sources at the end of the volume, and the information there provided has been chosen with the needs of the non-specialist in mind.

The greatest difficulty in appreciating Hooker as a political thinker lies not in his style or sources, however, but in his great distance from the secular politics of the modern world. The "politicality" and the constructive relevance of the *Laws* to Hooker's own situation are the main topics of the introduction to this volume.

I am grateful to the editors of Cambridge Texts in the History of Political Thought for their encouragement and to Jeremy Mynott of Cambridge University Press and Margaretta Fulton of Harvard University Press for the diplomatic efforts which have made it possible to use as a basis for this volume the recently established Folger–Harvard text of Hooker, which is reprinted by permission of the publishers from The Works of Richard Hooker: The Folger Library Edition, W. Speed Hill, General Editor, Cambridge, Mass.; Harvard University Press © 1977, 1981 by the President and Fellows of Harvard University.

Only they themselves can fully understand what I owe my colleagues on the Folger edition, especially William P. Haugaard and Lee Gibbs, from whose notes to Hooker's Preface and First Book I have benefited greatly, and W. Speed Hill, John Booty, Paul Stanwood, and Georges Edelen, who have joined with Professors Haugaard and Gibbs over the years in helping me to think somewhat more clearly about Hooker. As is customary, I am happy to absolve these friends from responsibility for faults remaining, but I am happier still to be able to refer the reader to their own work, in the commentary volume on the *Laws* which is to conclude the Folger edition, for an authoritative fuller account of sources, circumstances, and turns of argument than is here provided. Finally, and from the beginning, I am happy to have had the good counsel of my wife in matters of both style and substance, and her help in proofreading and indexing.

Abbreviations

ACW	*Ancient Christian Writers, the works of the fathers in translation.*
ANF	*The Ante-Nicene Fathers.* American edition.
CR	*Corpus Reformatorum.*
CSEL	*Corpus scriptorum ecclesiasticorum latinorum.*
F	*The Folger Library Edition of the Works of Richard Hooker.*
FOTC	*Fathers of the Church, a new translation.*
K	*Keble.*
L	*Loeb Classical Library.*
N1	*A Select Library of the Nicene and Post-Nicene Father of the Christian Church.* First series.
N2	*A Select Library of the Nicene and Post-Nicene Fathers of the Christian Church.* Second series.
PG	*Patrologiae cursus completus.* Series Graeca. J. P. Migne, ed.
PL	*Patrologiae cursus completus.* Series Latina. J. P. Migne, ed.
SR	*The Statutes of the Realm, printed by command of his majesty George III.*
STC	*A Short-Title Catalogue of Books Printed in England, Scotland, and Ireland and of English Books Printed Abroad, 1475–1640.*
W	*The Works of John Whitgift.* John Ayre, ed., 3 vols. (Cambridge, 1851–53).

Introduction

Richard Hooker was born in or near Exeter in April 1554, less than six years before the accession of Elizabeth I and the reestablishment by statute of the religious and political order for which he himself was to attempt a coherent intellectual justification some forty years later. At an early age he came to the attention of John Jewel, Bishop of Salisbury, the first official defender of the English church in Elizabeth's reign. With Jewel's support, Hooker attended Oxford, where he became a Fellow of Corpus Christi College in 1579 and taught logic and Hebrew.

Hooker was made a deacon in 1579 and later ordained to the priesthood. In 1585 his appointment as Master of the Temple made him chief pastor of one of the principal centers of legal studies in London. Enough sermons survive from this period of his life to form the basis for a substantial volume in the Folger edition. However, Hooker's chief work – indeed, the chief English prose work of the sixteenth century – was *Of the Laws of Ecclesiastical Polity: Eight Books*.

Hooker gave up his place at the Temple to work on the *Laws* in 1591 and resided for the next few years in the home of his father-in-law, the London merchant John Churchman. He consulted frequently in the course of writing with two of his former students, Edwin Sandys, son of the Archbishop of York and a member of the parliament of 1593, and George Cranmer, grand-nephew of the martyred Archbishop of Canterbury. The Preface and first four books of the *Laws* were published in 1593 and Book v in 1597, all with financial assistance from Sandys. In 1595 Hooker was presented by the Queen to the living of Bishopsbourne in Kent, where he continued work on the last three books. He died at Bishopsbourne on All Souls' Day, *for* the feast of All Souls, 1600. He is remembered on the following day, November 3, in the calendars of many churches of the Anglican communion.

The last three books of the *Laws* are the ones most directly pertinent to the clashes over ecclesiastical jurisdiction and supreme political power leading to the English Civil War. There is evidence that Hooker finished all of them, but the surviving versions of Books VI and VIII are clearly partial or unfinished drafts, and none of the three was published for many years after Hooker's death: Books VI and VIII in 1648, Book VII in 1661. In the absence of these books from the public domain, all sides appealed to Hooker in the period leading up to the war, although it has been well argued that his influence on the politically moderate Great Tew group was especially significant. In the eighteenth century he was taken up into a somewhat self-satisfied Whig ideology. In the nineteenth, as edited by John Keble, a leader of the Oxford Movement, Hooker became the defender of catholic Christianity against the menace of extreme Protestantism. More recently he has been seen as a model of the balanced respect for Scripture, tradition, and reason thought to be distinctive of Anglicanism.

Praise has been the common note in response to Hooker through the centuries. This has now changed. From being a consistently admired but decreasingly read classic, the *Laws* has come to be seen in some studies as a partisan polemic of doubtful moral or theoretical integrity. Where the traditional view has been that Hooker was an angelic soul, above the brutal religious polemics of his day, he is now often presented as a deeply engaged controversialist who used every resource at his disposal to make a political case. Where his work has previously been regarded as one of the last coherent presentations of the religiously idealistic premodern western image of the human condition, it has more recently been seen as an inevitably disfiguring attempt to give that image some major features of modern secularism.

The parts of the *Laws* making up the present volume are central to the current debate about Hooker. Before considering them, however, it will be well to look briefly at the situation in which Hooker wrote, both the condition of English church and commonwealth and Hooker's personal situation.

In retrospect, the religious settlement promulgated in the 1559 Acts of Supremacy and Uniformity looks remarkably stable. For many of those who lived in it, however, the Elizabethan golden age was a time of bitter struggle. A great majority could, to be sure, accept the queen's leadership in the church and the forms of worship prescribed in the new *Book of Common Prayer* as a point of departure, but perhaps only the queen herself saw these arrangements as permanently satisfactory. Hooker's account of the laws and orders of the Elizabethan church cannot be understood, at any rate, unless we enter into what was clearly his perception of the age as a perilous one, a time in which persistent and conflicting discontents with the 1559 settlement threatened the most basic social and spiritual values.

Many of the young queen's subjects had been happy with the brief undoing of the Reformation under her sister Mary and hoped that Elizabeth, too, might in time bring the country back to the old forms of devotion and into a normal relationship with the papacy. Such hopes endured until 1570, when Pius V excommunicated Elizabeth and absolved her subjects from obedience to her. At that point, English Christians loyal to the pre-Reformation *ecclesia Anglicana* but unable to recognize their church in the current establishment entered an extraordinarily difficult period of existence. They were urged from one side to more or less direct rebellion, and, however they responded, became victims from the other side of an increasingly obsessive anti-papalism among English Protestants. There can be no doubt of Hooker's own commitment to the Reformation, but he conspicuously did not reject the previous millennium of Christianity as sheer perversion and error. Accordingly, although those who looked to Rome for spiritual leadership were excluded from civil or religious office under Elizabeth, they were an important and not entirely negative factor in his country's situation as Hooker perceived it.

A less obviously divisive movement of discontent with the 1559 settlement arose on the Protestant side. Many reform-minded clergy and laity, especially those with experience of Calvin's Geneva, hoped to find in Elizabeth a "godly prince", under whom they could complete the abolition of medieval idolatry and superstition and proceed to a thorough doctrinal, ceremonial, and moral renewal of English church and commonwealth. By his own account (Preface, 1.2), corroborated by his lasting friendship with John Rainolds, a leading Oxford proponent of further reformation, Hooker had at first found reformist zeal attractive. From the time of his appointment at the Temple, however, a different attitude becomes evident.

As Master, Hooker came into contention with the Temple Reader, Walter Travers, whose *Full and Plain Declaration of Ecclesiastical Discipline* of 1574 was the leading exposition of the presbyterian system of church government proposed by the more militant reformers to replace the regime of bishops. Travers had hoped to be appointed Master himself. He continued to assert his own theological views after Hooker's arrival, so that "the pulpit spake pure Canterbury in the morning and Geneva in the afternoon." Travers was alarmed, furthermore, by Hooker's apparent leniency towards Rome. He appealed to the queen's Privy Council against Hooker. Hooker replied. Travers' supplication was rejected, and he himself was forbidden to preach.

Hooker's personal situation at this point was a miniature of his church's. In both cases, official positions depended on acts of authority which were subject to question from theologically respectable and politically powerful quarters. There was nothing bizarre about Travers' attempt to displace Hooker. In the 1580s a proposal to remove a minister supported by the Archbishop of Canterbury in favour of a distinguished apostle of Geneva had some hope of success at the highest levels of government save one. Hooker succeeded in defending himself against Travers. In *Of the Laws of Ecclesiastical Polity* he attempted to defend "the present state of the Church of God established amongst us."

Against what or whom, exactly, was this larger defence directed? The safest answer here is a narrow one: Hooker opposed the congregationally centered presbyterianism fully and plainly declared in Travers' treatise of 1574 and yet more eminently championed by Thomas Cartwright, formerly Lady Margaret Professor of Divinity at Cambridge and tenacious defender of the reformist *Admonition* to the parliament of 1571. Although Hooker reserved his formal theological refutation of presbyterianism and defence of episcopacy for Books VI and VII of the Laws, the tenor of his preface suggests that the governmental or disciplinary side of the reform movement was uppermost in his mind from the beginning. In the absence of a completed Book VI, the Preface – the first selection in the present volume – is indeed the leading text for a reading of Hooker as political partisan, anxious above all else to defend an existing power structure against revolutionary challenge.

The Preface opens with a grave, conciliatory exordium (chapter 1), but in the ensuing account of the Genevan and English reformed cause Hooker employs shrewd political and psychological analysis to discredit his antagonists before even beginning a formal consideration of their position. He first presents Calvin's establishment of a clerical–lay consistory at Geneva in the 1540s as an astute response to chance circumstances, not the fulfillment of a divine imperative (chapter 2). He goes on to analyze the spread of enthusiasm for the Genevan model in England, both among the common people (chapter 3) and among intellectuals (chapter 4), as due to factors other than Biblical inspiration or rational persuasion. The Preface continues with an apparently open-handed profession of personal willingness to have the points at issue treated in public disputation (chapter 5). This is followed, however, by a demand for submission to some "definitive sentence" as the only way to settle matters (chapter 6), a demand which might seem to require a convinced presbyterian to obey man rather than God. The long and grim eighth chapter of the Preface (which follows a useful outline of all the following books in chapter 7) may seem unfair in another direction. Hooker begins chapter 8 with a constructed, albeit plausible, accusation of his opponents which he puts in the mouths of Christians more radical than they, men and women who have taken the presbyterian leaders' attacks on the established church so seriously that they have left it. The separatists reproach their teachers for inconsistency in conforming to the legally sanctioned religion while at the same time proclaiming its absolute unacceptability. But then Hooker continues with an account of radicalism gone wild in the rebellion of Thomas Münzer, a notorious but atypical episode from the history of Anabaptism. The chapter is intended to show "the manifold dangerous events" likely to result from putting the Disciplinarian program into practice. Given the thorough integration of presbyterian supporters with the rest of Elizabethan society, more than one perceptive reader has found Hooker's dire warnings of social upheaval grossly unfair.

Hooker's work opens, then, with an assault on the spiritual credentials and socially subversive implications of sixteenth-century presbyterianism. Book VI of the *Laws* was to have dealt with the proposed system of discipline on a more straightforwardly theological plane. An early draft refutation of lay-elders has been lost – we know of it only through notes made by Cranmer and Sandys. It is clear from the surviving version of Book VI, however, that Hooker considered the issues of ecclesiastical power remaining for discussion in the last three books to be the weightiest with which he had to contend: "For, let not any man imagine, that the bare and naked difference of a few ceremonies could either have kindled so much fire, or have caused it to flame so long; but that the parties which herein laboured mightily for change, and (as they say) for Reformation, had somewhat more than this mark only whereat to aim" (VI.I.I). The mark at which Hooker took his opponents to have been aiming was a seizure of power by the lower clergy and the eviction of bishops.

All of this is consistent with the idea that Hooker's own dominant aim was to provide ideological backing for the repression of presbyterianism which was being carried out, at the very time he was writing the early books of the *Laws*, in police actions directed by Cartwright's adversary in the *Admonition* controversy, John Whitgift, now archbishop of Canterbury and in 1597 the dedicatee of Hooker's Book V. Every line of the *Laws* does in fact have a controversial point. If one takes it that that point is always to support the existing command structure of the English church against a threat of change from below, Hooker can only be depicted as an arch-polemicist and establishment ideologue.

If this were the only or even the best likeness of Hooker, however, it would be difficult to explain the high regard in which he has been held through the centuries by readers wholly unconcerned with choosing between presbyteries and bishops as rulers of their spiritual lives. To provide a plausible explanation for the appeal of the *Laws* to a wider audience than the circle of dedicated episcopalians, we must move to a second question: what was Hooker defending?

Bishops, to be sure. Yet it is clear that the case made for episcopacy in Book VII does not stem from a love of hierarchy for its own sake. Hooker's position here is complex but largely functionalist. Whether divinely inspired or humanly invented in the early church, the office of bishop was, he argued, a highly effective means for sustaining the practice of the Christian religion.

To say that Hooker chiefly cared about the practice of Christianity may seem a platitude, but this statement of the positive aim of the *Laws* directs us to the central and largest part of the work, Book v, on "the public duties of religion." Here Hooker defends the manner of discharging those duties which was prescribed in the *Book of Common Prayer*. In that defence he in effect created Anglicanism as a self-consciously distinctive form of religious life. This is not to belittle the achievement of Thomas Cranmer and others in producing the English Prayer Book. The point is rather that Hooker was the first to make explicit the many ways in which Prayer Book devotional forms can establish and maintain connections between basic theological values and the needs and capacities of a broad Christian community, a community of all sorts and conditions, a nation. Hooker apparently intended his exposition of the Prayer Book to be shorter and less polemical than it became. Even with the inclusion of long passages meant only to refute Cartwrightian objections, however, Book v is an unsurpassed presentation of a distinctively public devotional theology. Here, then, along with answers to reformist complaints, we find Hooker undertaking a solidly constructive project.

Hooker's devotional theology is "public" in many ways that have little to do with politics in any strict sense, but at significant points Book v is also "politic." Each of the book's two major sections begins in an overtly political way by discussing the relation between religion and commonwealth. Hooker's argument in chapters 1–3, directed in part against Machiavelli, presents personal religion (in opposition to the contrary vices of atheism and superstition) as the root of all true virtues and the support of all well-ordered commonwealths. Chapter 76 justifies an ordained ministry as needed for happiness "not eternal only but also temporal."

As Book V is a defence of legally prescribed forms of worship, it is important to note Hooker's consistent focus on the mind and character, the intellectual and moral state of soul, of those participating in such worship. He does not suggest that some abstract righteousness accrues to individual or society by mere presence at officially approved liturgical events. Something is supposed to happen there. A specific trait of character, the virtue of godliness, is meant to be engendered and strengthened. The virtue of godliness is both the "chiefest top" and the "wellspring" of all true virtues.

It has an intelligible causal relation to such other virtues as justice, practical wisdom, and courage (v.1.2) and is itself, as Hooker attempts to show, an intelligible effect of instruction, prayer, and personal participation in the life of God through the Christian sacraments. Fostering these causal relationships is the point of the ceremonies Hooker classically defends in Book v.

Hooker presents the last four books of the *Laws* as a defence of "particular decisions," decisions about the public duties of religion (Book v) and decisions about the structures of ecclesiastical and secular power (Books vi–viii). The defence is based on four preceding books of "general meditations" (1.1.2). Book i is especially fundamental. Here, Hooker distills a remarkably large portion of Judaeo-Christian and classical western tradition to lay out a worldview in which disputed points of church polity are seldom visible. Book i is thus an especially promising text for reading Hooker as an Anglican angelic doctor, serenely above the controversies of his day. As we shall see, even this book has an important polemical function in the argument of the *Laws*, but its success in serving this function depends on its persuasiveness in articulating assumptions that were indeed acceptable to virtually all of Hooker's contemporaries.

Hooker's entire account of these assumptions is in terms of a single idea, the idea of law. He applies the term "law" to "any kind of rule or canon, whereby actions are framed" (1.3.1). This conception is distinctive in not requiring imposition by superior authority as an essential feature. Strictly speaking, only God has no superior, and Hooker's enlargement of the term is explicitly intended to make it relevant to God's actions. The enlargement also affects other cases, however. In making vows or contracts we impose laws on our own actions (1.10.7), and when the members of a political body participate in its legislative processes, they impose laws upon themselves as individuals (Preface, 5.2; and compare viii.8.9). The actions framed by law include, then, the voluntary operations of God (Book i, chapter 2) and the functioning of natural agents (chapter 3) and angels (chapter 4), as well as properly human conduct, both individual and social, civil and religious.

> All things that are, have some operation not violent or casual. Neither doth any thing ever begin to exercise the same, without some fore-conceived end for which it worketh. And the end which

it worketh for is not obtained, unless the work be also fit to obtain it by. For unto every end every operation will not serve. That which doth assign unto each thing the kind, that which doth moderate the force and power, that which doth appoint the form and measure of working, the same we term a *Law*. (1.2.1).

(The peculiar negative construction, "not violent or casual [that is, random]," where the positive term "natural" might be expected, preserves the distinction between operations wholly determined by an agent's nature and voluntary actions – a distinction more important for Hooker than for other defenders of established authority.) The idea of law has an extremely broad range for Hooker. Even in the voluntary part of the range, however, there is an element of necessity. Not every "sentence of reason" guiding human conduct is a law, properly speaking, but only those dictates which show what "must" be done (1.8.8). Law for Hooker is thus both a comprehensive notion and a forcefully pointed one. The term has never borne more meaning in the history of the English language.

Hooker's elaboration of the idea of law in Book I, his survey of "laws and their several kinds in general," is a masterpiece of philosophical theology but a Renaissance masterpiece. By the standards of medieval scholasticism or modern analytic philosophy, it seems loose and ungrounded. This is due in part, no doubt, to considerations of audience. Hooker wrote for readers ready to appreciate learning but not necessarily ready to follow sustained abstract argumentation. He considered his age to be "full of tongue and weak of brain" and accordingly declined to make any "curious or deep inquiry" into the "causes" of goodness but contented himself with adducing reliable "signs" (1.8.2). We can, to be sure, find indications of the sort of intellectual system he might have developed in other circumstances. He had a clear preference for Aristotelian demonstration over the quick-study method of Ramistry (1.6.4). He believed that the existence and some properties of God could be known even by "mere natural men" (1.8.7). One would guess from the ubiquitousness of Aristotelian ideas in the *Laws* that he sympathized with the sixteenth-century Thomistic revival. Even if we credit Hooker with a single preferred systematic philosophy or theology of his own, however, it would be a mistake to read Book I as an attempt to popularize that one system. The worldview he presents has room for many systems, hence also for a certain lack of system.

He takes pains, for example, to gather testimony from a wide range of sources for the sense that the First Cause of all things is in some way rational (1.2.3). He adduces a still larger collection to support his contention that "the general persuasion of mankind" is a reliable sign of goodness (1.8.3). He argues abstractly for the proposition that union with God is the only possible full satisfaction of human desires (1.11.1–2) and then makes a more experiential case for the same conclusion (1.11.4). Hooker is one of the first writers to use the term "law of nature" in the modern sense of a physical law, in contrast with the Stoic and medieval sense (which he also employs) of universally valid moral principles. He regards the nearly perfect lawfulness of nature's operations as a challenge to scientific inquiry (1.3.2; 1.6.3), but he makes no attempt to guarantee success in such inquiries by elaborating new canons of induction with Bacon or refuting skepticism with Descartes.

Hooker's purpose in the *Laws* was to gain willing compliance with English religious statutes which, in his own judgement, merited such compliance. An attempt to convert the world to a single philosophy would have contributed nothing or less than nothing to this purpose. The technical groundlessness of Book I is thus not merely a concession to the limitations of Hooker's readers. It is warranted by his paramount aim in writing.

In its scope and eclecticism Book I defies brief summary. Two points call for attention, however, because of their special bearing on Hooker's treatment of supreme ecclesiastical and political power in Book VIII. One concerns the broad range of capacities and purposes Hooker attributes to human nature and deliberate historical action. We are born without knowledge. Nevertheless, from this "utter vacuity" we may come by degrees to be, cognitively speaking, "even as the angels are" (1.6.1). Indeed, God is our model for imitation as we seek to possess truth and exercise virtue (1.5.3). The reason for forming societies is our individual insufficiency in furnishing ourselves with "things needful for such a life as our nature doth desire, a life fit for the dignity of man" (1.10.1). Hooker's priorities for social action take account of both basic needs and ideal possibilities. Temporally, the former come first. He cites St. Paul and Genesis to show that the necessities of life are the first things that must be provided for in political association. True, the kingdom of God must be the first thing in our purposes, but "righteous life presupposeth life," and so "the first impediment which naturally we endeavour to remove is penury and want of things without which we cannot live" (I.10.2). There are, however, human goods of greater "dignity", such as being wise, virtuous, and religious (*ibid.*). Finally, there is the prospect of an ultimate "felicity and bliss" in a union with God of which no other creature in the world is capable (I.11.3), which is discerned and approached by the virtues of faith, hope, and charity (I.11.6). On Hooker's principles, then, the "operation not violent or casual" to which human beings are directed, and in which they direct themselves, is a rich and attractive one. The rules framing the actions of a political community might reasonably be expected to take account of this wide range of human goals and activities.

The second point demanding our attention in Book I is Hooker's explicit break with his mentor Aristotle in requiring some form of consent by the governed as a basis for legitimate political power: "without which consent there were no reason that one man should take upon him to be lord or judge over another" (I.10.4). Again, "for any prince or potentate of what kind soever upon earth to exercise the same [i.e. legislative power] of himself, and not either by express commission immediately and personally received from God, or else by authority derived at the first from their consent upon whose persons they impose laws, it is no better than mere tyranny" (I.10.8). Hooker qualifies both of these statements, the second one quite drastically. Nevertheless, Locke was correct in principle when he cited the "judicious Hooker" near the beginning of the *Second Treatise of Government* to support his own conception of morality as based on a natural human equality without political subordination of one person to another.

In Book I of the *Laws* Hooker offers a wealth of reflection on the human condition that is suitable for meditation in circumstances far removed from the disputes of his age. In a sense, Book I can be seen as a contribution to the Elizabethan debate about religion and society just because of its generality, its lack of oppressively immediate relevance. The book also has a more polemical function in the debate. It is intended to demonstrate that there are more norms in heaven and earth than zealous reformers dream of. The controversial point of Hooker's survey of heaven and earth – of God and angels and the natural and human worlds – is to counter his opponents' rapid derivation of unconditional ecclesiastical imperatives from their own reading of the Bible. Books II–IV continue this complicating project. In Book II Hooker argues against the position that "Scripture is the only rule of all things which in this life may be done by men." In Book III he proceeds against the assertion that "in Scripture there must be of necessity contained a form of church polity, the laws whereof may in nowise be altered." Having sought in these books to neutralize what he took to be the major affirmative principles of the reform movement, he rejects the movement's chief negative principle, anti-Romanism, in Book IV, arguing that conformity with Roman usage is insufficient reason for the English church to abandon otherwise wholesome devotional forms.

The net result of the four "general" books of Hooker's *Laws* was not to provide a foundation which *necessitated* the Prayer Book, the authority of bishops, or the royal headship of the English church. These books did, however, set up a complex array of normative considerations which could be drawn on to assess the reasonableness of particular decisions on such matters. On the basis of these considerations, Hooker was able to give good reasons in Book V for the Prayer Book's devotional forms and for related practices of the English church. Good reasons, but not compelling ones. To understand how the particular decisions at issue in the later books could come to have the constraining force of law, we must turn to Hooker's distinctive construal of English political institutions in Book VIII, his defence of the royal supremacy.

The chief prerequisite for understanding Hooker's conception of the royal supremacy is a recognition that the whole question of politically supreme religious power arose for him from the comprehensive scope of human community. The broad range of activities and potentialities considered in Book I of the *Laws* implies an equally broad range of purposes for human association. Individuals may reasonably associate for economic ends, but also for what they take to be higher ends – for living, but also for "living well." If all the individuals making up a physically independent multitude profess the same religion and hence the same fundamental idea of living well, the coordination of their pursuit of secular and spiritual goals will be an inescapable communal task. The long opening chapter of Hooker's Book VIII is intended to make just this point.

The published title of the chapter – "an admonition concerning men's judgements about the question of regal power" – gives little indication of what to expect. We know from recently discovered working notes for the book that Hooker had considered a more informative title: "of the distinction of the church and the commonwealth in a Christian kingdom." The central thesis of the chapter is that the distinction is formal, not substantial. In one of the most widely quoted passages in the *Laws*, Hooker argues by geometrical analogy that just as the same line of a triangle can be either a base or a side, depending on its position, so the same independent multitude of Christians may properly be described as either a church or a commonwealth, depending on whether it is considered generally as a politic society or specifically as a politic society embracing the true religion, Christianity (VIII.I.2). Following Aristotle, Hooker argues that a political community will normally be more than an economic association. It will involve the pursuit of distinctively human psychological goods, goods of the soul. Deepening Aristotle's acknowledgment of religion as part of a complete *polis*, Hooker makes it the *chief* good of the soul for which a body politic will naturally "care" (VIII.I.4). Accordingly, he is able to acknowledge both that the religious is different from the secular (in the sense that different offices and activities will be specifically concerned with each) and that they are unavoidably related (in the sense that the same body of individuals has both secular and religious ends).

The concrete or extensional identity of church and commonwealth did not, however, automatically vindicate the royal supremacy. Quite the contrary. For Hooker this identity posed the problem for which a royal supremacy was one possible solution. The legitimacy of that solution to the problem of coordinating secular and religious communal purposes remained to be shown. The rest of Book VIII is devoted to that task. In chapter 2 Hooker briefly states the nature and limitations of the spiritual–political power at issue, the power of ecclesiastical dominion, as he terms it. In the following chapters he seeks to justify the English crown's possession of such power, both in general and with regard to such particular prerogatives as the title "head of the church" (chapter 4); the right to call ecclesiastical assemblies (chapter 5); a share, largely negative, in legislation for the church (chapter 6); the right to appoint (but not consecrate) bishops (chapter 7); supreme judicial authority overarching the traditional dual system of secular and ecclesiastical courts (chapter

8); and exemption from ordinary processes of ecclesiastical censure (chapter 9).

In earlier editions of the *Laws*, the break between chapters 2 and 3 of Book VIII has been placed at various points, none corresponding with those indicated in Hooker's working notes. We can now see that Hooker planned to follow up his long discussion in chapter 1 of the distinction – and identity – of church and commonwealth in a Christian kingdom with a very short and pointed chapter laying out what the power of ecclesiastical dominion essentially is. Until the Folger edition, however, this chapter has always been merged with more or less of the long and dense next chapter, on the "manner" of the crown's dominion, a chapter consisting of sections on (1) the "right" or basis of royal religious authority – the human right of communal consent, Hooker argues, rather than the divine right of Biblical commandment; (2) the "sort" of communal consent needed to support the crown's power – original and "habitual" rather than recurrently active; (3) the "measure" of royal power – its limitation by human law as well as by natural and divine law; (4) the "conveniency" of such a power – its utility in preventing irresolvable conflicts between independent supreme jurisdictions in the same territory; and (5) the Biblical "example" according to which Christian kings may exercise such power.

When Hooker's brief statement of the essence of ecclesiastical dominion is clearly marked off from the elaborately subdivided material which follows it, one notices that fully a third of this strategically located chapter is taken up with three "exceptions" or limitations on supreme power. First, no one would be so "brainsick" as to imagine that a human king's power is superior to God's. Further, if a king's power is given by human law, it must be exercised in accordance with that law. Finally, although a king is rightfully supreme over any and every part of the community he rules, he is not supreme when standing over and against the whole community: he is greater than the particular members of the body politic but less than the whole. These three qualifications are important keys to understanding Hooker's remarkably republican conception of the Elizabethan settlement. Such keys to interpretation are all the more welcome, given the complexity of the rest of the book. For present purposes it will be convenient to consider the three qualifications in reverse order.

Hooker's emphasis on the whole body of the community as the source of political power represents a union of Aristotelian political theory with emerging English practice. If a doctrine of consent is added to Aristotle's conception of politics as intentional association for the sake of living well, the logical result is a requirement for broad communal participation in the processes by which important political decisions are made. The increasingly important role of the English parliament in the sixteenth century made it possible for Hooker to depict this institution as fulfilling that requirement. Stretching the makeup of parliament to include the clergy in convocation (and stretching the notion of "voluntary" personal representation well beyond the narrow limits of the contemporary suffrage), he writes:

> The parliament of England together with the convocation annexed thereunto, is that whereupon the very essence of all government within this kingdom doth depend; it is even the body of the whole realm; it consisteth of the king, and of all that within the land are subject unto him: for they all are there present, either in person or by such as they voluntarily have derived their very personal right unto. (VIII.6.13)

As this passage suggests, Hooker saw legislation as the chief sphere in which the whole body of the community was actively authoritative. He carefully distanced himself from contemporary advocates of elective monarchy (VIII.3.2) and never hinted that the representative assembly of the realm should exercise executive power. Yet on Hooker's account, the crown's executive power in religion was directly dependent on the consent of the community as given in parliament. Here he was happily in accord with the letter of the law. In contrast to the supremacy act passed under Henry VIII, which recognized the king's headship of the church as given by God, the Elizabethan act made the queen supreme governor "by the authority of this present parliament." Elizabeth was not especially fond of the difference, but to Hooker it was a blessing. It enabled him to present the royal supremacy as the *community*'s solution to the problem of coordinating the various ends pursued within it and by it.

The second "exception" to the supremacy of supreme spiritual power laid down in the brief second chapter of Book VIII is equally important: "Besides, where the law doth give *Dominion*, who doubteth but that the king who receiveth it must hold it of and under the law" (VIII.2.3). In his emphasis on the rule of law, which is especially evident in chapters 3, 6, and 8, Hooker again followed and articulated English practice and ideology, which was self-consciously legalistic. He is exceptionally forthright, however, in presenting law as a *restraint* on royal action, and not only divine and natural law but also "municipal" law. Hooker's refusal in the concluding ninth chapter of Book VIII to subject the monarch to ordinary processes of ecclesiastical censure is balanced, politically speaking, by his ringing statement in chapter 3 that "for the received laws and liberties of the *Church*, the *King* hath supreme authority and power but against them none." The statement is striking as it stands. It would gain in content if we had the detailed discussion of ecclesiastical law that Hooker's working notes show he planned for Book VI. At the time he wrote, it was not entirely clear what the "received" laws of the church were, a situation Hooker evidently had some interest in remedying.

In an age when contending English Christians thought each other worse than infidels, Hooker tried to give politics a good name. The burden of the preceding pages has been that he made extraordinary efforts to construct an idea of "supreme" power which would allow a community to operate in a genuinely political way and thus have the sort of self-legislating "operation not violent or casual" suggested as a possibility by his non-coercive definition of law at the beginning of Book I. In these terms, Hooker's idealized description of English public life near the end of Book VIII suggests the rule or canon by which his own actions were framed as a legitimating agent for the Elizabethan establishment:

> The whole body politic maketh laws, which laws give power unto the *King* and the *King* having bound himself to use according unto law that power, it so falleth out that the execution of the one is accomplished by the other in most religious and peaceable sort. (VIII.8.9)

The first and major limitation laid down in Hooker's initial account of the power of ecclesiastical dominion is the supremacy of God, "the king of all the kings of the earth." Hooker presents God's supremacy as something no one would be so mad as to deny. It is nevertheless the central theme in what is theologically Book VIII's most interesting and earnestly argued chapter, Hooker's defence of the sovereign's right to the title "head" of the church (chapter 4). The word "head" is not the point (it had in any case been abandoned by Elizabeth in favor of "governor"). The substantive question concerns the reality of Christ's lordship in a Christian community visibly governed in all things by the lay ruler. Hooker argues at length that in the English church–commonwealth of his day the crown is indeed appropriately subordinate to Christ, that Christ's lordship is effective in the sacraments, ceremonies, and flawed officials of the established order. The extended comparison of the headships of Christ and of the king in this chapter responds directly to the reformist challenge as Hooker had stated it at the beginning of Book I, a challenge which in the case of the royal supremacy was urged equally by Roman Catholics: "We are accused as men that will not have Christ Jesus to rule over them, but have wilfully cast his statutes behind their backs." "Behold," he had answered, "we offer the laws whereby we live unto the general trial and judgement of the whole world, heartily beseeching Almighty God ... that both we and others ... may have eyes to see and hearts to embrace the things that in his sight are most acceptable" (I.I.3).

On Hooker's account, "the laws whereby we live" both established and limited the crown's power in religious matters, and these laws were themselves established by "the whole body politic." If, as he had argued at the beginning of Book VIII, spiritual as well as secular activities are included in the natural ends of political association, then this order of legitimation had a good claim to moral authority. A good claim but not an absolute one. In the last analysis, for all parties concerned – for Thomas Cartwright and for the Roman Catholic Thomas Stapleton, who opposed the supremacy by citing the same patristic texts, and for Hooker himself – the decision to be a part of any community had to be consistent with "laws" prior to the community, constraining moral and theological norms which could not in conscience be violated for the sake of social tranquillity. Hooker's distinctively political treatment of "supreme" spiritual power must be understood in the context of such prior norms.

A polemical preface, a philosophical survey of the normative, an inclusive political treatment of supreme ecclesiastical authority – how do these sum up? Was Hooker above the bitter spiritual warfare of his day, or was he a deeply engaged partisan? Did he offer an integrating response to the disintegration of Christianity in the west, or was his own integrity broken in the attempt to construe a chance political arrangement as the acceptable service of the Lord? Surely, each side of the first antithesis has something to be said for it. Hooker's breadth of vision was unique among sixteenth-century religious writers. He was master of vast intellectual resources for placing the most divisive issues of the day in a larger, less divisive historical and doctrinal context. But he also took sides. The *Laws* is decidedly "partisan" in the sense that it is written to refute the positions of presbyterians, militant liturgical reformers, and Roman Catholics on a host of specific issues, some relatively unimportant, others momentous.

What of coherence, then? Could Hooker coherently combine speculative breadth and partisan polemic? If the coherence required is a matter of deducing the particular decisions of the last four books as necessary consequences from the normative principles of the first four, one may wonder whether Hooker would wish to be thought coherent. His avowed intent was only to show that there was "great reason" to observe the ecclesiastical laws of the land and "no necessity" to impugn them (Preface, 7.1). It is truer to his spirit and his text to read him, even in his most conservative moments, as defending "the present state" of the English church as a more than minimally acceptable solution to the problems of his community, but not as establishing a new distinction between the godly and the ungodly, the holy and the unholy, the loyal and the subversive, based on unqualified devotion to the establishment as the most perfect arrangement that could possibly be had. The fraternal tone in which Hooker addresses his opponents has often been noted. It is not a pretense. Hooker is often ironic, sometimes sarcastic and angry, but never self-righteous. The English law he defends demands obedience. It does not merely request it. In the last analysis, however, the move from "great reason" to the acceptance of legal constraint is a matter of willing participation in a given communal order. Accordingly, Hooker's own appeal is to a judgement of conscience, for he sees that unless his own party and opposing parties can live together in good conscience, there will be no law or community left to defend.

Principal dates in Hooker's life and the publication of his work

1554 *April:* Born in or near Exeter.

1557 *September:* Scholar (probationary Fellow) of Corpus Christi
College, Oxford.

1579 *August:* Ordained Deacon by John Aylmer at Fulham Palace,
London.
September: Gives bond as full Fellow of Corpus Christi
College.

1585 *March:* Appointed Master of the Temple.

1591 *July:* Instituted Subdean of Salisbury, Prebend of Nether-
avon, Rector of Boscombe.

1593 *March:* Preface and Books I–IV of *Of the Laws of Ecclesiastical
Polity* published.

1595 *July:* Presented by the Queen to the living of Bishopsbourne,
Kent.

1597 Publication of Book V of the *Laws*.

1600 *November 2:* Dies at Bishopsbourne.

1648 First publication of Books VI and VIII of the *Laws*.

1661 First publication of Book VII.

Bibliographical note

Text: *The Folger Library Edition of the Works of Richard Hooker*, W. Speed Hill, general editor (The Belknap Press of Harvard University Press: Cambridge, Mass. and London, England: 1977–). Vol. 1, ed. Georges Edelen, *Of the Laws of Ecclesiastical Polity, Preface, Books I–IV* (1977). Vol. 2, ed. W. Speed Hill, *Of the Laws of Ecclesiastical Polity, Book V* (1977). Vol. 3, ed. P. G. Stanwood, *Of the Laws of Ecclesiastical Polity, Books VI, VII, VIII* (1981) (includes first publication of autograph working notes for Books VI and VIII discovered among Archbishop Ussher's papers at Trinity College, Dublin in 1974). Vol. 4, ed. John E. Booty, *Of the Laws of Ecclesiastical Polity, Attack and Response* (1982) (the anonymous *Christian Letter* of 1599, with Hooker's marginal comments on his copy and some additional notes for a reply). Vol. 5, ed. Laetitia Yeandle and Egil Grislis, *Tractates and Sermons* (1989).

Pending publication of the sixth and final volume of the Folger edition, which will be devoted primarily to commentary on the *Laws*, see for bibliography W. Speed Hill, ed., *Studies in Richard Hooker: Essays Preliminary to an Edition of His Works* (Cleveland, 1972), pp. 279–320.

Izaak Walton's *Life* of Hooker, printed with earlier editions of Hooker's works as well as with Walton's lives of Donne, Herbert, and others, needs revision in the light of criticism by C. J. Sisson (*The Judicious Marriage of Mr. Hooker and the Birth of The Laws of Ecclesiastical Polity*, Cambridge, 1940) and David Novarr (*The Making of Walton's Lives*, Ithaca, New York, 1958). Recent research by Georges Edelen, as yet unpublished, suggests that Sisson may have gone too far in discounting the evidence that Hooker completed Books VI–VIII before his death.

For Hooker's influence, see Hugh Trevor-Roper in *Catholics, Anglicans, and Puritans* (London, 1987); Robert Eccleshall, "Richard Hooker and the Peculiarities of the English: The Reception of the *Ecclesiastical Polity* in the Seventeenth and Eighteenth Centuries," *History of Political Thought*, 2 (1981): 63–117; and H. R. McAdoo, *The Spirit of Anglicanism* (London, 1965).

The situation of the English church under Elizabeth is presented from various perspectives in the following works:

William P. Haugaard, *Elizabeth and the English Reformation* (Cambridge, 1968). Assumes a more substantial parliamentary opposition to the queen's policy than now seems warranted but properly emphasizes Elizabeth's importance in forming her church's character.

Norman L. Jones, *Faith by Statute* (London, 1982). The establishment of the establishment. Based on fuller evidence than the above.

Patrick Collinson, *The Elizabethan Puritan Movement* (London, 1967) and *The Religion of Protestants* (Oxford, 1982). The first is the classic account of the period from the standpoint of Hooker's immediate opponents. The second presents the Elizabethan and Jacobean church as not radically divided by Puritanism.

Peter Lake, *Puritan and Anglican? Presbyterianism and English Conformist Thought from Whitgift to Hooker* (London, 1988). Another account emphasizing similarities of outlook within Elizabethan Protestantism, but in a valuable chapter on Hooker Lake argues for his originality in relation to previous conformists as well as Puritans.

Christopher Haigh, ed., *The English Reformation Revisited* (Cambridge, 1987). Essays revising the view of the Reformation as a broad national movement. "The Reformation had created not a united Protestant England but a deeply divided England."

On Hooker's political thought see:

W. D. J. Cargill Thompson, "The Philosopher of the Politic Society: Richard Hooker as a Political Thinker" in Hill, *Studies in Richard Hooker*, pp. 3–76; reprinted in Cargill Thompson, *Studies in the Reformation*, ed. C. W. Dugmore (London, 1980). A brilliant, sympathetic, ultimately negative assessment of the moral coherence of Hooker's work.

Robert Eccleshall, *Order and Reason in Politics: Theories of Absolute and Limited Monarchy in Early Modern England* (Oxford, 1978). A good account of the range of contemporary positions, including Hooker's. Perceptive comparison of Hooker with Hegel.

Robert K. Faulkner, *Richard Hooker and the Politics of a Christian England* (Berkeley, 1981). A relatively ahistorical but morally intense account of Hooker's project.

J. P. Sommerville, "Richard Hooker, Hadrian Saravia, and the Advent of the Divine Right of Kings," *History of Political Thought*, 4 (1983): 229–246. Documents radical differences between thinkers often thrown together as establishment apologists.

J. M. Finnis, *Natural Law and Natural Rights* (Oxford, 1980) is hardly at all concerned with Hooker but admirably presents a natural law position akin to his.

The text and notes of this edition

The text for this volume is a modern-spelling version of the text of the Preface and Books I and VIII of the *Laws* published in volumes I and 3 of the *Folger Library Edition of the Works of Richard Hooker*, which includes a number of substantive variants from earlier editions. Hooker regularly wrote "self," "thing," and "time" separately in compound expressions ("my self," "any thing," "some time," etc.). Other changes in spelling from the Folger edition seem inconsequential. The Folger text follows the first edition in printing Hooker's Preface, addressed to the reformist critics of the establishment, in italics and in setting off with quotation marks down both margins (as if each line were a separate quotation) the reproach to non-separating reformers which Hooker voices from a separatist standpoint at Preface, 8.1. It has not been feasible to retain these features of typography in the present volume. Where it can be identified with some certainty (that is, in the Preface and Book I), Hooker's punctuation has been preserved. It will give the reader trouble in some passages but on the whole makes for a more involving experience than the somewhat mechanical partitioning of nineteenth-century editions. I have preferred the first edition's "sounder" to the Folger "founder" at Preface, 8.7 (p. 43) and have made a small number of corrections and emendations in Book VIII (noted as they occur) in the interests of accuracy and clearer sense. The bracketed section numbers within chapters in the Preface and Book I are Keble's, retained in the Folger edition. In chapters 2–4 and 6 of Book VIII, the order of the material in the Folger text differs from Keble's arrangement. Keble's section numbers are indicated with a "K" where they differ from the Folger numbers.

I have taken a much freer hand with Hooker's notes, with the aim of making them as useful as possible to the contemporary reader. In his notes, Hooker regularly quotes Greek and Latin authors in the original and occasionally offers an observation of his own in Latin. These passages have been translated or (if meant only to support an English version in the text) dropped. Many titles are filled out, and nearly all are given in English, even when no English translation of the cited work exists. Hooker's references to canon law and to the Roman civil law of Justinian have been altered to conform to the numbered sections and subsections of the standard modern editions: for the *Corpus juris canonici* A. Friedberg's edition, for the *Corpus juris civilis* the editions of Paul Krueger and Theodore Mommsen. Abbreviated references to modern editions of other works are occasionally added in brackets. Chapter numbers in current editions are added in brackets when these differ from the numbers Hooker gives. Page numbers of the Berlin Academy edition of Aristotle serve this function for Hooker's major philosophical source. Stephanus numbers are added for references to Plato.

So as not to occupy space in the midst of Hooker's own presentation, all further information has been placed in the Guide to Hooker's Sources beginning on page 227. Editions cited by date in the notes are identified more fully in the Guide.

Hooker's vocabulary is not as difficult as his syntax. The following short glossary may, however, be of use:

> conceit, conceipt/misconceipt = conceiving, conception, concept/misconception
> convenience, conveniency/inconvenient = appropriateness (in a stronger sense than our current one)/inappropriate, causing significant difficulty.
> emprese = a personal emblem or motto.
> glosc = explain away.
> happily = haply, perhaps.
> loover = a turret-like erection on the roof of a medieval building.
> ure/inure = use (*n.*)/make used to, become used to.

A PREFACE

To them that seek (as they term it) the reformation of Laws, and orders Ecclesiastical, in the Church of ENGLAND.

The cause and occasion of handling these things, and what might be wished in them for whose sakes so much pain is taken.

1. Though for no other cause, yet for this; that posterity may know [1.1] we have not loosely through silence permitted things to pass away as in a dream, there shall be for men's information extant thus much concerning the present state of the Church of God established amongst us, and their careful endeavor which would have upheld the same. At your hands beloved in our Lord and Saviour Jesus Christ (for in him the love which we bear unto all that would but seem to be born of him, it is not the sea of your gall and bitterness that shall ever drown) I have no great cause to look for other than the selfsame portion and lot, which your manner hath been hitherto to lay on them that concur not in opinion and sentence with you. But our hope is that the God of peace shall (notwithstanding man's nature too impatient of contumelious malediction) enable us quietly and even gladly to suffer all things, for that work's sake which we covet to perform. The wonderful zeal and fervour wherewith [1.2] ye have withstood the received orders of this Church was the first thing which caused me to enter into consideration, whether (as all your published books and writings peremptorily maintain) every christian man fearing God stand bound to join with you for the furtherance of that which ye term *the Lord's Discipline.* Wherein I must plainly confess unto you, that before I examined your sundry declarations in that behalf, it could not settle in my head to think but that undoubtedly such numbers of otherwise right well affected

I

and most religiously inclined minds, had some marvelous reasonable inducements which led them with so great earnestness that way. But when once, as near as my slender ability would serve, I had with travail and care performed that part of the Apostle's advice and counsel in such cases whereby he willeth to *try all things*, and was come at the length so far, that there remained only the other clause to be satisfied, wherein he concludeth that *what good is must be held*: there was in my poor understanding no remedy, but to set down this as my final resolute persuasion, *Surely the present form of Church government which the laws of this land have established, is such, as no law of God, nor reason of man hath hitherto been alleged of force sufficient to prove they do ill, who to the uttermost of their power withstand the alteration thereof.* Contrariwise, *The other which instead of it we are required to accept, is only by error and misconceipt named the ordinance of Jesus Christ, no one proof as yet brought forth whereby* [1.3] *it may clearly appear to be so in very deed.* The explication of which two things I have here thought good to offer into your own hands, heartily beseeching you even by the meekness of Jesus Christ, whom I trust ye love; that, as ye tender the peace and quietness of this Church, if there be in you that gracious humility which hath ever been the crown and glory of a christianly disposed mind, if your own souls, hearts, and consciences, (the sound integrity whereof can but hardly stand with the refusal of truth in personal respects) be, as I doubt not but they are, things most dear and precious unto you, [a]*Let not the faith which ye have in our Lord Jesus Christ*, be blemished *with partialities*, regard not who it is which speaketh, but weigh only what is spoken. Think not that ye read the words of one, who bendeth himself as an adversary against the truth which ye have already embraced; but the words of one, who desireth even to embrace together with you the selfsame truth, if it be the truth, and for that cause (for no other God he knoweth) hath undertaken the burdensome labour of this painful kind of conference. For the plainer access whereunto, let it be lawful for me to rip up to the very bottom, how and by whom your Discipline was planted, at such time as this age we live in began to make first trial thereof.

[a] *James 2:1.*

The first establishment of new discipline by Mr. Calvin's industry in the Church of Geneva, and the beginning of strife about it amongst ourselves.

2. A founder it had, whom, for mine own part, I think incomparably [2.1] the wisest man that ever the French Church did enjoy, since the hour it enjoyed him. His bringing up was in the study of the Civil Law. Divine knowledge he gathered, not by hearing or reading so much, as by teaching others. For, though thousands were debtors to him, as touching knowledge in that kind; yet he to none but only to God, the author of that most blessed fountain, the book of life, and of the admirable dexterity of wit, together with the helps of other learning which were his guides: till being occasioned to leave France, he fell at the length upon Geneva; which City, the Bishop and Clergy thereof had a little before, (as some do affirm) forsaken, being of likelihood frighted with the people's sudden attempt for abolishment of popish religion: the event of which enterprise they thought it not safe for themselves to wait for in that place. At the coming of Calvin thither, the form of their civil regiment was popular, as it continueth at this day; neither King, nor Duke, nor nobleman of any authority or power over them, but officers chosen by the people yearly out of themselves, to order all things with public consent. For spiritual government, they had no laws at all agreed upon, but did what the Pastors of their souls by persuasion could win them unto. Calvin, being admitted one of their Preachers, and a divinity reader amongst them, considered how dangerous it was that the whole estate of that Church should hang still on so slender a thread, as the liking of an ignorant multitude is, if it have power to change whatsoever itself listeth. Wherefore taking unto him two of the other ministers for more countenance of the action (albeit the rest were all against it) they moved, and in the end persuaded with much ado the people to bind themselves by solemn oath, first never to admit the Papacy amongst them again; and secondly, to live in obedience unto such orders concerning the exercise of their religion, and the form of their ecclesiastical government, as those their true and faithful Ministers of God's word had agreeably to Scripture set down for that end and purpose. When these things began to be put in ure, the people also (what [2.2]

3

causes moving them thereunto, themselves best know) began to repent them of that they had done, and irefully to champ upon the bit they had taken into their mouths; the rather for that they grew by means of this innovation into dislike with some Churches near about them, the benefit of whose good friendship their state could not well lack. It was the manner of those times (whether through men's desire to enjoy alone the glory of their own enterprises, or else because the quickness of their occasions required present dispatch,) so it was, that every particular Church did that within itself, which some few of their own thought good, by whom the rest were all directed. Such number of Churches then being, though free within themselves, yet small, common conference beforehand might have eased them of much aftertrouble. But a greater inconvenience it bred, that every later endeavoured to be certain degrees more removed from conformity with the Church of Rome, than the rest before had been: whereupon grew marvelous great dissimilitudes, and by reason thereof, jealousies, heartburnings, jars and discords amongst them. Which notwithstanding might have easily been prevented, if the orders which each Church did think fit and convenient for itself, had not so peremptorily been established under that high commanding form, which tendered them unto the people, as things everlastingly required by the law of that Lord of Lords, against whose statutes there is no exception to be taken. For by this mean it came to pass, that one Church could not but accuse and condemn another of disobedience to the will of Christ, in those things where manifest difference was between them: whereas the selfsame orders allowed, but yet established in more wary and suspense manner, as being to stand in force till God should give the opportunity of some general conference what might be best for every of them afterwards to do; this I say had both prevented all occasion of just dislike which others might take, and reserved a greater liberty unto the authors themselves of entering into further consultation afterwards. Which though never so necessary they could not easily now admit, without some fear of derogation from their credit: and therefore that which once they had done, they became forever after resolute to maintain. Calvin therefore and the other two his associates stiffly refusing to administer the holy Communion to such as would not quietly without contradiction and murmur submit themselves unto the orders which their solemn oath had bound them to obey, were in that quarrel banished the town. A few years after (such was the levity of that people) the places [2.3] of one or two of their Ministers being fallen void, they were not before so willing to be rid of their learned Pastor, as now importunate to obtain him again from them who had given him entertainment, and which were loath to part with him, had not unresistable earnestness been used. One of the town ministers that saw in what manner the people were bent for the revocation of Calvin, gave him notice of their affection in this sort. *bThe Senate of two hundred being assembled, they all crave Calvin. The next day a general convocation. They cry in like sort again all: We will have Calvin that good and learned man Christ's Minister. This*, saith he, *when I understood I could not choose but praise God, nor was I able to judge otherwise than that this was the Lord's doing, and that it was marvelous in our eyes*, and *cThat the stone which the builders refused, was now made the head of the corner.* The other two whom they had thrown out (together with Calvin) they were content should enjoy their exile. Many causes might lead them to be more desirous of him. First, his yielding unto them in one thing, might happily put them in hope, that time would breed the like easiness of condescending further unto them. For in his absence he had persuaded them, with whom he was able to prevail, that albeit himself did better like of common bread to be used in the Eucharist, yet the other they rather should accept, than cause any trouble in the Church about it. Again they saw that the name of Calvin waxed every day greater abroad, and that, together with his fame, their infamy was spread, which had so rashly and childishly ejected him. Besides it was not unlikely but that his credit in the world, might many ways stand the poor town in great stead: as the truth is, their ministers' foreign estimation hitherto hath been the best stake in their hedge. But whatsoever secret respects were likely to move them, for contenting of their minds Calvin returned (as it had been another Tully) to his old home. He ripely considered [2.4] how gross a thing it were for men of his quality, wise and grave men, to live with such a multitude, and to be tenants at will under them, as their ministers, both himself and others, had been. For the remedy of which inconvenience he gave them plainly to understand, that if he did become their teacher again, they must be content

---

b Calvin, Epistle 24 [*CR*, 39:148–149].   c Luke 20:17.

to admit a complete form of discipline, which both they, and also their pastors should now be solemnly sworn to observe forever after. Of which discipline the main and principal parts were these: A standing ecclesiastical Court to be established; perpetual Judges in that Court to be their ministers, others of the people annually chosen twice so many in number as they to be judges together with them in the same Court: these two sorts to have the care of all men's manners, power of determining all kind of Ecclesiastical causes, and authority to convent, to control, to punish, as far as with excommunication, whomsoever they should think worthy, none either small or great excepted. This device I see not how the wisest at that time living could have bettered, if we duly consider what the present estate of Geneva did then require. For their Bishop and his Clergy being (as it is said) departed from them by moonlight, or howsoever, being departed; to choose in his room any other Bishop, had been a thing altogether impossible. And for their ministers to seek that themselves alone might have coercive power over the whole Church, would perhaps have been hardly construed at that time. But when so frank an offer was made, that for every one minister there should be two of the people to sit and give voice in the Ecclesiastical Consistory, what inconvenience could they easily find which themselves might not be able always to remedy? Howbeit (as evermore the simpler sort are, even when they see no apparent cause, jealous notwithstanding over the secret intents and purposes of wiser men) this proposition of his did somewhat trouble them. Of the Ministers themselves, which had stayed behind in the City when Calvin was gone, some, upon knowledge of the people's earnest intent to recall him to his place again, had beforehand written their letters of submission, and assured him of their allegiance forever after, if it should like him to hearken unto that public suit. But yet misdoubting what might happen, if this discipline did go forward; they objected against it the example of other reformed Churches living quietly and orderly without it. Some of chiefest place and countenance amongst the laity professed with greater stomach their judgements, that such a discipline was little better than popish tyranny disguised and tendered unto them under a new form. This sort, it may be, had some fear that the filling up of the seats in the Consistory with so great a number of laymen, was but to please the minds of the people, to the end they might think their own sway somewhat; but when things came to trial of practice their Pastors' learning would be at all times of force to overpersuade simple men, who knowing the time of their own Presidentship to be but short, would always stand in fear of their Ministers' perpetual authority: and among the Ministers themselves, one being so far in estimation above the rest, the voices of the rest were likely to be given for the most part respectively with a kind of secret dependency and awe: so that in show a marvelous indifferently composed Senate Ecclesiastical was to govern, but in effect one only man should, as the Spirit and soul of the residue, do all in all. But what did these vain surmises boot? Brought they were now to so strait an issue, that of two things they must choose one: namely whether they would to their endless disgrace, with ridiculous lightness, dismiss him whose restitution they had in so impotent manner desired; or else condescend unto that demand, wherein he was resolute either to have it or to leave them. They thought it better to be somewhat hardly yoked at home, than forever abroad discredited. [d]Wherefore in the end those orders were on all sides assented unto: with no less alacrity of mind, than Cities unable to hold out longer are wont to show, when they take conditions such as it liketh him to offer them which hath them in the narrow straits of advantage. Not many years were overpassed, before these twice sworn men [2.5] adventured to give their last and hottest assault to the fortress of the same discipline; childishly granting by common consent of their whole Senate, and that under their town seal, a relaxation to one Bertelier whom the Eldership had excommunicated; further also decreeing, with strange absurdity, that to the same Senate it should belong to give final judgement in matter of excommunication, and to absolve whom it pleased them: clean contrary to their own former deeds and oaths. The report of which decree being forthwith brought unto Calvin; *Before* (saith he) *this decree take place, either my blood or banishment shall sign it.* Again two days before the Communion should be celebrated, his speech was publicly to like effect, *Kill me if ever this hand do reach forth the things that are holy to them whom* THE CHURCH *hath judged despisers.* Whereupon, for fear of tumult, the forenamed Bertelier was by his friends advised for that time not to use the liberty granted him by the Senate, nor to

[d] A.D. 1541.

7

present himself in the Church, till they saw somewhat further what would ensue. After the Communion quietly ministered, and some likelihood of peaceable ending these troubles without any more ado, that very day in the afternoon, besides all men's expectation, concluding his ordinary sermon, he telleth them, that because he neither had learned nor taught to strive with such as are in authority, therefore (saith he) *the case so standing as now it doth, let me use these words of the Apostle unto you, I commend you unto God and the word*

[2.6] *of his grace,* and so bade them heartily all *Adieu.* It sometimes cometh to pass that the readiest way, which a wise man hath to conquer, is to fly. This voluntary and unexpected mention of sudden departure caused presently the Senate (for according to their wonted manner they still continued only constant in unconstancy) to gather themselves together, and for a time to suspend their own decree, leaving things to proceed as before till they had heard the judgement of four Helvetian Cities concerning the matter which was in strife. This to have done at the first before they gave assent unto any order had showed some wit and discretion in them: but now to do it was as much as to say in effect, that they would play their parts on a stage. Calvin therefore dispatcheth with all expedition his letters unto some principal pastor in every of those cities, craving earnestly at their hands, to respect this cause as a thing whereupon the whole state of religion and piety in that church did so much depend, that God and all good men were now inevitably certain to be trampled under foot, unless those four Cities by their good means might be brought to give sentence with the ministers of Geneva, when the cause should be brought before them: yea so to give it, that two things it might effectually contain; the one an absolute approbation of the discipline of Geneva as consonant unto the word of God without any cautions, qualifications, ifs or ands; the other an earnest admonition not to innovate or change the same. His vehement request herein as touching both points was satisfied. For albeit the said Helvetian Churches did never as yet observe that discipline, nevertheless the Senate of Geneva having required their judgement concerning these three questions: ʿFirst, *after what manner by God's commandment according to the Scripture, and unspotted religion excommunication is to be exercised:* Secondly, *whether it may*

ᵉ Calvin, Epistle 166 [*CR*, 42:697].

not be exercised some other way than by the Consistory: thirdly, *what the use of their Churches was to do in this case:* answer was returned from the said Churches, *That they had heard already of those consistorial laws, and did acknowledge them to be* godly *ordinances* drawing towards *the prescript of the word of God, for which cause that they did not think it good for* the Church of Geneva *by innovation to change the same, but rather to keep them as they were.* Which answer, although not answering unto the former demands, but respecting what Mr. Calvin had judged requisite for them to answer, was notwithstanding accepted without any further reply: inasmuch as they plainly saw that when stomach doth strive with wit, the match is not equal. And so the heat of their former contentions began to slake. The [2.7] present inhabitants of Geneva, I hope, will not take it in evil part that the faultiness of their people heretofore, is by us so far forth laid open, as their own learned guides and Pastors have thought necessary to discover it unto the world. For out of their books and writings it is that I have collected this whole narration, to the end it might thereby appear in what sort amongst them that discipline was planted, for which so much contention is raised amongst ourselves. The reason which moved Calvin herein to be so earnest, was, as Beza himself testifieth, *ffor that he saw how needful these bridles were to be put in the jaws of that City.* That which by wisdom he saw to be requisite for that people, was by as great wisdom compassed. But wise men are men, and the truth is truth. That which Calvin did for establishment of his discipline, seemeth more commendable than that which he taught for the countenancing of it established. Nature worketh in us all a love to our own counsels. The contradiction of others is a fan to inflame that love. Our love set on fire to maintain that which once we have done, sharpeneth the wit to dispute, to argue, and by all means to reason for it. Wherefore a marvel it were if a man of so great capacity, having such incitements to make him desirous of all kind of furtherances unto his cause, could espy in the whole Scripture of God nothing which might breed at the least a probable opinion of likelihood, that divine authority itself was the same way somewhat inclinable. And all which the wit even of Calvin was able from thence to draw, by sifting the very utmost sentence and syllable, is no more than that certain

---

f [Beza, *Life of Calvin* (*CR*, 49:131).]

speeches there are which to him did seem to intimate that all Christian Churches ought to have their Elderships endowed with power of excommunication, and that a part of those Elderships everywhere should be chosen out from amongst the laity after that form which himself had framed Geneva unto. But what argument are ye able to show, whereby it was ever proved by Calvin, that any one sentence of Scripture doth necessarily enforce these things, or the rest wherein your opinion concurreth with his against the orders of your [2.8] own Church? We should be injurious unto virtue itself, if we did derogate from them whom their industry hath made great. Two things of principal moment there are which have deservedly procured him honour throughout the world: the one his exceeding pains in composing the Institutions of Christian religion; the other his no less industrious travails for exposition of holy Scripture according unto the same institutions. In which two things whosoever they were that after him bestowed their labour; he gained the advantage of prejudice against them if they gainsaid; and of glory, above them, if they consented. His writings published after the question about that discipline was once begun omit not any the least occasion of extolling the use and singular necessity thereof. Of what account the Master of sentences was in the Church of Rome, the same and more amongst the preachers of reformed Churches Calvin had purchased: so that the perfectest divines were judged they, which were skilfullest in Calvin's writings. His books almost the very canon to judge both doctrine and discipline by. French Churches, both under others abroad and at home in their own Country, all cast according unto that mould which Calvin had made. The Church of Scotland in erecting the fabric of their reformation took the self-same pattern. Till at length the discipline, which was at the first so weak, that without the staff of their approbation, who were not subject unto it themselves, it had not brought others under subjection; began now to challenge universal obedience, and to enter into open conflict with those very Churches which in desperate extremity [2.9] had been relievers of it. To one of those Churches which lived in most peaceable sort, and abounded as well with men for their learning in other professions singular, as also with divines whose equals were not elsewhere to be found, a Church ordered by Gualter's discipline, and not by that which Geneva adoreth: unto this Church, the Church of Heidelberg, there cometh one who craving leave to dispute publicly defendeth with open disdain of their government, that *To a Minister with his Eldership power is given by the law of God to excommunicate whomsoever, yea even kings and princes themselves.* Here were the seeds sown of that controversy which sprang up between Beza and Erastus about the matter of excommunication, whether there ought to be in all Churches an Eldership having power to excommunicate, and a part of that Eldership to be of necessity certain chosen out from amongst the laity for that purpose. In which disputation they have, as to me it seemeth, divided very equally the truth between them; Beza most truly maintaining the necessity of excommunication, Erastus as truly the non-necessity of layelders to be ministers thereof. Amongst ourselves, there was [2.10] in King Edward's days some question moved by reason of a few men's scrupulosity touching certain things. And beyond Seas, of them which fled in the days of Queen Mary, some contenting themselves abroad with the use of their own Service book at home authorized before their departure out of the Realm; others liking better the Common prayer book of the Church of Geneva translated, those smaller contentions before begun were by this mean somewhat increased. Under the happy reign of her Majesty which now is, the greatest matter a while contended for was the wearing of the Cap and Surplice, till there came Admonitions directed unto the high Court of Parliament, by men who concealing their names thought it glory enough to discover their minds and affections, which now were universally bent even against all the orders and laws wherein this Church is found unconformable to the platform of Geneva. Concerning the defender of which admonitions, all that I mean to say is but this: *There will come a time when three words uttered with charity and meekness shall receive a far more blessed reward than three thousand volumes written with disdainful sharpness of wit.* But the manner of men's writing must not alienate our hearts from the truth if it appear they have the truth: as the followers of the same defender do think he hath, and in that persuasion they follow him, no otherwise than himself doth Calvin, Beza and others with the like persuasion that they in this cause had the truth. We being as fully persuaded otherwise, it resteth that some kind of trial be used to find out which part is in error.

By what means so many of the people are trained into the liking of that discipline.

[3.1] *3.* The first mean whereby nature teacheth men to judge good from evil as well in laws as in other things, is the force of their own discretion. Hereunto therefore Saint Paul referreth oftentimes his own speech to be considered of by them that heard him, *[g]I speak as to them which have understanding, judge ye what I say.* Again afterward, *[h]Judge in your selves, is it comely that a woman pray uncovered?* *[i]*The exercise of this kind of judgement our Saviour requireth in the Jews. In them of Berea the Scripture commendeth it. Finally whatsoever we do, if our own secret judgement consent not unto it as fit and good to be done; the doing of it to us is sin, although the thing itself be allowable. Saint Paul's rule therefore generally is, *[j]Let every man in his own mind be fully persuaded* of that thing [3.2] which he either alloweth or doth. Some things are so familiar and plain, that truth from falsehood, and good from evil is most easily discerned in them, even by men of no deep capacity. And of that nature, for the most part are things absolutely unto all men's salvation necessary, either to be held or denied, either to be done or avoided. For which cause Saint Augustine acknowledgeth that they are not only set down, but also plainly set down in Scripture: so that he which heareth or readeth may, without any great difficulty, understand. Other things also there are belonging (though in a lower degree of importance) unto the offices of Christian men: which, because they are more obscure, more intricate and hard to be judged of, therefore God hath appointed some to spend their whole time principally in the study of things divine, to the end that in these more doubtful cases their understanding might be a light to direct others. *[k]If the understanding power or faculty of the soul be* (saith the grand Physician) *like unto bodily sight not of equal sharpness in all, what can be more convenient than that, even as the dark-sighted man is directed by the clear about things visible, so likewise in matters of deeper discourse the wise in heart do show the simple where his way lieth?* In our doubtful cases of law, what man is there who seeth not how requisite it is that professors of skill in that faculty be

[g] 1 Cor. 10:15.   *[h]* 1 Cor. 11:13.   *[i]* Luke 12:56–57.
[j] Rom. 14:5.   *[k]* Galen, *Of the Best Kind of Teaching* [ed. 1965, 1:52].

our directors? So it is in all other kinds of knowledge. And even in this kind likewise the Lord hath himself appointed, that [l]*the Priest's lips should preserve knowledge, and that other men should seek the truth at his mouth,* because *he is the messenger of the Lord of Hosts.* Gregory Nazianzen offended at the people's too great presumption in controlling the judgement of them to whom in such cases they should have rather submitted their own, seeketh by earnest entreaty to stay them within their bounds: [m]*Presume not ye that are sheep to make yourselves guides of them that should guide you, neither seek ye to overskip the fold which they about you have pitched. It sufficeth for your part, if ye can well frame yourselves to be ordered. Take not upon you to judge your judges, nor to make them subject to your laws who should be a law to you. For God is not a God of sedition and confusion but of order and of peace.* But ye will say that [n]if the guides of the [3.3] people be blind, the common sort of men must not close up their own eyes and be led by the conduct of such; [o]if the Priest be partial in the law, the flock must not therefore depart from the ways of sincere truth, and in simplicity yield to be followers of him for his place's sake and office over them. Which thing, though in itself most true, is in your defence notwithstanding weak: because the matter, wherein ye think that ye see and imagine that your ways are sincere, is of far deeper consideration than any one amongst five hundred of you conceiveth. Let the vulgar sort amongst you know that there is not the least branch of the cause wherein they are so resolute, but to the trial of it a great deal more appertaineth than their conceipt doth reach unto. I write not this in disgrace of the simplest that way given, but I would gladly they knew the nature of that cause wherein they think themselves thoroughly instructed and are not; by means whereof they daily run themselves, without feeling their own hazard, upon the dint of the [p]Apostle's sentence against evil speakers as touching things wherein they are ignorant. [q]If it be granted a thing unlawful for private men, not [3.4] called unto public consultation, to dispute which is the best state of civil Polity (with a desire of bringing in some other kind than that under which they already live, for of such disputes I take it

[l] Mal. 2:7.
[m] Gregory of Nazianzen, *The Oration by Which He Excuses Himself* [*PG*, 35:1053].
[n] Matt. 15:14. [o] Mal. 2:9. [p] Jude 10. 2 Pet. 2:12.
[q] Calvin, *Institutes*, Bk 4, ch. 20, sect. 8.

his meaning was), if it be a thing confessed that of such questions they cannot determine without rashness, inasmuch as a great part of them consisteth in special circumstances, and for one kind as many reasons may be brought as for another; is there any reason in the world why they should better judge what kind of regiment Ecclesiastical is the fittest? For in the Civil state more insight, and in those affairs more experience a great deal must needs be granted them, than in this they can possibly have. When they which write in defence of your discipline and commend it unto the *Highest* not in the least cunning manner, are forced notwithstanding to acknowledge, that 'with whom the truth is they know not,' they are not certain;

[3.5] what certainty or knowledge can the multitude have thereof? Weigh what doth move the common sort so much to favour this innovation, and it shall soon appear unto you, that the force of particular reasons which for your several opinions are alleged is a thing whereof the multitude never did nor could so consider as to be therewith wholly carried; but certain general inducements are used to make saleable your Cause in gross; and when once men have cast a fancy towards it, any slight declaration of specialties will serve to lead forward

[3.6] inclinable and prepared minds. The method of winning the people's affection unto a general liking of *the Cause* (for so ye term it) hath been this. First in the hearing of the multitude, the faults especially of higher callings are ripped up with marvelous exceeding severity and sharpness of reproof; which being oftentimes done begetteth a great good opinion of integrity, zeal and holiness, to such constant reprovers of sin, as by likelihood would never be so much offended

[3.7] at that which is evil, unless themselves were singularly good. The next thing hereunto is to impute all faults and corruptions wherewith the world aboundeth, unto the kind of Ecclesiastical government established. Wherein, as before by reproving faults, they purchased unto themselves with the multitude a name to be virtuous; so by finding out this kind of cause they obtain to be judged wise above others; whereas in truth unto the form even of Jewish government, which the Lord himself (they all confess) did establish, with like show of reason they might impute those faults which the Prophets condemn in the governors of that commonwealth, as to the English kind of regiment Ecclesiastical (whereof also God himself though

---

ʳ The author of the *petition directed to her Majesty* [*STC* 1521], p. 3.

in other sort is author) the stains and blemishes found in our State, which springing from the root of human frailty and corruption, not only are, but have been always more or less, yea and (for anything we know to the contrary) will be till the world's end complained of, what form of government soever take place. Having gotten thus [3.8] much sway in the hearts of men, a third step is to propose their own form of Church government, as the only sovereign remedy of all evils; and to adorn it with all the glorious titles that may be. And the nature, as of men that have sick bodies, so likewise of the people in the crazedness of their minds possessed with dislike and discontentment at things present, is to imagine that anything (the virtue whereof they hear commended) would help them; but that most, which they least have tried. The fourth degree of induce- [3.9] ment is by fashioning the very notions and conceipts of men's minds in such sort, that when they read the Scripture, they may think that everything soundeth towards the advancement of that discipline, and to the utter disgrace of the contrary. 'Pythagoras, by bringing up his Scholars in the speculative knowledge of numbers, made their conceipts therein so strong, that when they came to the contemplation of things natural they imagined that in every particular thing they even beheld as it were with their eyes, how the elements of number gave essence and being to the works of nature. A thing in reason impossible; which notwithstanding through their mis-fashioned preconceipt, appeared unto them no less certain, than if nature had written it in the very foreheads of all the creatures of God. When they of the family of love have it once in their heads, that *Christ* doth not signify any one person but a quality whereof many are partakers; that to be *raised* is nothing else but to be regenerated or endowed with the said quality; and that when separation of them which have it from them which have it not is here made, this is *judgement*; how plainly do they imagine that the Scripture everywhere speaketh in the favour of that sect? And assuredly the very cause which maketh the simple and ignorant to think they even see how the word of God runneth currently on your side, is that their minds are forestalled and their conceits perverted beforehand by being taught, that an *Elder* doth signify a layman admitted only to the office of rule or government in the Church; a *Doctor*

---

⁵ Aristotle, *Metaphysics*, Bk 1, ch. 5 [985b].

15

one which may only teach and neither preach nor administer the Sacraments; a *Deacon* one which hath charge of the alms box and of nothing else: that the *Scepter*, the *rod*, the *throne* and *kingdom* of Christ are a form of regiment, only by Pastors, Elders, Doctors and Deacons: that by mystical resemblance mount Sion and Jerusalem are the Churches which admit, Samaria and Babylon the Churches which oppugn the said form of regiment. And in like sort they are taught to apply all things spoken of repairing the walls and decayed parts of the City and temple of God, by Esdras, Nehemiah, and the rest: as if purposely the holy ghost had therein meant to foresignify, what the authors of admonitions to the Parliament, of supplications to the Council, of petitions to her Majesty, and of such other like writs, should either do or suffer in behalf of

[3.10] this their cause. From hence they proceed to an higher point, which is the persuading of men credulous and over-capable of such pleasing errors, that it is the special illumination of the holy Ghost, whereby they discern those things in the word, which others reading yet discern them not. *'Dearly beloved* saith St. John, *Give not credit unto every Spirit.* There are but two ways whereby the spirit leadeth men into all truth: the one extraordinary, the other common; the one belonging but unto some few, the other extending itself unto all that are of God; the one that which we call by a special divine excellency *Revelation*, the other *Reason*. If the Spirit by such revelation have discovered unto them the secrets of that discipline out of Scripture, they must profess themselves to be all (even men, women, and children) Prophets. Or if reason be the hand which the Spirit hath led them by, forasmuch as persuasions grounded upon reason are either weaker or stronger according to the force of those reasons whereupon the same are grounded, they must every of them from the greatest to the least be able for every several article to show some special reason as strong as their persuasion therein is earnest. Otherwise how can it be but that some other sinews there are from which that overplus of strength in persuasion doth arise? Most sure it is, that when men's affections do frame their opinions, they are in defence of error more earnest a great deal, than (for the most part) sound believers in the maintenance of truth apprehended according to the nature of that evidence which scripture yieldeth:

' 1 John 4:1.

16

which being in some things plain, as in the principles of Christian doctrine; in some things, as in these matters of discipline, more dark and doubtful, frameth correspondently that inward assent which God's most gracious Spirit worketh by it as by his effectual instrument. It is not therefore the fervent earnestness of their persuasion, but the soundness of those reasons whereupon the same is built, which must declare their opinions in these things to have been wrought by the holy Ghost, and not by the *"fraud* of that evil Spirit which is even in his illusions strong. After that the fancy [3.11] of the common sort hath once thoroughly apprehended the Spirit to be author of their persuasion concerning discipline, then is instilled into their hearts, that the same Spirit leading men into this opinion, doth thereby seal them to be God's children, and that as the state of the times now standeth, the most special token to know them that are God's own from others, is an earnest affection that way. This hath bred high terms of separation between such and the rest of the world, whereby the one sort are named *The* brethren, *The* godly, and so forth, the other worldlings, timeservers, pleasers of men not of God, with such like. From hence, they are [3.12] easily drawn on to think it exceeding necessary, for fear of quenching that good Spirit, to use all means whereby the same may be both strengthened in themselves, and made manifest unto others. This maketh them diligent hearers of such as are known that way to incline; this maketh them eager to take and to seek all occasions of secret conference with such; this maketh them glad to use such as counsellors and directors in all their dealings which are of weight, as contracts, testaments, and the like; this maketh them, through an unweariable desire of receiving instruction from the masters of that company, to cast off the care of those very affairs which do most concern their estate, and to think that then they are like unto Mary, commendable for making choice of the better part. Finally, this is it which maketh them willing to charge, yea, oftentimes even to overcharge themselves for such men's sustenance and relief, lest their zeal to the cause should any way be unwitnessed. For what is it which poor beguiled souls will not do through so powerful incitements? In which respect it is also noted, that most labor hath [3.13] been bestowed to win and retain towards this cause them whose judgements are commonly weakest by reason of their sex. And

" 2 Thess. 2:11.

although not *women laden with sins*, as the Apostle St. Paul speaketh, but (as we verily esteem of them for the most part) women propense and inclinable to holiness be otherwise edified in good things, rather than carried away as captives into any kind of sin and evil by such as enter into their houses, with purpose to plant there a zeal and a love towards this kind of discipline: yet some occasion is hereby ministered for men to think, that if the cause which is thus furthered did gain by the soundness of proof, whereupon it doth build itself, it would not most busily endeavor to prevail where least ability of judgement is: and therefore that this so eminent industry in making proselytes more of that sex than of the other groweth, for that they are deemed apter to serve as instruments and helps in the cause. Apter they are through the eagerness of their affection, that maketh them which way soever they take, diligent in drawing their husbands, children, servants, friends and allies the same way; apter through that natural inclination unto pity which breedeth in them a greater readiness than in men, to be bountiful towards their Preachers who suffer want; apter through sundry opportunities which they especially have, to procure encouragements for their brethren; finally, apter through a singular delight which they take in giving very large and particular intelligence how all near about them stand
[3.14] affected as concerning the same cause. But be they women or be they men, if once they have tasted of that cup, let any man of contrary opinion open his mouth to persuade them, they close up their ears, his reasons they weigh not, all is answered with rehearsal of the words of John, *ᵂWe are of God, he that knoweth God, heareth us*, as for the rest, ye are of the world, for this world's pomp and vanity it is that ye speak, and the world whose ye are heareth you. Which cloak sitteth no less fit on the back of their cause, than of the Anabaptists', when the dignity, authority and honor of God's Magistrate is upheld against them. Show these eagerly affected men their inability to judge of such matters; their answer is, *ˣGod hath chosen the simple.* Convince them of folly, and that so plainly, that very children upbraid them with it; they have their bucklers of like defence. *ʸChrist's own Apostle was accounted mad. ᶻThe best men evermore by*

ᵛ 2 Tim. 3:6.   ᵂ 1 John 4:6.   ˣ 1 Cor. 1:27.

ʸ Acts 26:24. Wisdom 5:4. *We fools thought his life madness.*

ᶻ Mercurius Trismegistus, *Concerning Thought and Sense Perception, to Asclepius* [ed. 1924, 1:178–179, 181]. See Lactantius on justice, Bk 5, ch. 16 [or 17, of *The Divine Institutes*].

the sentence of the world have been judged to be out of their right minds. When instruction doth them no good, let them feel but the least [3.15] degree of most mercifully tempered severity, they fasten on the head of the Lord's vicegerents here on earth whatsoever they anywhere find uttered against the cruelty of bloodthirsty men, and to themselves they draw all the sentences which scripture hath in the favour of innocence persecuted for the truth; yea, they are of their due and deserved sufferings no less proud, than those ancient disturbers, to whom St. Augustine writeth, saying: *ªMartyrs rightly so named are they not which suffer for their disorder, and for the ungodly breach they have made of christian unity, but which for righteousness' sake are persecuted. For Hagar also suffered persecution at the hands of Sarah, wherein, she which did impose was holy, and she unrighteous which did bear the burden. In like sort, with thieves was the Lord himself crucified, but they who were matched in the pain which they suffered, were in the cause of their suffering disjoined. If that must needs be the true Church which doth endure persecution, and not that which persecuteth, let them ask of the Apostle what Church Sarah did represent, when she held her maid in affliction. For even our mother which is free, the heavenly Jerusalem, that is to say the true Church of God was, as he doth affirm, prefigured in that very woman by whom the bondmaid was so sharply handled. Although, if all things be thoroughly scanned, she did in truth more persecute Sarah by proud resistance, than Sarah her, by severity of punishment.* These are the paths wherein ye have walked that [3.16] are of the ordinary sort of men, these are the very steps ye have trodden, and the manifest degrees whereby ye are of your guides and directors trained up in that school: a custom of inuring your ears with reproof of faults especially in your governors; an use to attribute those faults to the kind of spiritual regiment under which ye live; boldness in warranting the force of their discipline for the cure of all such evils; a slight of framing your conceipts to imagine that Scripture everywhere favoureth that discipline; persuasion that the cause why ye find it in Scripture is the illumination of the spirit, that the same Spirit is a seal unto you of your nearness unto God, that ye are by all means to nourish and witness it in yourselves, and to strengthen on every side your minds against whatsoever might be of force to withdraw you from it.

ª Augustine, Epistle 50 [*PL*, 33:796–797; *NI*, 4:636–637; *FOTC*, 30:149–151].

What hath caused so many of the learneder sort
to approve the same discipline.

[4.1] *4.* Wherefore to come unto you whose judgement is a lantern of direction for all the rest, you that frame thus the people's hearts, not altogether (as I willingly persuade myself) of a politic intent or purpose, but yourselves being first overborn with the weight of greater men's judgements: on your shoulders is laid the burden of upholding the cause by argument. For which purpose sentences out of the word of God ye allege diverse: but so, that when the same are discussed, thus it always in a manner falleth out, that what things by virtue thereof ye urge upon us as altogether necessary, are found to be thence collected only by poor and marvelous slight conjectures. I need not give instance in any one sentence so alleged, for that I think the instance in any alleged otherwise a thing not easy to be given. A very strange thing sure it were that such a discipline as ye speak of should be taught by Christ and his Apostles in the word of God, and no Church ever have found it out, nor received it till this present time; contrariwise, the government against which ye bend yourselves be observed everywhere throughout all generations and ages of the Christian world, no Church ever perceiving the word of God to be against it. We require you to find out but one Church upon the face of the whole earth, that hath been ordered by your discipline, or hath not been ordered by ours, that is to say, by episcopal regiment, since the time that the blessed
[4.2] Apostles were here conversant. Many things out of antiquity ye bring, as if the purest times of the Church had observed the selfsame orders which you require; and as though your desire were, that the Churches of old should be patterns for us to follow, and even glasses, wherein we might see the practice of that which by you is gathered out of scripture. But the truth is ye mean nothing less. All this is done for fashion's sake only: for ye complain of it as of an injury, that men should be willed to seek for examples and patterns of government in any of those times that have been before. *b*Ye plainly hold that from the very Apostles' times till this present

b T.C., Bk I, p. 97 [*W*, 2:181–184].

age wherein yourselves imagine ye have found out a right pattern of sound discipline, there never was any time safe to be followed. Which thing ye thus endeavour to prove. Out of Egesippus ye say that ᶜEusebius writeth, how although as long as the Apostles lived, the Church did remain a pure virgin, yet after the death of the Apostles, and after they were once gone whom God vouchsafed to make hearers of the divine wisdom with their own ears, the placing of wicked error began to come into the Church. ᵈClement also in a certain place, to confirm that there was corruption of doctrine immediately after the Apostles' times, allegeth the proverb, that *There are few sons like their fathers.* ᵉSocrates saith of the Church of Rome and Alexandria, the most famous Churches in the Apostles' times, that about the year 430 the Roman and Alexandrian Bishops leaving the sacred function, were degenerate to a secular rule or dominion. Hereupon ye conclude, that it is not safe to fetch our government from any other than the Apostles' times. Wherein by the way it [4.3] may be noted, that in proposing the Apostles' times as a pattern for the Church to follow, though the desire of you all be one, the drift and purpose of you all is not one. The chiefest thing which lay reformers yawn for is, that the Clergy may through conformity in state and condition be Apostolical, poor as the Apostles of Christ were poor. In which one circumstance if they imagine so great perfection, they must think that Church which hath such store of mendicant Friars, a Church in that respect most happy. Were it for the glory of God and the good of his Church indeed that the Clergy should be left even as bare as the Apostles when they had neither staff nor scrip, that God which should lay upon them the condition of his Apostles, would I hope, endow them with the selfsame affection which was in that holy Apostle whose words concerning his own right virtuous contentment of heart, ᶠ*As well how to want as how to abound*, are a most fit episcopal emprese. The Church of Christ is a body mystical. A body cannot stand, unless the parts thereof be proportionable. Let it therefore be required on both parts, at the hands of the Clergy, to be in meanness of state like the Apostles; at the hands of the laity to be as they were who lived under the Apostles: and in this reformation there will be though little wisdom,

---

ᶜ Eusebius, *Ecclesiastical History*, Bk 3, ch. 32.
ᵈ Clement of Alexandria, *Miscellanies*, somewhat after the beginning.
ᵉ Socrates, *Ecclesiastical History*, Bk 7, ch. 11.   ᶠ Philip. 4:12.

[4.4] yet some indifferency. But your reformation which are of the Clergy (if yet it displease you not that I should say ye are of the Clergy) seemeth to aim at a broader mark. Ye think that he which will perfectly reform, must bring the form of Church discipline unto the state which then it was at. A thing neither possible, nor certain, nor absolutely convenient. Concerning the first, what was used in the Apostles' times, the scripture fully declareth not, so that making their times the rule and canon of Church polity, ye make a rule which being not possible to be fully known, is as impossible to be kept. Again, since the later even of the Apostles' own times had that which in the former was not thought upon, in this general proposing of the Apostolical times, there is no certainty which should be followed, especially seeing that ye give us great cause to doubt how far ye allow those times. For albeit the loover of Antichristian building were not, ye say, as then set up, yet the foundations thereof were secretly and under the ground laid in the Apostles' times: so that all other times ye plainly reject, and the Apostles' own times ye approve with marvelous great suspicion, leaving it intricate and doubtful, wherein we are to keep ourselves unto the pattern of their times. Thirdly, whereas it is the error of the common multitude to consider only what hath been of old, and, if the same were well, to see whether still it continue; if not, to condemn that presently which is, and never to search upon what ground or consideration the change might grow: such rudeness cannot be in you so well borne with, whom learning and judgement hath enabled much more soundly to discern how far the times of the Church, and the orders thereof may alter without offence. True it is, *g*the ancienter, the better ceremonies of religion are; howbeit, not absolutely true and without exception, but true only so far forth as those different ages do agree in the state of those things for which at the first those rites, orders, and ceremonies, were instituted. In the Apostles' times that was harmless, which being now revived, would be scandalous, as their *h*oscula sancta. Those *i*feasts of charity, which being insti-

---

g Arnobius, p. 746 [Minucius Felix, *Octavius*; *L*, pp. 328–329].

h Rom. 16:16. 2 Cor. 13:12. 1 Thess. 5:26. 1 Pet. 5:14. In their meetings to serve God, their manner was in the end to salute one another with a kiss, using these words, *Peace be with you*. For which cause Tertullian doth call it *signaculum orationis, the seale of prayer. On Prayer* [*ANF*, 3:686].

i Jude, verse 12. Concerning which feasts, St. Chrysostom says, *On stated days, they*

tuted by the Apostles, were retained in the Church long after, are not now thought anywhere needful. What man is there of understanding, unto whom it is not manifest how the way of providing for the Clergy by tithes, the device of alms-houses for the poor, the sorting out of the people into their several parishes, together with sundry other things which the Apostles' times could not have, (being now established) are much more convenient and fit for the Church of Christ, than if the same should be taken away for conformity's sake with the ancientest and first times? The orders there- [4.5] fore which were observed in the Apostles' times, are not to be urged as a rule universally either sufficient or necessary. If they be, nevertheless on your part it still remaineth to be better proved, that the form of discipline which ye entitle Apostolical, was in the Apostles' times exercised. For of this very thing ye fail even touching that which ye make most account of, as being matter of substance in discipline, I mean the power of your lay-elders, and the difference of your Doctors from the Pastors in all Churches. So that in sum, we may be bold to conclude, that besides these last times, which for insolence, pride, and egregious contempt of all good order are the worst, there are none wherein ye can truly affirm, that the complete form of your discipline, or the substance thereof was practised. The evidence therefore of antiquity failing you, ye fly to the judge- [4.6] ments of such learned men, as seem by their writings to be of opinion that all Christian Churches should receive your discipline, and abandon ours. Wherein, as ye heap up the names of a number of men not unworthy to be had in honor, so there are a number whom when ye mention, although it serve you to purpose with the ignorant and vulgar sort, who measure by tale and not by weight, yet surely they who know what quality and value the men are of, will think ye draw very near the dregs. But were they all of as great account as the best and chiefest amongst them, with us notwithstanding neither are they, neither ought they to be of such reckoning, that their opinion or conjecture should cause the laws of the Church

made the table common, and when the liturgical service was completed, after the communion of the mysteries, they would begin a feast, with the rich, indeed, supplying foods, and with the poor and those who had nothing being, contrariwise, invited. Homilies on 1 Corinthians, 27 [PG, 61:223–224; Nr, 12:157]. Of the same feasts in like sort Tertullian, *Our dinner exhibits its nature in its name. For it is called* ἀγάπη, *which is, among the Greeks, love. However great the expense may be, it is reckoned a gain in the name of piety.* Apology, ch. 39 [PL, 1:538; ANF, 3:47].

of England to give place. Much less when they neither do all agree in that opinion, and of them which are at agreement, the most part through a courteous inducement have followed one man as their guide, finally that one therein not unlikely to have swerved. If any chance to say it is probable that in the Apostles' times there were lay-elders, or not to mislike the continuance of them in the Church, or to affirm that Bishops at the first were a name, but not a power distinct from presbyters, or to speak anything in praise of those Churches which are without episcopal regiment, or to reprove the fault of such as abuse that calling, all these ye register for men, persuaded as you are, that every christian Church standeth bound by the law of God to put down Bishops, and in their rooms to erect an Eldership so authorized as you would have it for the government of each parish. Deceived greatly they are therefore, who think that all they whose names are cited amongst the favourers of this

[4.7] cause, are on any such verdict agreed. Yet touching some material points of your discipline, a kind of agreement we grant there is amongst many Divines of reformed Churches abroad. For first to do as the Church of Geneva did, the learned in some other Churches must needs be the more willing, who having used in like manner not the slow and tedious help of proceeding by public authority, but the people's more quick endeavour for alteration, in such an exigency I see not well how they could have stayed to deliberate about any other regiment than that which already was devised to their hands, that which in like case had been taken, that which was easiest to be established without delay, that which was likeliest to content the people by reason of some kind of sway which it giveth them. When therefore the example of one Church was thus at the first almost through a kind of constraint or necessity followed by many, their concurrence in persuasion about some material points belonging to the same polity is not strange. For we are not to marvel greatly, if they which have all done the same thing, do easily embrace

[4.8] the same opinion as concerning their own doings. Besides, mark I beseech you that which Galen in matter of philosophy noteth, for the like falleth out even in questions of higher knowledge. *j*It fareth many times with men's opinions as with rumors and reports. That which a credible person telleth is easily thought probable by

---

j Galen, *Concerning the Diagnosis and Cure of the Errors of Every Soul* [ed. 1965, 5:96–97].

such as are well persuaded of him. But if two, or three, or four, agree all in the same tale, they judge it then to be out of controversy, and so are many times overtaken, for want of due consideration; either some common cause leading them all into error, or one man's oversight deceiving many through their too much credulity and easiness of belief. Though ten persons be brought to give testimony in any cause, yet if the knowledge they have of the thing whereunto they come as witnesses appear to have grown from some one amongst them, and to have spread itself from hand to hand, they all are in force but as one testimony. Nor is it otherwise here where the daughter Churches do speak their mother's dialect, here where so many sing one song, by reason that he is the guide of the choir concerning whose deserved authority amongst even the gravest divines, we have already spoken at large. Will ye ask what should move those many learned to be followers of one man's judgement, no necessity of argument forcing them thereunto? [k]your demand is answered by yourselves. Loath ye are to think that they whom ye judge to have attained as sound knowledge in all points of doctrine, as any since the Apostles' time should mistake in discipline. Such is naturally our affection, that whom in great things we mightily admire; in them we are not persuaded willingly that anything should be amiss. The reason whereof is, [l]for that as dead flies putrify the ointment of the Apothecary, so a little folly him that is in estimation for wisdom. This in every profession hath too much authorized the judgements of a few. This with Germans hath caused Luther, and with many other Churches, Calvin to prevail in all things. Yet are we not able to define, whether the wisdom of that God (who setteth before us in holy Scripture so many admirable patterns of virtue, and no one of them without somewhat noted wherein they were culpable, to the end that to him alone it might always be acknowledged, *Thou only art holy thou only art just*) might not permit those worthy vessels of his glory to be in some things blemished with the stain of human frailty, even for this cause, lest we should esteem of any man above that which behoveth.

---

[k] *A Petition to her Majesty* [STC 1521], p. 14.   [l] Eccles. 10:1.

Their calling for trial by disputation.

[5.1] 5. Notwithstanding, as though ye were able to say a great deal more than hitherto your books have revealed to the world, earnest challengers ye are of trial by some public disputation. Wherein if the thing ye crave be no more than only leave to dispute openly about those matters that are in question, the schools in Universities (for anything I know) are open unto you: they have their yearly Acts and Commencements, besides other disputations both ordinary and upon occasion, wherein the several parts of our own Ecclesiastical discipline are oftentimes offered unto that kind of examination; the learnedest of you have been of late years noted seldom or never absent from thence at the time of those greater assemblies; and the favor of proposing there in convenient sort whatsoever ye can object (which thing myself have known them to grant of Scholastical courtesy unto strangers) neither hath (as I think) nor ever will (I [5.2] presume) be denied you. If your suit be to have some great extraordinary confluence, in expectation whereof the laws that already are should sleep and have no power over you, till in the hearing of thousands ye all did acknowledge your error and renounce the further prosecution of your cause; happily they whose authority is required unto the satisfying of your demand, do think it both dangerous to admit such concourse of divided minds, and unmeet that laws which being once solemnly established, are to exact obedience of all men, and to constrain thereunto, should so far stoop as to hold themselves in suspense from taking any effect upon you, till some disputer can persuade you to be obedient. A law is the deed of the whole body politic, whereof if ye judge yourselves to be any part, then is the law even your deed also. And were it reason in things of this quality to give men audience pleading for the overthrow of that which their own very deed hath ratified? Laws that have been approved may be (no man doubteth) again repealed, and to that end also disputed against, by the authors thereof themselves. But this is when the whole doth deliberate what laws each part shall observe, and not when a part refuseth the laws which the [5.3] whole hath orderly agreed upon. Notwithstanding, forasmuch as the cause we maintain is (God be thanked) such as needeth not to shun any trial, might it please them on whose approbation the matter dependeth to condescend so far unto you in this behalf, I wish heartily that proof were made even by solemn conference in orderly and quiet sort, whether you would yourselves be satisfied, or else could by satisfying others draw them to your part. Provided always, first inasmuch as ye go about to destroy a thing which is in force, and to draw in that which hath not as yet been received; to impose on us that which we think not ourselves bound unto, and to overthrow those things whereof we are possessed; that therefore ye are not to claim in any such conference other than the plaintiff's or opponent's part, which must consist altogether in proof and confirmation of two things, the one, that our orders by you condemned we ought to abolish, the other that yours, we are bound to accept in the stead thereof: secondly, because the questions in controversy between us are many, if once we descend unto particularities, that for the easier and more orderly proceeding therein, the most general be first discussed, nor any question left off, nor in each question the prosecution of any one argument given over and another taken in hand, till the issue whereunto by replies and answers both parts are come be collected, read and acknowledged as well on the one side as on the other to be the plain conclusion which they are grown unto: thirdly for avoiding of the manifold inconveniences whereunto ordinary and extemporal disputes are subject, as also because if ye should singly dispute one by one, as every man's own wit did best serve, it might be conceived by the rest that happily some other would have done more, the chiefest of you do all agree in this action, that whom ye shall then choose your speaker, by him that which is publicly brought into disputation be acknowledged by all your consents not to be his allegation but yours, such as ye all are agreed upon, and have required him to deliver in all your names; the true copy whereof being taken by a notary, that a reasonable time be allowed for return of answer unto you in the like form. Fourthly, whereas a number of conferences have been had in other causes with the less effectual success, by reason of partial and untrue reports published afterwards unto the world, that to prevent this evil, there be at the first a solemn declaration made on both parts of their agreement to have that very book and no other set abroad, wherein their present authorized notaries do write those things fully and only, which being written and there read, are by their own open testimony acknowledged to be their own. Other circumstances hereunto belonging, whether for the choice of time, place, and language, or for prevention of impertinent and needless speech, or to any end and purpose else, they may be thought on when occasion serveth. In this sort to broach my private conceit for the ordering of a public action, I should be loath (albeit I do it not otherwise than under correction of them whose gravity and wisdom ought in such cases to overrule) but that so venturous boldness I see is a thing now general, and am thereby of good hope, that where all men are licensed to offend, no man will show himself a sharp accuser.

No end of contention without submission of both parts unto some definitive sentence.

[6.1] 6. What success God may give unto any such kind of conference or disputation, we cannot tell. But of this we are right sure, that nature, scripture, and experience itself, have all taught the world to seek for the ending of contentions by submitting itself unto some judicial and definitive sentence, whereunto neither part that contendeth may under any pretense or color refuse to stand. This must needs be effectual and strong. As for other means without this, they seldom prevail. I would therefore know whether for the ending of these irksome strifes wherein you and your followers do stand thus formally divided against the authorized guides of this Church, and the rest of the people subject unto their charge, whether I say ye be content to refer your cause to any other higher judgement than your own, or else intend to persist and proceed as ye have begun, till yourselves can be persuaded to condemn yourselves. If your determination be this, we can be but sorry that ye should deserve to be reckoned with such, of whom God himself pronounceth, *"The*
[6.2] *way of peace they have not known.* Ways of peaceable conclusion there are, but these two certain: the one, a sentence of judicial decision given by authority thereto appointed within ourselves; the other, the like kind of sentence given by a more universal authority. The former of which two ways God himself in the law prescribeth; and his Spirit it was which directed the very first Christian Churches

" Rom. 3:17.

in the world to use the latter. The ordinance of God in the law was this. *"If there arise a matter too hard for thee in judgement between blood and blood, between plea etc. then shalt thou arise, and go up unto the place which the Lord thy God shall choose, and thou shalt come unto the Priests of the Levites, and unto the Judge that shall be in those days, and ask, and they shall show thee the sentence of judgement, and thou shalt do according to that thing which they of that place which the Lord hath chosen show thee, and thou shalt observe to do according to all that they inform thee, according to the law which they shall teach thee, and according to the judgement which they shall tell thee shalt thou do, thou shalt not decline from the thing which they shall show thee to the right hand nor to the left. And that man that will do presumptuously, not hearkening unto the Priest (that standeth before the Lord thy God to minister there) or unto the Judge, that man shall die, and thou shalt take away evil from Israel.* When there grew in the Church of Christ a question, *°Whether the Gentiles believing might be saved, although they were not circumcised after the manner of Moses, nor did observe the rest of those legal rites and ceremonies whereunto the Jews were bound;* After great dissension and disputation about it, their conclusion in the end was, to have it determined by sentence at Jerusalem: which was accordingly done in a Council there assembled for the same purpose. Are ye able to allege any just and sufficient cause wherefore absolutely ye should not condescend in this controversy to have your judgements overruled by some such definitive sentence, whether it fall out to be given with or against you, that so these tedious contentions may cease? Ye will perhaps make answer, that [6.3] being persuaded already as touching the truth of your cause, ye are not to hearken unto any sentence, no not though Angels should define otherwise, as the blessed Apostle's own example teacheth; again that men, yea, Councils may err; and that, unless the judgement given do satisfy your minds, unless it be such as ye can by no further argument oppugn; in a word, unless you perceive and acknowledge it yourselves consonant with God's word, to stand unto it not allowing it, were to sin against your own consciences. But consider I beseech you first as touching the Apostle, how that wherein he was so resolute and peremptory, our Lord Jesus Christ made manifest unto him even by intuitive revelation, wherein there

---

ⁿ Deut. 17:8.   *°* Acts 15.

was no possibility of error. That which you are persuaded of, ye have it no otherwise than by your own only probable collection, and therefore such bold asseverations as in him were admirable, should in your mouths but argue rashness. God was not ignorant that the Priests and Judges, whose sentence in matters of controversy he ordained should stand, both might and oftentimes would be deceived in their judgement. Howbeit, better it was in the eye of his understanding, that sometime an erroneous sentence definitive should prevail, till the same authority perceiving such oversight, might afterwards correct or reverse it, than that strifes should have respite to grow, and not come speedily unto some end. Neither wish we that men should do anything which in their hearts they are persuaded they ought not to do, but this persuasion ought (we say) to be fully settled in their hearts, that in litigious and contro-versed causes of such quality, the will of God is to have them do whatsoever the sentence of judicial and final decision shall deter-mine, yea, though it seem in their private opinion to swerve utterly from that which is right: as no doubt many times the sentence amongst the Jews did seem unto one part or other contending, and yet in this case God did then allow them to do that which in their private judgement it seemed, yea and perhaps truly seemed that the law did disallow. For if God be not the author of confusion but of peace, then can he not be the author of our refusal, but of our contentment, to stand unto some definitive sentence, without which almost impossible it is that either we should avoid confusion, or ever hope to attain peace. To small purpose had the Council of Jerusalem been assembled, if once their determination being set down, men might afterwards have defended their former opinions. When therefore they had given their definitive sentence, all contro-versy was at an end. Things were disputed before they came to be determined; men afterwards were not to dispute any longer, but to obey. The sentence of judgement finished their strife, which their disputes before judgement could not do. This was ground sufficient for any reasonable man's conscience to build the duty of obedience upon, whatsoever his own opinion were as touching the matter before in question. So full of wilfulness and self-liking is our nature, that without some definitive sentence, which being given may stand, and a necessity of silence on both sides afterward imposed, small hope there is that strifes thus far prosecuted, will

in short time quietly end. Now it were in vain to ask you whether [6.4]
ye could be content that the sentence of any Court already erected,
should be so far authorized, as that among the Jews established
by God himself, for the determining of all controversies: *That man
which will do presumptuously not hearkening unto the Priest that standeth
before the Lord to minister there, nor unto the Judge, let him die.* Ye
have given us already to understand, what your opinion is in part
concerning her sacred Majesty's Court of high Commission, the
nature whereof is the same with that amongst the Jews, albeit the
power be not so great. The other way happily may like you better,
because [p]Master Beza in his last book save one written about these
matters, professeth himself to be now weary of such combats and
encounters, whether by word or writing, inasmuch as he findeth
that controversies thereby are made but brawls, and therefore
wisheth *that in some common lawful assembly of Churches, all these
strifes may at once be decided.* Shall there be then in the meanwhile no [6.5]
doings? Yes. There are [q]*the weightier matters of the law, judgement
and mercy and fidelity.* These things we ought to do; and these things,
while we contend about less, we leave undone. Happier are they
whom the Lord when he cometh, shall find *doing* in these things,
than disputing about *Doctors, Elders,* and *Deacons.* Or if there be
no remedy but somewhat needs ye must do which may tend to the
setting forward of your discipline; do that which wise men, who
think some Statute of the realm more fit to be repealed, than to
stand in force, are accustomed to do before they come to Parliament
where the place of enacting is; that is to say, spend the time in
reexamining more duly your cause, and in more thoroughly considering of that which ye labour to overthrow. As for the orders
which are established, since equity and reason, the law of nature,
God and man, do all favour that which is in being, till orderly judgement of decision be given against it; it is but justice to exact of you,
and perverseness in you it should be to deny thereunto your willing
obedience. Not that I judge it a thing allowable for men to observe [6.6]
those laws which in their hearts they are steadfastly persuaded to
be against the law of God: but your persuasion in this case ye are
all bound for the time to suspend, and in otherwise doing, ye offend

---

[p] Beza, *Tract on Excommunication and the Presbytery*, Preface.
[q] Matt. 23:23.

against God by troubling his Church without any just or necessary cause. Be it that there are some reasons inducing you to think hardly of our laws. Are those reasons demonstrative, are they necessary, or but mere probabilities only? An argument necessary and demonstrative is such, as being proposed unto any man and understood, the mind cannot choose but inwardly assent. Any one such reason dischargeth, I grant the conscience, and setteth it at full liberty. For the public approbation given by the body of this whole Church unto those things which are established, doth make it but probable that they are good. And therefore unto a necessary proof that they are not good, it must give place. But if the skilfullest amongst you can show that all the books ye have hitherto written be able to afford any one argument of this nature, let the instance be given. As for probabilities, what thing was there ever set down so agreeable with sound reason, but some probable show against it might be made? Is it meet that when publicly things are received, and have taken place, general obedience thereunto should cease to be exacted, in case this or that private person led with some probable conceipt, should make open protestation, *I Peter or John disallow them, and pronounce them nought?* In which case your answer will be, that concerning the laws of our Church, they are not only condemned in *'the opinion of a private man, but of thousands,* yea and even *of those amongst which divers are in public charge and authority.* As though when public consent of the whole hath established anything, every man's judgement being thereunto compared, were not private, howsoever his calling be to some kind of public charge. So that of peace and quietness there is not any way possible, unless the probable voice of every entire society or body politic overrule all private of like nature in the same body. Which thing effectually proveth, that God being author of peace and not of confusion in the Church, must needs be author of those men's peaceable resolutions, who concerning these things, have determined with themselves to think and do as the Church they are of decreeth, till they see necessary cause enforcing them to the contrary.

<hr />

' T.C., Bk 2, p. 181.

The matter contained in these eight books.

7. Nor is mine own intent any other in these several books of dis- [7.1]
course, than to make it appear unto you, that for the ecclesiastical
laws of this land, we are led by great reason to observe them, and
ye by no necessity bound to impugn them. It is no part of my secret
meaning to draw you hereby into hatred or to set upon the face
of this cause any fairer glass, than the naked truth doth afford:
but my whole endeavour is to resolve the conscience, and to show
as near as I can what in this controversy the heart is to think, if
it will follow the light of sound and sincere judgement, without
either cloud of prejudice, or mist of passionate affection. Wherefore [7.2]
seeing that laws and ordinances in particular, whether such as we
observe, or such as yourselves would have established; when the
mind doth sift and examine them, it must needs have often recourse
to a number of doubts and questions about the nature, kinds, and
qualities of laws in general, whereof unless it be thoroughly
informed, there will appear no certainty to stay our persuasion upon:
I have for that cause set down in the first place an introduction
on both sides needful to be considered. Declaring therein what
law is, how different kinds of laws there are, and what force they
are of according unto each kind. This done, because ye suppose [7.3]
the laws for which ye strive are found in scripture; but those not,
against which ye strive; and upon this surmise are drawn to hold
it as the very main pillar of your whole cause, that *scripture ought
to be the only rule of all our actions*, and consequently that the Church-
orders which we observe being not commanded in scripture, are
offensive and displeasant unto God: I have spent the second book
in sifting of this point, which standeth with you for the first and
chiefest principle whereon ye build. Whereunto the next in degree [7.4]
is, that as God will have always a Church upon earth while the
world doth continue, and that Church stand in need of government,
of which government it behoveth himself to be both the author and
teacher: so it cannot stand with duty that man should ever presume
in any wise to change and alter the same; and therefore *That in
Scripture there must of necessity be found some particular form of polity
Ecclesiastical, the laws whereof admit not any kind of alteration.* The [7.5]

33

first three books being thus ended, the fourth proceedeth from the general grounds and foundations of your cause unto your general accusations against us, as having in the orders of our Church (for so you pretend) *corrupted the right form of Church polity with manifold popish rites and ceremonies, which certain reformed Churches have banished from amongst them, and have thereby given us such example as* (you think) *we ought to follow.* This your assertion hath herein drawn us to make search, whether these be just exceptions against the customs of our Church, when ye plead that they are the same which the Church of Rome hath, or that they are not the same

[7.6] which some other reformed Churches have devised. Of those four books which remain and are bestowed about the specialities of that cause which lieth in controversy, the first examineth the causes by you alleged, wherefore the public duties of Christian religion, as our prayers our Sacraments and the rest, should not be ordered in such sort as with us they are; nor that power whereby the persons of men are consecrated unto the ministry, be disposed of in such manner as the laws of this Church do allow. The second and third are concerning the power of jurisdiction: the one, whether laymen, such as your governing Elders are, ought in all congregations forever to be invested with that power; the other, whether Bishops may have that power over other Pastors, and therewithal that honour which with us they have. And because besides the power of order which all consecrated persons have, and the power of jurisdiction which neither they all nor they only have, there is a third power, a power of Ecclesiastical Dominion, communicable as we think, unto persons not Ecclesiastical, and most fit to be restrained unto the Prince or Sovereign commander over the whole body politic: the eighth book we have allotted unto this question, and have sifted therein your objections against those preeminences royal which thereunto

[7.7] appertain. Thus have I laid before you the brief of these my travails, and presented under your view the limbs of that cause litigious between us: the whole entire body whereof being thus compact, it shall be no troublesome thing for any man to find each particular controversy's resting place, and the coherence it hath with those things, either on which it dependeth, or which depend on it.

How just cause there is to fear the manifold dangerous events likely to ensue upon this intended reformation, if it did take place.

8. The case so standing therefore my brethren as it doth, the wisdom [8.1] of governors ye must not blame, in that they further also forecasting the manifold strange and dangerous innovations which are more than likely to follow if your discipline should take place, have for that cause thought it hitherto a part of their duty to withstand your endeavors that way. The rather, for that they have seen already some small beginnings of the fruits thereof, in them who concurring with you in judgement about the necessity of that discipline, have adventured without more ado, to separate themselves from the rest of the Church, and to put your speculations in execution. These men's hastiness the warier sort of you doth not commend, ye wish they had held themselves longer in, and not so dangerously flown abroad before the feathers of the cause had been grown, their error with merciful terms ye reprove naming them in great commiseration of mind, your *poor brethren*. They on the contrary side more bitterly accuse you as their *false brethren*, and against you they plead saying: "From your breasts it is that we have sucked those things which when ye delivered unto us ye termed that heavenly, ʿsincere, and wholesome milk of God's word, howsoever ye now abhor as poison that which the virtue thereof hath wrought and brought forth in us. You sometime our ʿcompanions, guides and familiars, with whom we have had most sweet consultations, are now become our professed adversaries, because we think the statute-congregations in England to be no true Christian Churches; because we have severed ourselves from them; and because without their leave or licence that are in Civil authority, we have secretly framed our own Churches according to the platform of the word of God. For of that point between you and us there is no controversy. Alas what would ye have us to do? At such time as ye were content to accept us in the number of your own, your teachings we heard, we read your writings: and though we would, yet able we are not to forget with what zeal ye have ever professed, that in the English congre-

ˢ 1 Pet. 2:2.   ʿ Ps. 55:13.

gations (for so many of them as be ordered according unto their own laws) the very public service of God is fraught, as touching matter with heaps of intolerable pollutions, and, as concerning form, borrowed from the shop of Antichrist; hateful both ways in the eyes of the most holy: the kind of their government by Bishops and Archbishops Antichristian; "that discipline which Christ hath essentially tied, that is to say, so united unto his Church, that we cannot account it really to be his Church which hath not in it the same discipline, that very discipline no less there despised, than in the highest throne of Antichrist; all such parts of the word of God as do any way concern that discipline no less unsoundly taught and interpreted by all authorized English Pastors, than by Antichrist's factors themselves; at baptism crossing, at the supper of the Lord kneeling, at both a number of other the most notorious badges of Antichristian recognisance usual. Being moved with these and the like your effectual discourses, whereunto we gave most attentive ear, till they entered even into our souls, and were as fire within our bosoms; we thought we might hereof be bold to conclude, that since no such Antichristian synagogue may be accounted a true Church of Christ, you by accusing all congregations ordered according to the laws of England as Antichristian, did mean to condemn those congregations, as not being any of them worthy the name of a true Christian Church. Ye tell us now it is not your meaning. But what meant your often threatenings of them, who professing themselves the inhabitants of mount Sion, were too loath to depart wholly as they should out of Babylon? Whereat our hearts being fearfully troubled, we durst not, we durst not continue longer so near her confines, lest her plagues might suddenly overtake us, before we did cease to be partakers with her sins: for so we could not choose but acknowledge with grief that we were, when, they doing evil, we by our presence in their assemblies seemed to like thereof, or at leastwise not so earnestly to dislike, as became men heartily zealous of God's glory. For adventuring to erect the discipline of Christ without the leave of the Christian Magistrate, happily ye may condemn us as fools, in that we hazard thereby our estates and persons, further than you which are that way more wise think necessary: but of any offence or sin therein committed against God,

u Preface against Dr. Bancroft [*STC* 19603, sig. A3ᵛ–A4ʳ].

with what conscience can you accuse us, when your own positions are, that the things we observe should every of them be dearer unto us than ten thousand lives; that they are the peremptory commandments of God; that no mortal man can dispense with them, and that the Magistrate grievously sinneth in not constraining thereunto? Will ye blame any man for doing that of his own accord, which all men should be compelled to do that are not willing of themselves? When God commandeth, shall we answer that we will obey, if so be Cæsar will grant us leave? Is discipline an Ecclesiastical matter or a Civil? If an Ecclesiastical, it must of necessity belong to the duty of the Minister. And the Minister (you say) holdeth all his authority of doing whatsoever belongeth unto the spiritual charge of the house of God even immediately from God himself, without dependency upon any Magistrate. Whereupon it followeth, as we suppose, that the hearts of the people being willing to be under the Scepter of Christ, the minister of God, into whose hands the Lord himself hath put that Scepter, is without all excuse if thereby he guide them not. Nor do we find that hitherto greatly ye have disliked those Churches abroad where the people with direction of their godly ministers have even against the will of the Magistrate brought in either the doctrine or discipline of Jesus Christ. For which cause we must now think the very same thing of you, which our Saviour did sometime utter concerning falsehearted Scribes and Pharisees, *ʷThey say and do not.*" Thus the foolish Barrowist deriveth his schism by way of conclusion, as to him it seemeth, directly and plainly out of your principles. Him therefore we leave to be satisfied by you from whom he hath sprung. And if such [8.2] by your own acknowledgement be persons dangerous, although as yet the alterations which they have made are of small and tender growth; the changes likely to ensue throughout all states and vocations within this land, in case your desire should take place, must be thought upon. First concerning the supreme power of the highest, they are no small prerogatives which now thereunto belonging the form of your discipline will constrain it to resign, as in the last book of this treatise we have showed at large. Again it may justly be feared whether our English Nobility, when the matter came in trial, would contentedly suffer themselves to be always at the

ᵛ Matt. 23:3.

call, and to stand to the sentence of a number of mean persons assisted with the presence of their poor teacher, a man (as sometimes it happeneth) though better able to speak, yet little or no whit apter to judge than the rest: from whom, be their dealings never so absurd (unless it be by way of complaint to a Synod) no appeal may be made unto anyone of higher power, inasmuch as the order of your discipline admitteth no standing inequality of Courts, no spiritual judge to have any ordinary superior on earth, but as many suprema-[8.3] cies as there are parishes and several Congregations. Neither is it altogether without cause that so many do fear the overthrow of all learning as a threatened sequel of this your intended discipline. For if the *ʷworld's preservation* depend upon *the multitude of the wise;* and of that sort the number hereafter be not likely to wax over great, *when* (that wherewith the son of Sirach professeth himself *ˣat the heart grieved) men of understanding are* already so *little set by:* how should their minds whom the love of so precious a jewel filleth with secret jealousy even in regard of the least things which may any way hinder the flourishing estate thereof, choose but misdoubt lest this discipline, which always you match with divine doctrine as her natural and true sister, be found unto all kinds of knowledge a stepmother; seeing that the greatest worldly hopes, which are proposed unto the chiefest kind of learning, ye seek utterly to extirpate as weeds, and have grounded your platform on such propositions as do after a sort undermine those most renowned habitations, where through the goodness of almighty God all commendable arts and sciences are with exceeding great industry hitherto (and so may they forever continue) studied, proceeded in, and professed. To charge you as purposely bent to the overthrow of that wherein so many of you have attained no small perfection, were injurious. Only therefore I wish that yourselves did well consider how opposite certain your positions are unto the state of Collegiate societies, whereon the two Universities consist. Those degrees which their statutes bind them to take, are by your laws taken away; yourselves who have sought them ye so excuse, as that ye would have men to think ye judge them not allowable, but tolerable only, and to be borne with, for some help which ye find in them unto the furtherance of your purposes, till the corrupt estate of the Church

ʷ Wisdom 6:24.　　ˣ Ecclus. 26:29 [28].

38

may be better reformed. Your laws forbidding Ecclesiastical persons utterly the exercise of Civil power must needs deprive the Heads and Masters in the same Colleges of all such authority as now they exercise, either at home by punishing the faults of those, who not as children to their parents by the law of Nature, but altogether by civil authority are subject unto them: or abroad by keeping Courts amongst their tenants. Your laws making permanent inequality amongst Ministers a thing repugnant to the word of God, enforce those Colleges, the Seniors wherof are all or any part of them Ministers under the government of a master in the same vocation, to choose as oft as they meet together a new president. For if so ye judge it necessary to do in Synods, for the avoiding of permanent inequality amongst Ministers, the same cause must needs even in these Collegiate assemblies enforce the like. Except peradventure ye mean to avoid all such absurdities, by dissolving those Corporations, and by bringing the Universities unto the form of the School of Geneva. Which thing men the rather are inclined to look for, inasmuch as the Ministry, whereinto their founders with singular providence have by the same statutes appointed them necessarily to enter at a certain time, your laws bind them much more necessarily to forbear, till some parish abroad call for them. [y]Your [8.4] opinion concerning the law Civil is that the knowledge thereof might be spared, as a thing which this land doth not need. Professors in that kind being few ye are the bolder to spurn at them, and not to dissemble your minds as concerning their removal: in whose studies although myself have not much been conversant, nevertheless exceeding great cause I see there is to wish that thereunto more encouragement were given, as well for the singular treasures of wisdom therein contained, as also for the great use we have thereof both in decision of certain kinds of causes arising daily within ourselves, and especially for commerce with Nations abroad, whereunto that knowledge is most requisite. The reasons wherewith ye would persuade that Scripture is the only rule to frame all our actions by, are in every respect as effectual for proof that the same is the only law whereby to determine all our Civil controversies. And then what doth let, but that as those men may have their desire, who frankly broach it already

[y] *Humble Motion to the Lords of Her Majesty's Privy Council* [STC 7754], p. 50.

that the work of reformation will never be perfect, till the law of Jesus Christ be received alone; so pleaders and counsellors may bring their books of the Common law, and bestow them [z]as the students of curious and needless arts did theirs in the Apostles' time? I leave them to scan how far those words of yours may reach, wherein ye declare that, [a]whereas now many houses lie waste through inordinate suits of law, *This one thing will show the excellency of Discipline for the wealth of the Realm, and quiet of Subjects, that the Church is to censure such a party who is apparently troublesome and contentious, and without* REASONABLE CAUSE *upon a mere will and stomach doth vex and molest his brother and trouble the Country.* For mine own part I do not see but that it might very well agree with your principles, if your discipline were fully planted, even to send out your writs of surcease unto all Courts of England besides, [8.5] for the most things handled in them. A great deal further I might proceed and descend lower. But forasmuch as against all these and the like difficulties your answer is, [b]that we ought to search what things are consonant to God's will, not which be most for our own ease; and therefore that your discipline being (for such is your error) the absolute commandment of almighty God, it must be received although the world by receiving it should be clean turned upside down; herein lieth the greatest danger of all. For whereas the name of divine authority is used to countenance these things, which are not the commandments of God, but your own erroneous collections; on him ye must father whatsoever ye shall afterwards be led, either to do in withstanding the adversaries of your Cause, or to think in maintenance of your doings. And what this may be, God doth know. In such kinds of error the mind once imagining itself to seek the execution of God's will, laboureth forthwith to remove both things and persons which any way hinder it from taking place; and in such cases if any strange or new thing seem requisite to be done, a strange and new opinion concerning the lawfulness thereof, is withal [8.6] received and broached under countenance of divine authority. One example herein may serve for many, to show that false opinions, touching the will of God to have things done, are wont to bring forth mighty and violent practices against the hindrances of them; and those practices new opinions more pernicious than the first, yea most extremely

---

[z] Acts 19:19. [a] *Humble Motion*, p. 74. [b] *Counter-Poison* [*STC* 10770], p. 108.

sometimes opposite to that which the first did seem to intend. Where the people took upon them the reformation of the Church by casting out popish superstition, they having received from their Pastors a general instruction that 'whatsoever the heavenly father hath not planted must be rooted out, proceeded in some foreign places so far that down went oratories and the very temples of God themselves. For as they chanced to take the compass of their commission stricter or larger, so their dealings were accordingly more or less moderate. Amongst others there sprang up presently one kind of men, with whose zeal and forwardness the rest being compared, were thought to be marvelous cold and dull. These, grounding themselves on rules more general; that whatsoever the law of Christ commandeth not, thereof Antichrist is the author: and that whatsoever Antichrist or his adherents did in the world, the true professors of Christ are to undo; found out many things more than others had done, the extirpation whereof was in their conceit as necessary as of any thing before removed. Hereupon they secretly made their doleful complaints everywhere as they went, that albeit the world did begin to profess some dislike of that which was evil in the kingdom of darkness, yet fruits worthy of a true repentance were not seen; and that if men did repent as they ought, they must endeavor to purge the earth of all manner evil, to the end there might follow a new world afterward, wherein righteousness only should dwell. Private repentance they said must appear by every man's fashioning his own life contrary unto the customs and orders of this present world, both in greater things and in less. [d]To this purpose they had always in their mouths those greater things, charity, faith, the true fear of God, the Cross, the mortification of the flesh. All their exhortations were to set light of the things in this world, to count riches and honours vanity, and in token thereof not only to seek neither, but if men were possessors of both, even to cast away the one and resign the other, that all men might see their unfeigned conversion unto Christ. [e]They were solicitors of men to fasts, to often meditations of heavenly things, and as it were conferences in secret with God by prayers, not framed according to the frozen manner of the world, but expressing such fervent desires as might even force

[c] Matt. 15:13.
[d] Guy de Brès, *The Rise, Spring and Foundation of the Anabaptists*, p. 4.
[e] p. 5.

God to hearken unto them. *ʃ*Where they found men in diet, attire, furniture of house, or any other way observers of civility and decent order, such they reproved as being carnally and earthly minded. *ᵍ*Every word otherwise than severely and sadly uttered, seemed to pierce like a sword through them. *ʰ*If any man were pleasant, their manner was presently with deep sighs to repeat those words of our Saviour Christ, *Woe be to you which now laugh, for ye shall lament.* *ⁱ*So great was their delight to be always in trouble, that such as did quietly lead their lives, they judged of all other men to be in most dangerous case. *ʲ*They so much affected to cross the ordinary custom in everything, that when other men's use was to put on better attire, they would be sure to show themselves openly abroad in worse; the ordinary names of the days in the week they thought it a kind of profaneness to use, and therefore accustomed themselves to make no other distinction than by numbers, The First, Second, Third day. From this they proceeded unto public reformation, first Ecclesiastical, and then Civil. Touching the former, *ᵏ*they boldly avouched, that themselves only had the truth, which thing upon peril of their lives they would at all times defend; and that since the Apostles lived, the same was never before in all points sincerely taught. Wherefore that things might again be brought to that ancient integrity which Jesus Christ by his word requireth, they began to control the ministers of the Gospel for attributing so much force and virtue unto the scriptures of God read, whereas the truth was, that when the word is said to engender faith in the heart, and to convert the soul of man, or to work any such spiritual divine effect, these speeches are not thereunto applicable as it is read or preached, but as it is engrafted in us by the power of the holy Ghost opening the eyes of our understanding, and so revealing the mysteries of God, according to that which Jeremiah promised before should be, saying, *ˡI will put my law in their inward parts, and I will write it in their hearts.* The book of God they notwithstanding for the most part so admired, that *ᵐ*other disputation against their opinions than only by allegation of scripture they would not hear; besides it, they thought no other writings in the world should be studied, insomuch

[8.7]

ʃ p. 16. p. 118.   *ᵍ* 119. 120.   *ʰ* p. 116. Luke 6:12.
ⁱ De Brès, p. 124.   *ʲ* p. 117.   *ᵏ* p. 40.   *ˡ* Jer. 31:34.
ᵐ De Brès, p. 29.

as "one of their great Prophets exhorting them to cast away all respect unto human writings, so far to his motion they condescended, that as many as had any books save the holy Bible in their custody, they brought and set them publicly on fire. When they and their Bibles were alone together, what strange fantastical opinion soever at any time entered into their heads, their use was to think the Spirit taught it them. Their frenzies concerning our Saviour's incarnation, the state of souls departed, and such like, are things needless to be rehearsed. And forasmuch as they were of the same suit with those of whom the Apostle speaketh, saying, *°They are still learning, but never attain to the knowledge of truth*, it was no marvel to see them every day broach some new thing, not heard of before. Which restless levity they did interpret to be their growing to spiritual perfection, and a proceeding from faith to faith. *°The differences amongst them grew by this mean in a manner infinite, so that scarcely was there found any one of them, the forge of whose brain was not possessed with some special mystery. Whereupon, *^qalthough their mutual contentions were most fiercely prosecuted amongst themselves, yet when they came to defend the cause common to them all against the adversaries of their faction, they had ways to lick one another whole, *'the sounder in his own persuasion, excusing THE DEAR BRETHREN, which were not so far enlightened, and professing a charitable hope of the mercy of God towards them notwithstanding their swerving from him in some things. *°Their own ministers they highly magnified as men whose vocation was from God: *'the rest their manner was to term disdainfully Scribes and Pharisees, to account their calling an human creature, and to detain the people as much as might be from hearing them. As touching Sacraments, *"baptism administered in the church of Rome, they judged to be but an execrable mockery and no baptism: both because the Ministers thereof in the papacy are wicked idolaters, lewd persons, thieves, and murderers, cursed creatures, ignorant beasts, and also for that to baptize is a proper action belonging unto none but the Church of Christ, whereas Rome is Antichrist's synagogue. *°The custom of using Godfathers and Godmothers at Christenings they scorned. *"Baptizing of infants, although confessed by themselves

" 27.   ° 2 Tim. 3:7. De Brès, p. 65.   *^p 66.   *^q p. 135.
*^r p. 25.   *^s p. 71.   *^t 124.   *^u 764.   *^v 748.   *^w 512.

to have been continued even since the very Apostles' own times, yet they altogether condemned: partly because sundry errors are of no less antiquity, and partly *for that there is no commandment in the Gospel of Christ which saith, *Baptize infants*, but *he contrariwise in saying, *Go preach and Baptize*, doth appoint that the minister of Baptism shall in that action first administer doctrine, and then Baptism, as also in saying, *whosoever doth believe and is baptized*, he appointeth that the party to whom baptism is administered shall first believe, and then be baptized; to the end that believing may go before this sacrament in the receiver, no otherwise than preaching in the giver, since equally in both, the law of Christ declareth not only what things are required, but also in what order they are required. *The Eucharist they received (pretending our Lord and Saviour's example) after supper, and for avoiding all those impieties which have been grounded upon the mystical words of Christ *This is my body, This is my blood*, they thought it not safe to mention either body or blood in that Sacrament, but rather to abrogate both, and to use no words but these, *Take, eat, declare the death of our Lord: drink, show forth our Lord's death*. In rites and ceremonies their profession was hatred of all conformity with the Church of Rome: *for which cause they would rather endure any torment than observe the solemn festivals which others did, inasmuch as Antichrist (they

[8.8] said) was the first inventor of them. The pretended end of their civil reformation was that Christ might have dominion over all, that all crowns and scepters might be thrown down at his feet, that no other might reign over Christian men but he, no regiment keep them in awe, but his discipline, amongst them no sword at all be carried, besides his, the sword of spiritual excommunication. For this cause they laboured with all their might in overturning the seats of Magistracy, because Christ hath said, *Kings of Nations*; in abolishing the execution of justice, because Christ hath said, *Resist not evil*; *in forbidding oaths the necessary means of judicial trial, because Christ hath said, *Swear not at all*; finally *in bringing in community of goods, because Christ by his Apostles hath given the world such example, to the end that men might excel one another

[8.9] not in wealth the pillar of secular authority, but in virtue. These

---

*722. 726.   *518. 688.   *p. 38   *p. 122.
*p. 841.   *833.   *849.   *40.

44

men at the first were only pitied in their error, and not much withstood by any, the great humility, zeal, and devotion which appeared
to be in them, was in all men's opinion a pledge of their harmless
meaning. The hardest that men of sound understanding conceived
of them was but this, *[f]O quam honesta voluntate miseri errant? With
how good a meaning these poor souls do evil.* *[g]*Luther made request
unto Frederick Duke of Saxony, that within his dominion they might
be favourably dealt with and spared, for that (their error excepted)
they seemed otherwise right good men. By means of which merciful
toleration they gathered strength, much more than was safe for the
state of the commonwealth wherein they lived. *[h]*They had their
secret corner-meetings and assemblies in the night, the people
flocked unto them by thousands. *[i]*The means whereby they both   [8.10]
allured and retained so great multitudes were most effectual; first
a wonderful show of zeal towards God, wherewith they seemed
to be even rapt in everything they spake: secondly an hatred of
sin, and a singular love of integrity, which men did think to be
much more than ordinary in them, by reason of the custom which
they had to fill the ears of the people with invectives against their
authorized guides, as well spiritual as civil: thirdly the bountiful
relief wherewith they eased the broken estate of such needy creatures, as were in that respect the more apt to be drawn away: fourthly,
*[j]*a tender compassion which they were thought to take upon the
miseries of the common sort, over whose heads their manner was
even to pour down showers of tears in complaining that no respect
was had unto them, that their goods were devoured by wicked cor-
morants, their persons had in contempt, *[k]*all liberty both temporal
and spiritual taken from them, that it was high time for God now
to hear their groans, and to send them deliverance: lastly a cunning
slight which they had to stroke and smooth up the minds of their
followers, as well by appropriating unto them all the favourable titles,
the good words, and the gracious promises in Scripture, as also
be casting the contrary always on the heads of such as were severed
from that retinue. Whereupon the people's common acclamation
unto such deceivers was, *[l]*These are verily the men of God, these
are his true and sincere Prophets. *[m]*If any such Prophet or man

---

[f] Lactantius On Justice, Bk 5, ch. 19 [or 20, of *The Divine Institutes*].
[g] De Brès, p. 6.   *[h]* p. 4. 20.   *[i]* 55.   *[j]* p. 6.   *[k]* 7.   *[l]* 7.   *[m]* 27.

of God did suffer by order of law condign and deserved punishment; were it for felony, rebellion, murder, or what else, the people (so strangely were their hearts enchanted) as though blessed St. Stephen had been again martyred, did lament that God took away his most [8.11] dear servants from them. In all these things being fully persuaded that what they did, it was obedience to the will of God, and that all men should do the like: there remained after speculation practice, whereby the whole world thereunto (if it were possible) might be framed. "This they saw could not be done, but with mighty opposition and resistance: against which to strengthen themselves, they secretly entered into league of association. And peradventure considering, that although they were many, yet long wars would in time waste them out, they began to think whether it might not be that God would have them do for their speedy and mighty increase, the same which sometime God's own chosen people, the people of Israel did. Glad and fain they were to have it so, which very desire was itself apt to breed both an opinion of possibility, and a willingness to gather arguments of likelihood that so God himself would have it. Nothing more clear unto their seeming, than that a new Jerusalem being often spoken of in Scripture, they undoubtedly were themselves that new Jerusalem, and the old did by way of a certain figurative resemblance signify what they should both be and do. Here they drew in a Sea of matter by applying all things unto their own company which are anywhere spoken concerning divine favors and benefits bestowed upon the old commonwealth of Israel, concluding that as Israel was delivered out of Egypt, so they spiritually out of the Egypt of this world's servile thraldom unto sin and superstition; as Israel was to root out the Idolatrous nations, and to plant in stead of them a people which feared God, so the same Lord's good will and pleasure was now, that these new Israelites should under the conduct of other Joshuas, Sampsons, and Gideons perform a work no less miraculous in casting out violently the wicked from the earth, and establishing the kingdom of Christ with perfect liberty: and therefore as the cause why the children of Israel took unto one man many wives, might be lest the casualties of war should any way hinder the promise of God concerning their multitude from taking effect in them; so it was

" 6.

not unlike that for the necessary propagation of Christ's kingdom under the Gospel the Lord was content to allow as much. Now [8.12] whatsoever they did in such sort collect out of Scripture when they came to justify or persuade it unto others, all was the heavenly father's appointment, his commandment, his will and charge. Which thing is the very point in regard whereof I have gathered this declaration. For my purpose herein is to show that when the minds of men are once erroneously persuaded that it is the will of God to have those things done which they fancy, their opinions are as thorns in their sides never suffering them to take rest till they have brought their speculations into practice: the lets and impediments of which practice their restless desire and study to remove leadeth them every day forth by the hand into other more dangerous opinions, sometimes quite and clean contrary to their first pretended meanings: so as what will grow out of such errors as go masked under the cloak of divine authority, impossible it is that ever the wit of man should imagine, till time have brought forth the fruits of them: for which cause it behoveth wisdom to fear the sequels thereof, even beyond all apparent cause of fear. These men in whose mouths at the first, sounded nothing but only mortification of the flesh, were come at the length to think they might lawfully have their six or seven wives apiece; they which at the first thought judgement and justice itself to be merciless cruelty, accounted at the length their own hands sanctified with being imbrued in Christian blood; they who at the first were wont to beat down all dominion, and to urge against poor Constables, *Kings of Nations*, had at the length both Consuls and kings of their own erection amongst themselves: finally they which could not brook at the first that any man should seek, no not by law, the recovery of goods injuriously taken or withheld from him, were grown at the last to think they could not offer unto God more acceptable sacrifice, than by turning their adversaries clean out of house and home, and by enriching themselves with all kind of spoil and pillage; [o]which thing being laid to their charge they had in a readiness their answer, that now the time was come, when according to our Saviour's promise, [p]*The meek ones must inherit the earth*, and that their title hereunto was the same which [q]the righteous Israelites had unto the goods of the wicked Egyptians. Wherefore since the world hath had in these [8.13]

[o] p. 41. [p] Matt. 5:5. [q] Exod. 11:2.

men so fresh experience, how dangerous such active errors are, it must not offend you though touching the sequel of your present mispersuasions much more be doubted, than your own intents and purposes do happily aim at. And yet your words already are somewhat when ye affirm that your Pastors, Doctors, Elders, and Deacons, ought to be in this Church of England, *'whether her Majesty and our state will or no*; when for the animating of your confederates ye publish the musters which ye have made of your own bands, and proclaim them to amount I know not to how many thousands; when ye threaten that *'since neither your suits to the Parliament, nor supplications to our Convocation house, neither your defences by writing, nor challenges of disputation in behalf of that cause are able to prevail, we must blame ourselves if to bring in discipline some such means hereafter be used as shall cause all our hearts to ache. That *things doubtful are to be construed in the better part*, is a principle not safe to be followed in matters concerning the public state of a commonweal. But howsoever these and the like speeches be accounted as arrows idly shot at random, without either eye had to any mark, or regard to their lighting place: hath not your longing desire for the practice of your discipline, brought the matter already unto this demurrer amongst you, whether the people and their godly pastors that way affected, ought not to make separation from the rest, and to begin the exercise of discipline without the licence of Civil powers, which licence they have sought for, and are not heard? Upon which question as ye have now divided yourselves, the warier sort of you taking the one part, and the forwarder in zeal the other; so in case these earnest ones should prevail, what other sequel can any wise man imagine but this, that having first resolved that attempts for discipline without superiors are lawful, it will follow in the next place to be disputed what may be attempted against superiors which will not have the scepter of that discipline to rule over them? Yea even by you which have stayed yourselves from running headlong with the other sort, somewhat notwithstanding there hath been done without the leave or liking of your lawful superiors, for the exercise of a part of your discipline amongst the Clergy thereunto addicted. And lest examination of principal parties therein should bring those things to light, which might hinder and

---

r Martin Marprelate in his 3rd libel, p. 28 [*STC* 17456, p. 26].
s *A Demonstration of Discipline* in the preface [*STC* 24499, sig. B2^{r-v}].

let your proceedings; behold for a bar against that impediment, one opinion ye have newly added unto the rest even upon this occasion, an opinion to exempt you from taking oaths which may turn to the molestation of your brethren in that cause. The next neighbour opinion whereunto, when occasion requireth, may follow for dispensation with oaths already taken, if they afterwards be found to import a necessity of detecting aught which may bring such good men into trouble or damage, whatsoever the cause be. O merciful God, what man's wit is there able to sound the depth of those dangerous and fearful evils, whereinto our weak and impotent nature is inclinable to sink itself, rather than to show an acknowledgement of error in that which once we have unadvisedly taken upon us to defend, against the stream as it were of a contrary public resolution! Where- [8.14] fore if we anything respect their error, who being persuaded even as you are, have gone further upon that persuasion than you allow; if we regard the present state of the highest governor placed over us, if the quality and disposition of our Nobles, if the orders and laws of our famous Universities, if the profession of the Civil or the practice of the Common law amongst us, if the mischiefs whereinto even before our eyes so many others have fallen headlong from no less plausible and fair beginnings than yours are: there is in every of these considerations most just cause to fear lest our hastiness to embrace a thing of so perilous consequence should cause posterity to feel those evils, which as yet are more easy for us to prevent than they would be for them to remedy.

The conclusion of all.

9. The best and safest way for you therefore my dear brethren [9.1] is, to call your deeds past to a new reckoning, to reexamine the cause ye have taken in hand, and to try it even point by point, argument by argument, with all the diligent exactness ye can; to lay aside the gall of that bitterness wherein your minds have hitherto overabounded, and with meekness to search the truth. Think ye are men, deem it not impossible for you to err: sift unpartially your own hearts, whether it be force of reason, or vehemency of affection, which hath bred, and still doth feed these opinions in you. If truth do anywhere manifest itself, seek not to smother it with glosing

49

delusions, acknowledge the greatness thereof, and think it your best

[9.2] victory when the same doth prevail over you. That ye have been earnest in speaking or writing again and again the contrary way, shall be no blemish or discredit at all unto you. Amongst so many so huge volumes as the infinite pains of Saint Augustine have brought forth, what one hath gotten him greater love, commendation and honor, than the book wherein he carefully collecteth his own oversights, and sincerely condemneth them? Many speeches there are of Job's whereby his wisdom and other virtues may appear: but the glory of an ingenuous mind he hath purchased by these words only. *'Behold, I will lay mine hand on my mouth; I have spoken once, yet will I not therefore maintain argument; yea twice, howbeit for that*

[9.3] *cause further I will not proceed.* Far more comfort it were for us (so small is the joy we take in these strifes) to labour under the same yoke, as men that look for the same eternal reward of their labours, to be joined with you in bands of indissoluble love and amity, to live as if our persons being many our souls were but one, rather than in such dismembered sort to spend our few and wretched days in a tedious prosecuting of wearisome contentions: the end whereof, if they have not some speedy end, will be heavy even on both sides. Brought already we are even to that estate which Gregory Nazianzen mournfully describeth, saying. *"My mind leadeth me* (since there is no other remedy) *to fly and to convey myself into some corner out of sight, where I may escape from this cloudy tempest of maliciousness, whereby all parts are entered into a deadly war amongst themselves, and that little remnant of love which was, is now consumed to nothing. The only godliness we glory in, is to find out somewhat whereby we may judge others to be ungodly. Each other's faults we observe as matter of exprobration and not of grief. By these means we are grown hateful in the eyes of the Heathens themselves, and (which woundeth us the more deeply) able we are not to deny but that we have deserved their hatred. With the better sort of our own, our fame and credit is clean lost. The less we are to marvel if they judge vilely of us, who although we did well would hardly allow thereof. On our backs they also build that are lewd, and what we object one against another, the same they use to the utter scorn and disgrace of us all. This we have gained by our mutual home-dissensions. This we are worthily rewarded with which are more forward*

' Job 39:37 [40:4].   " Gregory Nazianzen, *Apology* [*PG*, 35:485, 489].

to strive, than becometh men of virtuous and mild disposition.
But our trust in the almighty is, that with us contentions are now [9.4]
at their highest float, and that the day will come (for what cause
of despair is there) when the passions of former enmity being allayed,
we shall with ten times redoubled tokens of our unfeignedly reconciled love, show ourselves each towards other the same which Joseph
and the brethren of Joseph were at the time of their interview in
Egypt. Our comfortable expectation and most thirsty desire whereof
what man soever amongst you shall any way help to satisfy (as we
truly hope there is no one amongst you but some way or other
will) the blessings of the God of peace both in this world and in
the world to come, be upon him more than the stars of the firmament
in number.

THE FIRST BOOK

Concerning Laws, and their several kinds in general.

The cause of writing this general discourse.

[1.1] 1. He that goeth about to persuade a multitude, that they are not so well governed as they ought to be, shall never want attentive and favourable hearers; because they know the manifold defects whereunto every kind of regiment is subject, but the secret lets and difficulties, which in public proceedings are innumerable and inevitable, they have not ordinarily the judgement to consider. And because such as openly reprove supposed disorders of state are taken for principal friends to the common benefit of all, and for men that carry singular freedom of mind; under this fair and plausible colour whatsoever they utter passeth for good and current. That which wanteth in the weight of their speech, is supplied by the aptness of men's minds to accept and believe it. Whereas on the other side, if we maintain things that are established, we have not only to strive with a number of heavy prejudices deeply rooted in the hearts of men, who think that herein we serve the time, and speak in favour of the present state, because thereby we either hold or seek preferment; but also to bear such exceptions as minds so averted beforehand usually take against that which they are loath

[1.2] should be poured into them. Albeit therefore much of that we are to speak in this present cause, may seem to a number perhaps tedious, perhaps obscure, dark, and intricate, (for many talk of the truth, which never sounded the depth from whence it springeth, and therefore when they are led thereunto they are soon weary, as men drawn from those beaten paths wherewith they have been inured) yet this may not so far prevail as to cut off that which the matter itself requireth, howsoever the nice humour of some be therewith pleased or no. They unto whom we shall seem tedious are in no wise injuried by us, because it is in their own hands to spare that labour which they are not willing to endure. And if any complain of obscurity, they must consider, that in these matters it cometh no otherwise to pass than in sundry the works both of art and also of nature, where that which hath greatest force in the very things we see, is notwithstanding itself oftentimes not seen. The stateliness of houses, the goodliness of trees, when we behold them delighteth the eye; but that foundation which beareth up the one, that root which ministereth unto the other nourishment and life, is in the bosom of the earth concealed: and if there be at any time occasion to search into it, such labour is then more necessary than pleasant both to them which undertake it, and for the lookers on. In like manner the use and benefit of good laws, all that live under them may enjoy with delight and comfort, albeit the grounds, and first original causes from whence they have sprung be unknown, as to the greatest part of men they are. But when they who withdraw their obedience pretend that the laws which they should obey are corrupt and vicious; for better examination of their quality, it behoveth the very foundation and root, the highest wellspring and fountain of them to be discovered. Which because we are not oftentimes accustomed to do, when we do it the pains we take are more needful a great deal, than acceptable, and the matters which we handle seem by reason of newness (till the mind grow better acquainted with them) dark, intricate and unfamiliar. For as much help whereof as may be in this case, I have endeavoured throughout the body of this whole discourse, that every former part might give strength unto all that follow, and every later bring some light unto all before. So that if the judgements of men do but hold themselves in suspense as touching these first more general meditations, till in order they have perused the rest that ensue: what may seem dark at the first will afterwards be found more plain, even as the later particular decisions will appear, I doubt not more strong, when the other have been read before. The laws of the Church, whereby for so many [1.3] ages together we have been guided in the exercise of Christian religion, and the service of the true God, our rites, customs, and orders of Ecclesiastical government are called in question, we are accused as men that will not have Christ Jesus to rule over them, but have wilfully cast his statutes behind their backs, hating to be reformed, and made subject unto the scepter of his discipline. Behold therefore we offer the laws whereby we live unto the general trial and judgement of the whole world, heartily beseeching Almighty God, whom we desire to serve according to his own will, that both we and others (all kind of partial affection being clean laid aside) may have eyes to see, and hearts to embrace the things that in his sight are most acceptable. And because the point about which we strive is the quality of our laws, our first entrance hereinto cannot better be made, than with consideration of the nature of law in general, and of that law which giveth life unto all the rest, which are commendable just and good, namely the law whereby the Eternal himself doth work. Proceeding from hence to the law first of nature, then of scripture, we shall have the easier access unto those things which come after to be debated, concerning the particular cause and question which we have in hand.

Of that law which God from before the beginning hath set for himself to do all things by.

[2.1] 2. All things that are have some operation not violent or casual. Neither doth anything ever begin to exercise the same without some foreconceived end for which it worketh. And the end which it worketh for is not obtained, unless the work be also fit to obtain it by. For unto every end every operation will not serve. That which doth assign unto each thing the kind, that which doth moderate the force and power, that which doth appoint the form and measure of working, the same we term a *Law*. So that no certain end could ever be attained, unless the actions whereby it is attained were regular, that is to say, made suitable fit and correspondent unto their end, by some canon, rule or law. Which thing doth first take place in [2.2] the works even of God himself. All things therefore do work after a sort according to law: all other things according to a law, whereof some superiors, unto whom they are subject, is author; only the works and operations of God have him both for their worker, and for the law whereby they are wrought. The being of God is a kind of law to his working: for that perfection which God is, giveth perfection to that he doth. Those natural, necessary, and internal operations of God, the *generation* of the Son, the *proceeding* of the Spirit, are without the compass of my present intent: which is to touch

54

only such operations as have their beginning and being by a voluntary purpose, wherewith God hath eternally decreed when and how they should be. Which eternal decree is that we term an eternal law. Dangerous it were for the feeble brain of man to wade far into the doings of the most High, whom although to know be life, and joy to make mention of his name: yet our soundest knowledge is to know that we know him not as in deed he is, neither can know him: and our safest eloquence concerning him is our silence, when we confess without confession that his glory is inexplicable, his greatness above our capacity and reach. He is above, and we upon earth, therefore it behoveth our words to be wary and few. Our God is one, or rather very *Oneness*, and mere unity, having nothing but itself in iself, and not consisting (as all things do besides God) of many things. In which essential unity of God a Trinity personal nevertheless subsisteth after a manner far exceeding the possibility of man's conceipt. The works which outwardly are of God, they are in such sort of him being one, that each person hath in them somewhat peculiar and proper. For being three, and they all subsisting in the essence of one deity; from the Father, by the Son, through the Spirit all things are. [a]That which the Son doth hear of the Father, and which the Spirit doth receive of the Father and the Son, the same we have at the hands of the Spirit as being the last, and therefore the nearest unto us in order, although in power the same with the second and the first. The wise and learned among [2.3] the very Heathens themselves, have all acknowledged some first cause, whereupon originally the being of all things dependeth. Neither have they otherwise spoken of that cause, than as an Agent, which knowing *what* and *why* it worketh, observeth in working a most exact *order* or *law*. Thus much is signified by that which *Homer* mentioneth, [b]Διὸς δ' ἐτελείτο βουλή. Thus much acknowledged by *Mercurius Trismegistus* [c]τὸν πάντα κόσμον ἐποίησεν ὁ δημιουργὸς οὐ χερσὶν ἀλλὰ λόγῳ. [d]Thus much confessed by *Anaxagoras* and *Plato*, terming the maker of the world an *Intellectual* worker. Finally the Stoics, although imagining the first cause of all things to be fire, held nevertheless that the same fire having

---

[a] John 16:13–15.   [b] *Jupiter's* Counsel *was accomplished* [*Iliad*, Bk 1, line 5].
[c] *The creator made the whole world not with hands, but by* Reason [ed. 1924, 1:148].
[d] Stobaeus, *Eclogues* [ed. 1958, 1:34 and 37].

art, did ῾ὁδῷ βαδίζειν ἐπὶ γενέσει κόσμον. They all confess therefore in the working of that first cause, that *counsel* is used, *reason* followed, a *way* observed, that is to say, constant *order* and *law* is kept, whereof itself must needs be author unto itself. Otherwise it should have some worthier and higher to direct it, and so could not itself be the first. Being the first, it can have no other than itself to be the author of that law which it willingly worketh by. God therefore is a law both to himself, and to all other things besides. To himself he is a law in all those things, whereof our Saviour speaketh, saying, *ʲMy Father worketh as yet, so I.* God worketh nothing without cause. All those things which are done by him, have some end for which they are done: and the end for which they are done, is a reason of his will to do them. His will had not inclined to create woman, but that he saw it could not be well if she were not created, *ᵍNon est bonum, It is not good man should be alone, Therefore let us make an helper for him.* That and nothing else is done by God, which to leave undone were not so good. If therefore it be demanded, why God having power and ability infinite, the effects notwithstanding of that power are all so limited as we see they are: the reason hereof is the end which he hath proposed, and the law whereby his wisdom hath stinted the effects of his power in such sort, that it doth not work infinitely but correspondently unto that end for which it worketh, even *ʰall things χρηστῶς*, in most decent

[2.4] and comely sort, *ⁱall things in measure, number, and weight.* The general end of God's external working, is the exercise of his most glorious and most abundant virtue: Which abundance doth show itself in variety, and for that cause this variety is oftentimes in scripture expressed by the name of *ʲriches.* *ᵏThe Lord hath made all things for his own sake.* Not that anything is made to be beneficial unto him, but all things for him to show beneficence and grace in them. The particular drift of every act proceeding externally from God, we are not able to discern, and therefore cannot always give the proper and certain reason of his works. Howbeit undoubtedly a proper and certain reason there is of every finite work of God, inasmuch as there is a law imposed upon it; which if there were

[2.5] not, it should be infinite even as the worker himself is. They err

ᵉ Proceed by a certain and a set Way in the making of the world [Stobaeus, ed. 1958, 1:37].
ᶠ John 5:17.   *ᵍ* Gen. 2:18.   *ʰ* Wisdom 8:1.
ⁱ Wisdom 11:17 [11.20].   *ʲ* Ephes. 1:7. Philip. 4:19. Col. 2:3.   *ᵏ* Prov. 16:4.

therefore who think that of the will of God to do this or that, there is no reason besides his will. Many times no reason known to us; but that there is no reason thereof, I judge it most unreasonable to imagine, inasmuch as he worketh all things [l]*κατὰ τὴν βουλὴν τοῦ θελήματος αὐτοῦ*, not only according to his own will, but *the counsel of his own will.* And whatsoever is done with counsel or wise resolution, hath of necessity some reason why it should be done, albeit that reason be to us in some things so secret, that it forceth the wit of man to stand, as the blessed Apostle himself doth, amazed thereat, [m]*O the depth of the riches both of the wisdom and knowledge of God, How unsearchable are his judgements, etc.* That law eternal which God himself hath made to himself, and thereby worketh all things whereof he is the cause and author, that law in the admirable frame whereof shineth with most perfect beauty the countenance of that wisdom which hath testified concerning herself, [n]*The lord possessed me in the beginning of his way, even before his works of old, I was set up etc.* That law which hath been the pattern to make, and is the card to guide the world by: that law which hath been of God, and with God everlastingly: that law the author and observer whereof is one only God to be blessed forever, how should either men or Angels be able perfectly to behold? The book of this law we are neither able nor worthy to open and look into. That little thereof which we darkly apprehend, we admire, the rest with religious ignorance we humbly and meekly adore. Seeing therefore [2.6]
that according to this law he worketh, [o]*of whom, through whom, and for whom are all things*, although there seem unto us confusion and disorder in the affairs of this present world: [p]*Tamen quoniam bonus mundum rector temperat, recte fieri cuncta ne dubites*, Let no man doubt but that everything is well done, because the world is ruled by so good a guide, as transgresseth not his own law, than which nothing can be more absolute, perfect and just. The law whereby he worketh, is eternal, and therefore can have no show or colour of mutability: for which cause a part of that law being opened in the promises which God hath made (because his promises are nothing else but declarations what God will do for the good of men) touching those promises the Apostle hath witnessed, [q]that God may as possibly deny himself and not be God, as fail to perform them. And concern-

[l] Ephes. 1:11. [m] Rom. 11:33. [n] Prov. 8:23. [o] Rom. 11:36.
[p] Boethius, *On the Consolation of Philosophy*, Bk 4 [Prose 6; *L*, p. 355]. [q] 2 Tim. 2:13.

ing the counsel of God; he termeth it likewise a thing ᵗ*unchangeable*, the counsel of God, and that law of God whereof now we speak being one. Nor is the freedom of the will of God any whit abated, let or hindered by means of this, because the imposition of this law upon himself is his own free and voluntary act. This law therefore we may name eternal, being *that order which God before all ages hath set down with himself, for himself to do all things by.*

The law which natural agents have given them to observe, and their necessary manner of keeping it.

[3.1] 3. I am not ignorant that by law eternal the learned for the most part do understand the order, not which God hath eternally purposed himself in all his works to observe, but rather that which with himself he hath set down as expedient to be kept by all his creatures, according to the several condition wherewith he hath endowed them. They who thus are accustomed to speak apply the name of *Law* unto that only rule of working which superior authority imposeth, whereas we somewhat more enlarging the sense thereof, term any kind of rule or canon whereby actions are framed a law. Now that law which as it is laid up in the bosom of God, they call *eternal*, receiveth according unto the different kinds of things which are subject unto it different and sundry kinds of names. That part of it which ordereth natural agents, we call usually *nature*'s law: that which Angels do clearly behold, and without any swerving observe is a law *celestial* and heavenly: the law of *reason* that which bindeth creatures reasonable in this world, and with which by reason they may most plainly perceive themselves bound; that which bindeth them, and is not known but by special revelation from God, *Divine* law; *human* law that which out of the law either of reason or of God, men probably gathering to be expedient, they make it a law. All things therefore, which are as they ought to be, are conformed unto *this second law eternal*, and even those things which to this *eternal* law are not conformable, are notwithstanding in some sort ordered by *the first eternal law*. For what good or evil is there under the sun, what action correspondent or repugnant unto the law which God hath imposed upon his creatures, but in or upon it God doth

ᵗ Heb. 6:17.

work according to the law which himself hath eternally purposed
to keep, that is to say, the *first law eternal*? So that a twofold law
eternal being thus made, it is not hard to conceive how they both
take place in ˢall things. Wherefore to come to the law of nature, [3.2]
albeit thereby we sometimes mean that manner of working which
God hath set for each created thing to keep: yet forasmuch as those
things are termed most properly natural agents, which keep the law
of their kind unwittingly, as the heavens and elements of the world,
which can do no otherwise than they do; and forasmuch as we
give unto intellectual natures the name of *voluntary* agents, that so
we may distinguish them from the other: expedient it will be, that
we sever the law of nature observed by the one from that which
the other is tied unto. Touching the former, their strict keeping
of one tenure statute and law is spoken of by all, but hath in it more
than men have as yet attained to know, or perhaps ever shall attain,
seeing the travail of wading herein is given of God to the sons
of men, that perceiving how much the least thing in the world hath
in it more than the wisest are able to reach unto, they may by this
means learn humility. *Moses* in describing the work of creation,
attributeth speech unto God, *God said, Let there be light, Let there
be a firmament: Let the waters under the heaven be gathered together
into one place: Let the earth bring forth: Let there be lights in the firmament
of heaven.* Was this only the intent of *Moses*, to signify the infinite
greatness of God's power by the easiness of his accomplishing such
effects, without travail, pain or labour? Surely it seemeth that *Moses*
had herein besides this a further purpose, namely, first to teach
that God did not work as a necessary, but a voluntary agent, intending beforehand and decreeing with himself that which did outwardly

---

ˢ *All that happens in created things is the matter of eternal law.* Thomas Aquinas, *Summa
Theologiae,* I–II, q. 93, arts. 4–6. *In no way does anything evade the laws of that most
high creator and orderer, by whom the peace of the universe is administered.* Augustine,
On the City of God, Bk 19, ch. 12. Even sin, insofar as it is justly permitted by God,
falls under the eternal law. Sin is also subject to the eternal law insofar as voluntary
transgression of the law implants a punishing unease in the soul, according to that
of Augustine, *You have appointed, Lord, and so it is, that every inordinate affection is
its own affliction. Confessions,* Bk 1, ch. 12. Nor do the scholastics say badly, *Just as
we see natural contingent things, when they exceed their own particular end and therefore
the eternal law, fall under that same eternal law insofar as they follow another end established
for them by the eternal law in a particular occurrence: so likewise it is when men sin and
revolt from the eternal law as commanding them, only to fall again into the order of the
eternal law as punishing them.*

proceed from him: secondly to show that God did then institute
a law natural to be observed by creatures, and therefore according
to the manner of laws, the institution thereof is described, as being
established by solemn injunction. His commanding those things
to be which are, and to be in such sort as they are, to keep that
tenure and course which they do, importeth the establishment of
nature's law. This world's first creation, and the preservation since
of things created, what is it but only so far forth a manifestation
by execution, what the eternal law of God is concerning things
natural? And as it cometh to pass in a kingdom rightly ordered,
that after a law is once published, it presently takes effect far and
wide, all states framing themselves thereunto; even so let us think
it fareth in the natural course of the world: since the time that
God did first proclaim the edicts of his law upon it, heaven and
earth have hearkened unto his voice, and their labour hath been
to do his will: He *made a law for the rain.* He gave his *decree unto
the sea, that the waters should not pass his commandment.* Now if nature
should intermit her course, and leave altogether, though it were
but for a while, the observation of her own laws: if those principal
and mother elements of the world, whereof all things in this lower
world are made, should lose the qualities which now they have,
if the frame of that heavenly arch erected over our heads should
loosen and dissolve itself: if celestial spheres should forget their
wonted motions and by irregular volubility, turn themselves any
way as it might happen: if the prince of the lights of heaven which
now 'as a Giant doth run his unwearied course, should as it were
through a languishing faintness begin to stand and to rest himself:
if the Moon should wander from her beaten way, the times and
seasons of the year blend themselves by disordered and confused
mixture, the winds breathe out their last gasp, the clouds yield no
rain, the earth be defeated of heavenly influence, the fruits of the
earth pine away as children at the withered breasts of their mother
no longer able to yield them relief, what would become of man
himself, whom these things now do all serve? See we not plainly
that obedience of creatures unto the law of nature is the stay of
[3.3] the whole world? Notwithstanding with nature it cometh sometimes
to pass as with art. Let *Phidias* have rude and obstinate stuff to

' Ps. 19:5.

carve, though his art do that it should, his work will lack that beauty which otherwise in fitter matter it might have had. He that striketh an instrument with skill, may cause notwithstanding a very unpleasant sound, if the string whereon he striketh chance to be uncapable of harmony. In the matter whereof things natural consist, that of Theophrastus taketh place, "Πολὺ τὸ οὐχ ὑπακοῦον οὐδὲ δεχόμενον τὸ εὖ, *much of it is oftentimes such as will by no means yield to receive that impression which were best and most perfect*: which defect in the matter of things natural, they who gave themselves unto the contemplation of nature amongst the heathen observed often: but the true original cause thereof divine malediction, laid for the sin of man upon these creatures which God had made for the use of man, this being an article of that saving truth which God hath revealed unto his Church, was above the reach of their merely natural capacity and understanding. But howsoever these swervings are now and then incident into the course of nature, nevertheless so constantly the laws of nature are by natural agents observed, that no man denieth but 'those things which nature worketh, are wrought either always or for the most part after one and the same manner. If [3.4] here it be demanded what that is which keepeth nature in obedience to her own law, we must have recourse to that higher law whereof we have already spoken, and because all other laws do thereon depend, from thence we must borrow so much as shall need for brief resolution in this point. Although we are not of opinion therefore, as some are, that nature in working hath before her certain exemplary draughts or patterns, which subsisting in the bosom of the Highest, and being thence discovered, she fixeth her eye upon them, as travelers by sea upon the pole-star of the world, and that according thereunto she guideth her hand to work by imitation: although we rather embrace the Oracle of *Hippocrates*, that *"Each thing both in small and in great fulfilleth the task which destiny hath set down*: and concerning the manner of executing and fulfilling the same. *What they do they know not, yet is it in show and appearance, as though they did know what they do, and the truth is they do not discern the things which they look on*: nevertheless, forasmuch as the works of nature are no less exact, than if she did both behold and study

---

" Theophrastus, *Metaphysics* [ed. 1929, pp. 34–35].
" Aristotle, *Rhetoric*, Bk I, ch. 39 [1369ab].
" [Hippocrates, *Regimen* (L, 4:236–237)].

how to express some absolute shape or mirror always present before her; yea, such her dexterity and skill appeareth, that no intellectual creature in the world were able by capacity to do that which nature doth without capacity and knowledge; it cannot be, but nature hath some director of infinite knowledge to guide her in all her ways. Who the guide of nature but only the God of nature? [x]*In him we live, move, and are.* Those things which nature is said to do, are by divine art performed, using nature as an instrument: nor is there any such art or knowledge divine in nature herself working, but in the guide of nature's work. Whereas therefore things natural which are not in the number of voluntary agents (for of such only we now speak, and of no other) do so necessarily observe their certain laws, that as long as they keep those [y]forms which give them their being, they cannot possibly be apt or inclinable to do otherwise than they do; seeing the kinds of their operations are both constantly and exactly framed according to the several ends for which they serve, they themselves in the meanwhile though doing that which is fit, yet knowing neither what they do, nor why: it followeth, that all which they do in this sort, proceedeth originally from some such agent as knoweth, appointeth, holdeth up, and even actually frameth the same. The manner of this divine efficiency being far above us, we are no more able to conceive by our reason, than creatures unreasonable by their sense are able to apprehend after what manner we dispose and order the course of our affairs. Only thus much is discerned, that the natural generation and process of all things receiveth order of proceeding from the settled stability of divine understanding. This appointeth unto them their kinds of working, the disposition whereof in the purity of God's own knowledge and will is rightly termed by the name of *Providence.* The same being referred unto the things themselves here disposed by it, was wont by the ancient to be called *natural destiny.* That law the performance whereof we behold in things natural, is as it were an authentical, or an original draught written in the bosom of God himself; whose spirit being to execute the same, useth every particular nature, every mere natural agent only as an instrument

---

[x] Acts 17:28.

[y] Form in other creatures is a thing proportionable unto the soul in living creatures. Sensible it is not, nor otherwise discernible, than only by effects. According to the diversity of inward forms, things of the world are distinguished into their kinds.

created at the beginning, and ever since the beginning used to work his own will and pleasure withal. ^zNature therefore is nothing else but God's instrument: in the course whereof *Dionysius* perceiving some sudden disturbance, is said to have cried out, *Aut Deus naturæ patitur aut mundi machina dissolvetur.* Either God doth suffer impediment, and is by a greater than himself hindered; or if that be impossible, then hath he determined to make a present dissolution of the world; the execution of that law beginning now to stand still, without which the world cannot stand. This workman, whose servitor nature is, being in truth but only one, the Heathens imagining to be more, gave him in the sky the name of *Jupiter*, in the air the name of *Juno*, in the water the name of *Neptune*, in the earth the name of *Vesta* and sometimes of *Ceres*, the name of *Apollo* in the Sun, in the Moon the name of *Diana*, the name of *Aeolus* and divers other in the winds, and to conclude even so many guides of nature they dreamed of, as they saw there were kinds of things natural in the world. These they honoured, as having power to work or cease accordingly as men deserved of them. But unto us there is one only guide of all agents natural, and he both the creator, and the worker of all in all, alone to be blessed, adored and honoured by all for ever. That which hitherto hath been spoken concerneth [3.5] natural agents considered in themselves. But we must further remember also (which thing to touch in a word shall suffice) that as in this respect they have their law, which law directeth them in the means whereby they tend to their own perfection: So likewise another law there is, which toucheth them as they are sociable parts united into one body, a law which bindeth them each to serve unto other's good, and all to prefer the good of the whole before whatsoever their own particular, as we plainly see they do, when things natural in that regard forget their ordinary natural wont, that which is heavy mounting sometimes upwards of its own accord, and forsaking the centre of the earth, which to itself is most natural, even as if it did hear itself commanded to let go the good it privately wisheth, and to relieve the present distress of nature in common.

---

^z See Thomas in the *Compendium of Theology*, ch. 3. *Everything which is moved by something is as it were a certain instrument of the first mover. But it is ridiculous even to the uneducated to suppose an instrument to be moved without some principal acting.*

The law which Angels do work by.

[4.1] 4. But now that we may lift up our eyes (as it were) from the footstool to the throne of God, and leaving these natural, consider a little the state of heavenly and divine creatures; *a*touching Angels which are spirits immaterial and intellectual, the glorious inhabitants of those sacred palaces, where nothing but light and blessed immortality, no shadow of matter for tears, discontentments, griefs and uncomfortable passions to work upon, but all joy, tranquillity, and peace, even forever and ever doth dwell; as in *b*number and order they are huge, mighty, and royal armies: so likewise in perfection of obedience unto that law, which the Highest, whom they adore, love, and imitate, hath imposed upon them, such observants they are thereof, that our Saviour himself being to set down the perfect *idea* of that which we are to pray and wish for on earth, *c*did not teach to pray or wish for more than only that here it might be with us, as with them it is in heaven. God which moveth mere natural agents as an efficient only, doth otherwise move intellectual creatures and especially his holy Angels. *d*For beholding the face of God, in admiration of so great excellency they all adore him; and being rapt with the love of his beauty, they cleave inseparably forever unto him. Desire to resemble him in goodness maketh them unweariable, and even unsatiable in their longing to do by all means all manner good unto all the creatures of God, but especially *e*unto the children of men; in the countenance of whose nature looking downward they behold themselves beneath themselves, even as upward in God, beneath whom themselves are, they see that character which is nowhere but in themselves and us resembled. Thus far even the Paynims have approached; thus far they have seen into the doings of the Angels of God; *Orpheus* confessing, *f*that the fiery throne of God is attended on by those most industrious Angels, careful how all things are performed amongst men; and the mirror of human wisdom plainly teaching, *g*that God moveth Angels, even as that thing doth stir man's heart, which is thereunto

---

a Ps. 104:4. Heb. 1:7. Ephes. 3:10.   *b* Dan. 7:10. Matt. 26:53. Heb. 12:22. Luke 2:13.
c Matt. 6:10.   *d* Matt. 18:10.
e Ps. 91:11–12. Luke 15:7. Heb. 1:14. Acts 10:3. Dan. 9:23. Matt. 18:10. Dan. 4:10.
f [Quoted by Clement of Alexandria, *Miscellanies*, Bk 5, ch. 14.]
g Aristotle, *Metaphysics*, Bk 12, ch. 7 [1072a].

presented amiable. Angelical actions may therefore be reduced unto these three general kinds; first, ^hmost delectable love arising from the visible apprehension of the purity, glory, and beauty of God, invisible saving only unto Spirits that are pure; secondly ⁱadoration grounded upon the evidence of the greatness of God, on whom they see how all things depend, thirdly ^jimitation bred by the presence of his exemplary goodness, who ceaseth not before them daily to fill heaven and earth with the rich treasures of most free and undeserved grace. Of Angels we are not to consider only what they [4.2] are, and do, in regard of their own being, but that also which concerneth them as they are linked into a kind of corporation amongst themselves, and of society or fellowship with men. Consider Angels each of them severally in himself, and their law is that which the Prophet David mentioneth, ^k*All ye his Angels praise him.* Consider the Angels of God associated, and their law is that which disposeth them as an ^l*Army*, one in order and degree above another. Consider finally the Angels as having with us ^mthat communion which the Apostle to the Hebrews noteth, and in regard whereof Angels have not disdained to profess themselves our ⁿ*fellowservants*; From hence there springeth up a third law which bindeth them to work of ministerial employment. Every of which their several functions are by them performed with joy. ^oA part of the Angels of God notwithstanding [4.3] (we know) have fallen, and that their fall hath been through the voluntary breach of that law, which did require at their hands continuance in the exercise of their high and admirable virtue. Impossible it was that ever their will should change or incline to remit any part of their duty, without some object having force to avert their conceit from God, and to draw it another way; and that before they attained that high perfection of bliss, wherein now the elect Angels are without possibility of falling. Of anything more than of God they could not by any means like, as long as whatsoever they knew besides God they apprehended it not in itself without dependency upon God; because so long God must needs seem infinitely better than anything which they so could apprehend. Things

^h Job 38:7. Matt. 18:10.   ⁱ Ps. 148:2. Heb. 1:6. Isa. 6:3.
^j This is intimated wheresoever we find them termed the sons of God: as Job 1:6 and 38:7.
^k Ps. 148:2.   ^l Luke 2:13. Matt. 26:53. Ps. 148:2.
^m Heb. 12:22.   ⁿ Rev. 22:9.   ^o 2 Pet. 2:4. Jude, verse 6.

beneath them could not in such sort be presented unto their eyes, but that therein they must needs see always how those things did depend on God. It seemeth therefore that there was no other way for Angels to sin, but by reflex of their understanding upon themselves; when being held with admiration of their own sublimity and honour, the memory of their subordination unto God and their dependency on him was drowned in this conceipt, whereupon their adoration, love, and imitation of God could not choose but be also interrupted. The fall of Angels therefore was pride. Since their fall, their practices have been the clean contrary unto those before mentioned. For being dispersed some in the air, some on the earth, some in the water, some amongst the minerals, dens, and caves, that are under the earth: *p*they have by all means laboured to effect an universal rebellion against the laws, and, as far as in them lieth, utter destruction of the works of God. These wicked Spirits the Heathens honoured instead of Gods, both generally under the name of *Dii inferi* Gods infernal; and particularly, some in oracles, some in Idols, some as household gods, some as Nymphs; in a word no foul and wicked spirit which was not one way or other honoured of men as God, till such time as light appeared in the world and dissolved the works of the devil. Thus much therefore may suffice for Angels, the next unto whom in degree are men.

The law whereby man is in his actions directed to the imitation of God.

[5.1] 5. God alone excepted, who actually and everlastingly is whatsoever he may be, and which cannot hereafter be that which now he is not; all other things besides are somewhat in possibility, which as yet they are not in act. And for this cause there is in all things an appetite or desire, whereby they incline to something which they may be: and when they are it, they shall be perfecter than now they are. All which perfections are contained under the general name of *Goodness*. And because there is not in the world anything whereby another may not some way be made the perfecter, therefore [5.2] all things that are, are good. Again since there can be no goodness

p John 8:44. 1 Pet. 5:8. Rev. 9:11. Gen. 3:15. 1 Chron. 21:1. Job 1:7 and 2:5. John 13:27. Acts 5:3. Rev. 20:8.

desired which proceedeth not from God himself, as from the supreme cause of all things; and every effect doth after a sort contain, at leastwise resemble the cause from which it proceedeth: ^{q}all things in the world are said in some sort to seek the highest, and to covet more or less the participation of God himself. Yet this doth nowhere so much appear as it doth in man: because there are so many kinds of perfections which man seeketh. The first degree of goodness is that general perfection which all things do seek, in desiring the continuance of their being. All things therefore coveting as much as may be to be like unto God in being ever, that which cannot hereunto attain personally, doth seek to continue itself another way, that is by offspring and propagation. The next degree of goodness is that which each thing coveteth by affecting resemblance with God, in the constancy and excellency of those operations which belong unto their kind. The immutability of God they strive unto, by working either always or for the most part after one and the same manner; his absolute exactness they imitate, by tending unto that which is most exquisite in every particular. Hence have risen a number of axioms in Philosophy showing, how ^{r}*The works of nature do always aim at that which cannot be bettered.* These two kinds of goodness [5.3] rehearsed are so nearly united to the things themselves which desire them, that we scarcely perceive the appetite to stir in reaching forth her hand towards them. But the desire of those perfections which grow externally is more apparent; especially of such as are not expressly desired unless they be first known or such as are not for any other cause, than for knowledge itself desired. Concerning perfections in this kind, that by proceeding in the knowledge of truth and by growing in the exercise of virtue, man amongst the creatures of this inferior world, aspireth to the greatest conformity with God, this is not only known unto us, ^{s}whom he himself hath so instructed, but even they do acknowledge, who amongst men are not judged the nearest unto him. With *Plato* what one thing more usual, than to excite men unto the love of wisdom, by showing how much wise men are thereby exalted above men; how knowledge doth raise them up into heaven; how it maketh them, though not Gods, yet as gods, high, admirable and divine? And *Mercurius*

---

^{q} Aristotle, *On the Soul*, Bk 2, ch. 4 [415ab].
^{r} Aristotle, *On the Heavens*, Bk. 2, ch. 5 [288a]. ^{s} Matt. 5:48. Wisdom 7:27.

Trismegistus speaking of the virtues of a righteous soul, '*Such spirits* (saith he) *are never cloyed with praising and speaking well of all men, with doing good unto every one by word and deed, because they study to frame themselves according to* THE PATTERN *of the father of spirits.*

Men's first beginning to grow to the knowledge of that law which they are to observe.

[6.1]   6. In the matter of knowledge, there is between the Angels of God and the children of men this difference. Angels already have full and complete knowledge in the highest degree that can be imparted unto them: "men if we view them in their spring, are at the first without understanding or knowledge at all. Nevertheless from this utter vacuity they grow by degrees, till they come at length to be even as the Angels themselves are. That which agreeth to the one now, the other shall attain unto in the end; they are not so far disjoined and severed, but that they come at length to meet. The soul of man being therefore at the first as a book, wherein nothing is, and yet all things may be imprinted; we are to search by what [6.2] steps and degrees it riseth unto perfection of knowledge. Unto that which hath been already set down concerning natural agents this we must add, that albeit therein we have comprised as well creatures living, as void of life, if they be in degree of nature beneath men; nevertheless a difference we must observe between those natural agents that work altogether unwittingly, and those which have, though weak, yet some understanding what they do, as fishes, fowls, and beasts have. Beasts are in sensible capacity as ripe even as men themselves, perhaps more ripe. For as stones, though in dignity of nature inferior unto plants, yet exceed them in firmness of strength or durability of being; and plants though beneath the excellency of creatures endowed with sense, yet exceed them in the faculty of vegetation and of fertility: so beasts though otherwise behind men, may notwithstanding in actions of sense and fancy go beyond them; because the endeavours of nature, when it hath an higher perfection to seek, are in lower the more remiss, not esteeming thereof so much as those things do, which have no better proposed [6.3] unto them. The soul of man therefore being capable of a more

' [Ed. 1924, 1:202–203].   " See Isa. 7:16.

divine perfection, hath (besides the faculties of growing unto sensible knowledge which is common unto us with beasts) a further ability, whereof in them there is no show at all, the ability of reaching [v]higher than unto sensible things. Till we grow to some ripeness of years, the soul of man doth only store itself with conceipts of things of inferior and more open quality, which afterwards do serve as instruments unto that which is greater: in the meanwhile above the reach of meaner creatures it ascendeth not. When once it comprehendeth anything above this, as the differences of time, affirmations, negations, and contradictions in speech; we then count it to have some use of natural reason. Whereunto if afterwards there might be added the right helps of [w]true art and learning (which helps I must plainly confess this age of the world, carrying the name of a learned age, doth neither much know nor greatly regard) there would undoubtedly be almost as great difference in maturity of judgement between men therewith inured, and that which now men are, as between men that are now and innocents. Which speech if any condemn, as being over-hyperbolical, let them consider but this one thing. No art is at the first finding out so perfect as industry may after make it. Yet the very first man that to any purpose knew the way we speak of and followed it, hath alone thereby performed more very near in all parts of natural knowledge, than since then in any one part thereof, the whole world besides hath done. In the poverty of [x]that other new devised aid two things there are notwithstanding singular. Of marvellous quick dispatch it is, and doth show them that have it as much almost in three days, as if it dwell threescore years with them. Again because the curiosity of man's wit, doth many times with peril wade farther in the search of things, than were convenient: the same is thereby restrained unto such generalities as everywhere offering themselves, are apparent unto men of the weakest conceipt that need be. So as following the rules and precepts thereof, we may define it to be, an Art which teacheth the way of speedy discourse, and restraineth the mind of man that it may not wax over-wise. Education and instruction are the means, the one by use, the other by precept to make our natural faculty of reason, both the better and the sooner able to judge rightly

[6.4]

[6.5]

---

[v] *But man ascends even to heaven and measures it. And what is more than all besides, he mounts to heaven without leaving the earth.* Mercurius Trismegistus [ed. 1924, 1:204–205].
[w] Aristotelical demonstration.   [x] Ramistry.

between truth and error, good and evil. But at what time a man may be said to have attained so far forth the use of reason, as sufficeth to make him capable of those laws, whereby he is then bound to guide his actions; this is a great deal more easy for common sense to discern, than for any man by skill and learning to determine: even as it is not in Philosophers, who best know the nature both of fire and of gold, to teach what degree of the one will serve to purify the other, so well as the artisan, who doth this by fire, discerneth by sense when the fire hath that degree of heat which sufficeth for his purpose.

Of man's will which is the thing that laws of action are made to guide.

[7.1] 7. By reason man attaineth unto the knowledge of things that are and are not sensible. It resteth therefore that we search how man attaineth unto the knowledge of such things unsensible as are to be known that they may be done. Seeing then that nothing can move unless there be some end, the desire whereof provoketh unto motion; how should that divine power of the soul, that *ySpirit of our mind* as the Apostle termeth it, ever stir itself unto action, unless it have also the like spur? The end for which we are moved to work, is sometimes the goodness which we conceive of the very working itself, without any further respect at all; and the cause that procureth action is the mere desire of action, no other good besides being thereby intended. Of certain turbulent wits it is said, *zIllis quieta movere magna merces videbatur*, They thought the very disturbance of things established an hire sufficient to set them on work. Sometimes that which we do is referred to a further end, without the desire whereof we would leave the same undone, *a*as in their actions that gave alms to purchase thereby the praise of [7.2] men. Man in perfection of nature being made according to the likeness of his maker resembleth him also in the manner of working; so that whatsoever we work as men, the same we do wittingly work and freely, neither are we according to the manner of natural agents any way so tied, but that it is in our power to leave the things we

y Ephes. 4:23. *z* Sallust [*The Catiline War*, ch. 21; *L*, pp. 38–39].
a Matt. 6:2.

do undone. The good which either is gotten by doing or which consisteth in the very doing itself, causeth not action, unless apprehending it as good we so like and desire it: that we do unto any such end, the same we choose and prefer before the leaving of it undone. Choice there is not unless the thing which we take be so in our power that we might have refused and left it. If fire consume the stubble, it chooseth not so to do, because the nature thereof is such that it can do no other. To choose is to will one thing before another. And to will is to bend our souls to the having or doing of that which they see to be good. Goodness is seen with the eye of the understanding. And the light of that eye, is reason. So that two principal fountains there are of human action, *Knowledge* and *Will*, which will in things tending towards any end is termed *Choice*. Concerning knowledge, Behold saith *Moses*, *[b]I have set before you this day good and evil, life and death*. Concerning Will, he addeth immediately, *Choose life*, that is to say, the things that tend unto life, them choose. But of one thing we must have special care, as [7.3] being a matter of no small moment, and that is, how the will properly and strictly taken, as it is of things which are referred unto the end that man desireth, differeth greatly from that inferior natural desire which we call appetite. The object of appetite is whatsoever sensible good may be wished for; the object of will is that good which reason doth lead us to seek. Affections, as joy, and grief, and fear, and anger, with suchlike; being as it were the sundry fashions and forms of appetite, can neither rise at the conceipt of a thing indifferent, nor yet choose but rise at the sight of some things. Wherefore it is not altogether in our power, whether we will be stirred with affections or no; whereas actions which issue from the disposition of the will are in the power thereof to be performed or stayed. Finally appetite is the will's solicitor, and the will is appetite's controller; what we covet according to the one, by the other we often reject, neither is any other desire termed properly will, but that where reason and understanding, or the show of reason prescribeth the thing desired. It may be therefore a question, whether those operations of men are to be counted voluntary, wherein that good which is sensible provoketh appetite, and appetite causeth action, reason being never called to council; as when we

[b] Deut. 30:19.

eat or drink, or betake ourselves unto rest, and such-like. The truth is, that such actions in men having attained to the use of reason are voluntary. For as the authority of higher powers hath force even in those things which are done without their privity, and are of so mean reckoning that to acquaint them therewith it needeth not: in like sort voluntarily we are said to do that also, which the will if it listed might hinder from being done, although about the doing thereof we do not expressly use our reason or understanding, and so immediately apply our wills thereunto. In cases therefore of such facility the will doth yield her assent, as it were with a kind of silence, by not dissenting; in which respect her force is not so apparent as in express mandates or prohibitions, especially

[7.4] upon advice and consultation going before. Where understanding therefore needeth, in those things reason is the director of man's will by discovering in action what is good. For the laws of well-doing are the dictates of right reason. Children which are not as yet come unto those years whereat they may have; again innocents which are excluded by natural defect from ever having; thirdly mad men which for the present cannot possibly have the use of right reason to guide themselves, have for their guide the reason that guideth other men, which are tutors over them to seek and to procure their good for them. In the rest there is that light of reason, whereby good may be known from evil, and which discovering the same

[7.5] rightly is termed right. The will notwithstanding doth not incline to have or do that which reason teacheth to be good, unless the same do also teach it to be possible. For albeit the appetite, being more general, 'may wish anything which seemeth good, be it never so impossible: yet for such things the reasonable will of man doth never seek. Let reason teach impossibility in anything, and the will of man doth let it go; a thing impossible it doth not affect, the

[7.6] impossibility thereof being manifest. There is in the will of man naturally that freedom, whereby it is apt to take or refuse any particular object whatsoever being presented unto it. Whereupon it followeth, that there is no particular object so good, but it may have the show of some difficulty or unpleasant quality annexed to it; in respect whereof the will may shrink and decline it: contrariwise (for so things are blended) there is no particular evil which hath not some

---

' *O if Jupiter would bring me back the years past* [Virgil, *Aeneid*, Bk 8, line 560].

appearance of goodness whereby to insinuate itself. *d*For evil as evil cannot be desired: if that be desired which is evil, the cause is the goodness which is, or seemeth to be joined with it. Goodness doth not move by being, but by being apparent; and therefore many things are neglected which are most precious, only because the value of them lieth hid. Sensible goodness is most apparent, near, and present, which causeth the appetite to be therewith strongly provoked. Now pursuit and refusal in the will do follow, the one the affirmation, the other the negation of goodness, which the understanding apprehendeth, grounding itself upon sense, unless some higher reason do chance to teach the contrary. And if reason have taught it rightly to be good, yet not so apparently that the mind receiveth it with utter impossibility of being otherwise; still there is place left for the will to take or leave. Whereas therefore amongst so many things as are to be done there are so few, the goodness whereof reason in such sort doth or easily can discover; we are not to marvel at the choice of evil, even then when the contrary is probably known. Hereby it cometh to pass, that custom inuring the mind by long practice, and so leaving there a sensible impression, prevaileth more than reasonable persuasion what way soever. Reason therefore may rightly discern the thing which is good, and yet the will of man not incline itself thereunto, as oft as the prejudice of sensible experience doth oversway. Nor let any man think that this [7.7] doth make anything for the just excuse of iniquity. For there was never sin committed, wherein a less good was not preferred before a greater, and that wilfully; which cannot be done without the singular disgrace of nature, and the utter disturbance of that divine order, whereby the preeminence of chiefest acceptation is by the best things worthily challenged. There is not that good reason which concerneth us, but it hath evidence enough for itself, if reason were diligent to search it out. Through neglect thereof, abused we are with the show of that which is not, sometimes the subtlety of Satan inveigling us as it did *e*Eve; sometimes the hastiness of our wills preventing the more considerate advice of sound reason, as in *f*the

---

d *If someone moves towards evil, he does not first move himself as towards evil, but rather as towards good. A little later, For it is impossible for anyone to move towards evil, willing to have it, without having the hope of a good or the fear of a greater evil.* Alcinous, *On Platonic Doctrines.*
e 2 Cor. 11:3.   *f* Luke 9:54.

apostles, when they no sooner saw what they liked not, but they forthwith were desirous of fire from heaven; sometimes the very custom of evil making the heart obdurate against whatsoever instructions to the contrary, as in them over whom our Saviour spake weeping, *[g]O Jerusalem, how often and thou wouldst not?* Still therefore that wherewith we stand blameable, and can no way excuse it is, In doing evil, we prefer a less good before a greater, the greatness whereof is by reason investigable, and may be known. The search of knowledge is a thing painful and the painfulness of knowledge is that which maketh the will so hardly inclinable thereunto. The root hereof divine malediction whereby the *[h]*instruments being weakened wherewithal the soul (especially in reasoning) doth work, it preferreth rest in ignorance before wearisome labour to know. For a spur of diligence therefore we have a natural thirst after knowledge ingrafted in us. But by reason of that original weakness in the instruments, without which the understanding part is not able in this world by discourse to work, the very conceipt of painfulness is as a bridle to stay us. For which cause the Apostle who knew right well, that the weariness of the flesh is an heavy clog to the will, striketh mightily upon this key, *[i]Awake thou that sleepest, Cast off all which presseth down, Watch, Labour, strive to go forward and to grow in knowledge.*

Of the natural way of finding out laws by reason to guide the will unto that which is good.

[8.1] 8. Wherefore to return to our former intent of discovering the natural way, whereby rules have been found out concerning that goodness wherewith the will of man ought to be moved in human actions; as every thing naturally and necessarily doth desire the utmost good and greatest perfection, whereof nature hath made it capable, even so man. Our felicity therefore being the object and accomplishment of our desire, we cannot choose but wish and covet it. All particular

[g] Matt. 23:37.

[h] Wisdom 9:15. *A corruptible body is heavy unto the soul, and the earthly mansion keeps down the mind that is full of cares. And hardly can we discern the things that are upon earth, and with great labour find we out the things which are before us. Who can then seek out the things that are in heaven?*

[i] Ephes. 5:14. Heb. 12:1–12. 1 Cor. 16:13. Prov. 2:4. Luke 13:24.

things, which are subject unto action, the will doth so far forth incline unto, as reason judgeth them the better for us, and consequently the more available to our bliss. If reason err, we fall into evil, and are so far forth deprived of the general perfection we seek. Seeing therefore that for the framing of men's actions the knowledge of good from evil is necessary; it only resteth that we search how this may be had. Neither must we suppose that there needeth one rule to know the good, and another the evil by. [j]For he that knoweth what is straight, doth even thereby discern what is crooked, because the absence of straightness in bodies capable thereof is crookedness. Goodness in actions is like unto straightness, wherefore that which is done well we term right. For as the straight way is most acceptable to him that traveleth, because by it he cometh soonest to his journey's end: so in action, that which doth lie the evenest between us and the end we desire, must needs be the fittest for our use. Besides which fitness for use there is also in rectitude, beauty; as contrariwise in obliquity deformity. And that which is good in the actions of men, doth not only delight as profitable, but as amiable also. In which consideration the Grecians most divinely have given to the active perfection of men, a [k]name expressing both beauty and goodness, because goodness in ordinary speech is for the most part applied only to that which is beneficial. But we in the name of goodness, do here imply both. And of discerning [8.2] goodness there are but these two ways; the one the knowledge of the causes whereby it is made such, the other the observation of those signs and tokens, which being annexed always unto goodness, argue that where they are found, there also goodness is, although we know not the cause by force whereof it is there. The former of these is the most sure and infallible way, but so hard that all shun it, and had rather walk as men do in the dark by haphazard, than tread so long and intricate mazes for knowledge sake. As therefore Physicians are many times forced to leave such methods of curing as themselves know to be the fittest, and being overruled by their patients' impatiency are fain to try the best they can, in taking that way of cure, which the cured will yield unto: in like sort, considering how the case doth stand with this present age

[j] [Aristotle, *On the Soul*, Bk I, ch. 5 (411a)].
[k] Καλοχα 'γαθία [Aristotle, *Magna Moralia*, Bk 2, ch. 9 (1207b); *Politics*, Bk 4, ch. 6 (1293b)].

full of tongue and weak of brain, behold we yield to the stream thereof; into the causes of goodness we will not make any curious or deep inquiry; to touch them now and then it shall be sufficient, when they are so near at hand that easily they may be conceived without any far removed discourse: that way we are contented to prove, which being the worse in itself, is notwithstanding now by reason of common imbecility the fitter and likelier to be brooked.

[8.3] Signs and tokens to know good by, are of sundry kinds: some more certain and some less. The most certain token of evident goodness is, if the general persuasion of all men do so account it. And therefore a common received error is never utterly overthrown, till such time as we go from signs unto causes, and show some manifest root or fountain thereof common unto all, whereby it may clearly appear how it hath come to pass that so many have been overseen. In which case surmises and slight probabilities will not serve, because the universal consent of men is the perfectest and strongest in this kind which comprehendeth only the signs and tokens of goodness. Things casual do vary, and that which a man doth but chance to think well of, cannot still have the like hap. Wherefore although we know not the cause, yet thus much we may know, that some necessary cause there is, whensoever the judgements of all men generally or for the most part run one and the same way, especially in matters of natural discourse. For of things necessarily and naturally done there is no more affirmed but this, *¹They keep either always or for the most part one tenure.* The general and perpetual voice of men is as the sentence of God himself. *ᵐFor that which all men have at all times learned, nature herself must needs have taught; and God being the author of nature, her voice is but his instrument. By her from him we receive whatsoever in such sort we learn.* Infinite duties there are, the goodness whereof is by this rule sufficiently

---

¹ Aristotle, *Rhetoric*, Bk 1, ch. 39 [1369ab].

ᵐ *Error cannot occur where all think the same.* Montecatini, on Book I of Aristotle's *Politics* [p. 3]. *Whatever is shared in common by all individuals of a species must have a common cause, which is the species and nature of those individuals.* The same. *What occurs in the whole of any species as universal also occurs by instinct of a particular nature.* Ficino, *On Christian Religion* [ch. 1]. *If you desire to make progress, first firmly regard as true that which the sound mind of all humanity attests.* Cusanus, *Compendium*, ch. 1. *It is not allowable to consider a natural and universal human judgement to be false and vain.* Telesio [*On the Nature of Things*, Bk 5, ch. 2]. *For what seems so to all, we say is so; and he who attacks this belief will certainly not be more believable.* Aristotle, *Nicomachean Ethics*, Bk 10, ch. 2 [1172b–1173a].

manifested, although we had no other warrant besides to approve them. The apostle St. Paul having speech concerning the Heathen saith of them, *"They are a law unto themselves.* His meaning is, that by force of the light of reason, wherewith God illuminateth everyone which cometh into the world, men being enabled to know truth from falsehood, and good from evil, do thereby learn in many things what the will of God is; which will himself not revealing by any extraordinary means unto them, but they by natural discourse attaining the knowledge thereof, seem the makers of those laws which indeed are his, and they but only the finders of them out. A law [8.4] therefore generally taken, is a directive rule unto goodness of operation. The rule of divine operations outward, is the definitive appointment of God's own wisdom set down within himself. The rule of natural agents that work by simple necessity, is the determination of the wisdom of God, known to God himself the principal director of them, but not unto them that are directed to execute the same. The rule of natural agents which work after a sort of their own accord, as the beasts do, is the judgement of common sense or fancy concerning the sensible goodness of those objects wherewith they are moved. The rule of ghostly or immaterial natures, as spirits and Angels, is their intuitive intellectual judgement concerning the amiable beauty and high goodness of that object, which with unspeakable joy and delight, doth set them on work. The rule of voluntary agents on earth is the sentence that reason giveth concerning the goodness of those things which they are to do. And the sentences which reason giveth are some more, some less general, before it come to define in particular actions what is good. The [8.5] main principles of reason are in themselves apparent. For to make nothing evident of itself unto man's understanding were to take away all possibility of knowing anything. And herein that of *Theophrastus* is true, *°They that seek a reason of all things do utterly overthrow reason.* In every kind of knowledge some such grounds there are, as that being proposed the mind doth presently embrace them as free from all possibility of error, clear and manifest without proof. In which kind axioms or principles more general are such as this, *That the greater good is to be chosen before the less.* If therefore it should be demanded, what reason there is why the will of man, which

---

ⁿ Rom. 2:14.   *°* Theophrastus, *Metaphysics* [ed. 1929, pp. 28–29].

doth necessarily shun harm and covet whatsoever is pleasant and sweet, should be commanded to count the pleasures of sin gall, and notwithstanding the bitter accidents wherewith virtuous actions are compassed, yet still to rejoice and delight in them; surely this could never stand with reason, but that wisdom thus prescribing, groundeth her laws upon an infallible rule of comparison, which is, that small difficulties, when exceeding great good is sure to ensue; and on the other side momentary benefits, when the hurt which they draw after them is unspeakable, are not at all to be respected. This rule is the ground whereupon the wisdom of the Apostle buildeth a law, enjoining patience unto himself; *PThe present lightness of our affliction worketh unto us even with abundance upon abundance an eternal weight of glory, while we look not on the things which are seen, but on the things which are not seen. For the things which are seen are temporal, but the things which are not seen eternal:* Therefore Christianity to be embraced, whatsoever calamities in those times it was accompanied withal. Upon the same ground our Saviour proveth the law most reasonable, that doth forbid those crimes which men for gain's sake fall into. *qFor a man to win the world, if it be with the loss of his soul, what benefit or good is it?* Axioms less general, yet so manifest that they need no further proof, are such as these, *God to be worshipped, Parents to be honoured, Others to be used by us as we ourselves would by them.* Such things, as soon as they are alleged, all men acknowledge to be good; they require no proof or further discourse to be assured of their goodness. Notwithstanding whatsoever such principle there is, it was at the first found out by discourse, and drawn from out of the very bowels of heaven and earth. For we are to note, that things in the world are to us discernible, not only so far forth as serveth for our vital preservation, but further also in a twofold higher respect. For first if all other uses were utterly taken away; yet the mind of man being by nature speculative and delighted with contemplation in itself, they were to be known even for mere knowledge and understanding's sake. Yea further besides this, the knowledge of every the least thing in the whole world, hath in it a second peculiar benefit unto us, inasmuch as it serveth to minister rules, canons, and laws for men to direct those actions by, which we properly term human.

p 2 Cor. 4:17.　　*q* Matt. 16:26.

This did the very Heathens themselves obscurely insinuate by making *Themis* which we call *Jus* or Right to be the daughter of heaven and earth. We know things either as they are in themselves, or [8.6] as they are in mutual relation one to another. The knowledge of that which man is in reference unto himself, and other things in relation unto man, I may justly term the mother of all those principles which are as it were edicts, statutes, and decrees in that law of nature, whereby human actions are framed. First therefore having observed that the best things, where they are not hindered, do still produce the best operations (for which cause where many things are to concur unto one effect, the best is in all congruity of reason to guide the residue, that it prevailing most, the work principally done by it may have greatest perfection) when hereupon we come to observe in ourselves, of what excellency our souls are in comparison of our bodies, and the diviner part in relation unto the baser of our souls; seeing that all these concur in producing human actions: it cannot be well unless the chiefest do command and direct the rest. ʳThe soul then ought to conduct the body, and the spirit of our minds the soul. This is therefore the first law, whereby the highest power of the mind requireth general obedience at the hands of all the rest concurring with it unto action. Touching the several [8.7] grand mandates which being imposed by the understanding faculty of the mind, must be obeyed by the will of man, they are by the same method found out, whether they import our duty towards God or towards man. Touching the one, I may not here stand to open by what degrees of discourse the minds, even of mere natural men, have attained to know, not only that there is a God, but also what power, force, wisdom, and other properties that God hath, and how all things depend on him. This being therefore presupposed, from that known relation which God hath unto us ˢas unto children, and unto all good things as unto effects, whereof himself is the ᵗprincipal cause, these axioms and laws natural concerning our duty, have arisen, *"That in all things we go about his aid, is by prayer to*

ʳ Aristotle, *Politics*, Bk I, ch. 5 [1254].
ˢ *No god is unkind to humans.* Plato, *Theaetetus* [151d].
ᵗ *For God is thought to be the cause of all and a kind of principle.* Aristotle, *Metaphysics*, Bk I, ch. 2 [983a].
ᵘ *But, O Socrates, all who have even a small share of sound-mindedness call upon God at the outset of every undertaking, small or great.* Plato, *Timaeus* [27c].

be craved, *That he cannot have sufficient honour done unto him, but the utmost of that we can do to honour him we must:* which is in effect the same that we read, *Thou shalt love the Lord thy God with all thy heart, with all thy soul, and with all thy mind.* Which law our Saviour doth term the *First and the great Commandment.* Touching the next, which as our Saviour addeth, is like unto this (he meaneth in amplitude and largeness inasmuch as it is the root out of which all laws of duty to men-ward have grown, as out of the former all offices of religion towards God) the like natural inducement hath brought men to know, that it is their duty no less to love others than themselves. For seeing those things which are equal, must needs all have one measure; if I cannot but wish to receive all good, even as much at every man's hand as any man can wish unto his own soul: how should I look to have any part of my desire herein satisfied, unless myself be careful to satisfy the like desire, which is undoubtedly in other men, we all being of one, and the same nature? To have anything offered them repugnant to this desire must needs in all respects grieve them as much as me, so that if I do harm, I must look to suffer; there being no reason that others should show greater measure of love to me, than they have by me showed unto them. My desire therefore to be loved of my equals in nature as much as possibly may be, imposeth upon me a natural duty of bearing to them-ward fully the like affection. From which relation of equality between ourselves and them that are as ourselves, what several rules and canons natural reason hath drawn for direction of life, no man is ignorant, as namely, *That because we would take no harm, we must therefore do none; That since we would not be in any thing extremely dealt with, we must ourselves avoid all extremity in our dealings; That from all violence and wrong we are utterly to abstain,* with such-like; which further to wade in would be tedious, and to our present purpose not altogether so necessary, seeing that on these *two general heads already mentioned all other specialties [8.8] are dependent. Wherefore the natural measure whereby to judge our doings, is the sentence of reason, determining and setting down

---

v Aristotle, *Nicomachean Ethics*, Bk 8, last chapter [1163b].
w Deut. 6:5.   *x* Matt. 22:38.
y *What anyone approves in himself he cannot reprove in another.* Justinian, *Code*, 3.28.11. *What anyone lays down as a law for another he ought also to abide by himself.* Justinian, *Digest*, 2.2. *One is entirely to abstain from all wrong and violence.* Justinian, *Digest*, 43.24.1.
z Matt. 22:40. *On these two commandments hangeth the whole law.*

what is good to be done. Which sentence is either mandatory, showing what must be done; or else permissive, declaring only what may be done; or thirdly admonitory, opening what is the most convenient for us to do. The first taketh place where the comparison doth stand altogether between doing and not doing of one thing which in itself is absolutely good or evil, *a*as it had been for *Joseph* to yield or not to yield to the impotent desire of his lewd mistress, the one evil, the other good simply. The second is when of diverse things evil, all being not evitable, we are permitted to take one, which one saving only in case of so great urgency were not otherwise to be taken, *b*as in the matter of divorce amongst the Jews. The last when of divers things good, one is principal and most eminent, *c*as in their act who sold their possessions and laid the price at the Apostles' feet, which possessions they might have retained unto themselves without sin; *d*again in the Apostle St. Paul's own choice to maintain himself by his own labour, whereas in living by the Church's maintenance, as others did, there had been no offence committed. In goodness therefore there is a latitude or extent, whereby it cometh to pass that even of good actions some are better than other some, whereas otherwise one man could not excel another, but all should be either absolutely good, as hitting jump that indivisible point or center wherein goodness consisteth; or else missing it they should be excluded out of the number of well-doers. Degrees of well-doing there could be none, except perhaps in the seldomness and oftenness of doing well. But the nature of goodness being thus ample, a law is properly that which reason in such sort defineth to be good that it must be done. And the law of reason or human nature is that which men by discourse of natural reason have rightly found out themselves to be all forever bound unto in their actions. Laws of reason have these marks to be known by. Such as keep [8.9] them, resemble most lively in their voluntary actions, that very manner of working which nature herself doth necessarily observe in the course of the whole world. The works of nature are all behoveful, beautiful, without superfluity or defect; even so theirs, if they be framed according to that which the law of reason teacheth. Secondly those laws are investigable by reason without the help of revelation supernatural and divine. Finally in such sort they are investigable,

---

a Gen. 39:9.   *b* Mark 10:4.   *c* Acts 4:37. Acts 5:4.   *d* 2 Thess. 3:8.

that the knowledge of them is general, the world hath always been acquainted with them, according to that which one in *Sophocles* observeth concerning a branch of this law, *'It is no child of today's or yesterday's birth, but hath been no man knoweth how long since.* It is not agreed upon by one, or two, or few, but by all: which we may not so understand, as if every particular man in the whole world did know and confess whatsoever the law of reason doth contain, but this law is such that being proposed no man can reject it as unreasonable and unjust. Again there is nothing in it but any man (having natural perfection of wit, and ripeness of judgement) may by labour and travail find out. And to conclude, the general principles thereof are such, as it is not easy to find men ignorant of them. Law rational therefore, which men commonly use to call the law of nature, meaning thereby the law which human nature knoweth itself in reason universally bound unto, which also for that cause may be termed most fitly the law of reason: this law, I say, comprehendeth all those things which men by the light of their natural understanding evidently know, or at leastwise may know, to be beseeming or unbeseeming, virtuous or vicious, good [8.10] or evil for them to do. Now although it be true, which some have said, *that whatsoever is done amiss, the law of nature and reason thereby is transgressed, because even those offences which are by their special qualities breaches of supernatural laws, do also, for that they are generally evil, violate in general that principle of reason, which willeth universally to fly from evil: yet do we not therefore so far extend the law of reason, as to contain in it all manner laws whereunto reasonable creatures are bound, but (as hath been shown) we restrain it to those only duties, which all men by force of natural wit either do or might understand to be such duties as concern all men. *Certain halfwaking men there are* (as Saint *Augustine* noteth) *who neither altogether asleep in folly, not yet thoroughly awake in the light of true understanding, have thought that there is not at all any thing just and righteous in itself: but look wherewith nations are inured, the same they take to be right and just. Whereupon their conclusion is,*

---

e Sophocles, *Antigone* [lines 456–457].

f Thomas Aquinas, *Summa Theologiae*, I–II, q. 94, art. 3. *All sins universally are against reason and the law of nature.* Augustine, *On the City of God*, Bk 12, ch. 1. *Every vice harms nature and is thus against nature.*

g *On Christian Teaching*, Bk 3, ch. 14.

that seeing each sort of people hath a different kind of right from other, and that which is right of its own nature must be everywhere one and the same, therefore in itself there is nothing right. These good folk (saith he, *that I may not trouble their wits with rehearsal of too many things*) *have not looked so far into the world as to perceive, that Do as thou wouldest be done unto, is a sentence which all nations under heaven are agreed upon. Refer this sentence to the love of God, and it extinguisheth all heinous crimes: refer it to the love of thy neighbour, and all grievous wrongs it banisheth out of the world.* Wherefore as touching the law of reason, this was (it seemeth) Saint *Augustine's* judgement, namely, that there are in it some things which stand as principles universally agreed upon: and that out of those principles, which are in themselves evident, the greatest moral duties we owe towards God or man, may without any great difficulty be concluded. If then it be [8.11] here demanded, by what means it should come to pass (the greatest part of the law moral being so easy for all men to know) that so many thousands of men notwithstanding have been ignorant even of principal moral duties, not imagining the breach of them to be sin: I deny not but lewd and wicked custom, beginning perhaps at the first amongst few, afterwards spreading into greater multitudes, and so continuing from time to time, may be of force even in plain things to smother the light of natural understanding, because men will not bend their wits to examine, whether things wherewith they have been accustomed, be good or evil. For example's sake that grosser kind of heathenish idolatry, whereby they worshipped the very works of their own hands, was an absurdity to reason so palpable, that the Prophet *David* comparing idols and idolaters together, maketh almost no odds between them, but the one in a manner as much without wit and sense as the other, [h]*They that make them are like unto them, and so are all that trust in them.* That wherein an idolater doth seem so absurd and foolish, is by the Wiseman thus expressed, [i]*He is not ashamed to speak unto that which hath no life, he calleth on him that is weak for health, he prayeth for life unto him which is dead, of him which hath no experience he requireth help, for his journey he sueth to him which is not able to go, for gain and work and success in his affairs he seeketh furtherance of him that hath no manner of power.* The cause of which senseless stupidity

---

[h] Ps. 135:18.   [i] Wisdom 13:17.

is afterwards imputed to custom. *ʲWhen a father mourned grievously for his son that was taken away suddenly, he made an image for him that was once dead, whom now he worshippeth as a God, ordaining to his servants ceremonies and sacrifices.* Thus by process of time this wicked custom prevailed, and was kept as a law; the authority of Rulers, the ambition of craftsmen, and such-like means thrusting forward the ignorant, and increasing their superstition. Unto this which the Wiseman hath spoken, somewhat besides may be added. For whatsoever we have hitherto taught, or shall hereafter, concerning the force of man's natural understanding, this we always desire withal to be understood, that there is no kind of faculty or power in man or any other creature, which can rightly perform the functions allotted to it, without perpetual aid and concurrence of that supreme cause of all things. The benefit whereof as oft as we cause God in his justice to withdraw, there can no other thing follow, than that which the Apostle noteth, even men endowed with the light of reason to walk notwithstanding *ᵏin the vanity of their mind, having their cogitations darkened, and being strangers from the life of God through the ignorance which is in them, because of the hardness of their hearts.* And this cause is mentioned by the prophet Isaiah, speaking of the ignorance of idolaters, who see not how the manifest law of reason condemneth their gross iniquity and sin. They have not in them, saith he, so much wit as to think, *ˡshall I bow to the stock of a tree? All knowledge and understanding is taken from them. For God hath shut their eyes that they cannot see.* That which we say in this case of idolatry, serveth for all other things, wherein the like kind of general blindness hath prevailed against the manifest laws of reason. Within the compass of which laws we do not only comprehend whatsoever may be easily known to belong to the duty of all men, but even whatsoever may possibly be known to be of that quality, so that the same be by *necessary* consequence deduced out of clear and manifest principles. For if once we descend unto probable collections what is convenient for men, we are then in the territory where free and arbitrary determinations, the territory where human laws take place, which laws are after to be considered.

ʲ Wisdom 14:14.   ᵏ Ephes. 4:17.   ˡ Isa. 44:19, 18.

The benefit of keeping that law
which reason teacheth.

9. Now the due observation of this law which reason teacheth us, [9.1] cannot but be effectual unto their great good that observe the same. For we see the whole world and each part thereof so compacted, that as long as each thing performeth only that work which is natural unto it, it thereby preserveth both other things, and also itself. Contrariwise, let any principal thing, as the Sun, the Moon, any one of the heavens or elements, but once cease or fail, or swerve, and who doth not easily conceive, that the sequel thereof would be ruin both to itself, and whatsoever dependeth on it? And is it possible that man being not only the noblest creature in the world, but even a very world in himself, his transgressing the law of his nature should draw no manner of harm after it? Yes, *tribulation and anguish unto every soul that doth evil*. Good doth follow unto all things, by observing the course of their nature, and on the contrary side evil by not observing it: but not unto natural agents that good which we call *Reward*, not that evil which we properly term *Punishment*. The reason whereof is, because amongst creatures in this world, only man's observation of the law of his nature is *Righteousness*, only man's transgression *Sin*. And the reason of this is the difference in his manner of observing or transgressing the law of his nature. He doth not otherwise than voluntarily the one or the other. What we do against our wills, or constrainedly, we are not properly said to do it, because the motive cause of doing it is not in ourselves, but carrieth us, as if the wind should drive a feather in the air, we no whit furthering that whereby we are driven. In such cases therefore the evil which is done, moveth compassion; men are pitied for it, as being rather miserable in such respect than culpable. Some things are likewise done by man, though not through outward force and impulsion, though not against, yet without their wills, as in alienation of mind, or any the like inevitable utter absence of wit and judgement. For which cause, no man did ever think the hurtful actions of furious men and innocents to be punishable. Again, some things we do neither against nor without, and yet not simply and merely with our wills, but with our wills in such sort moved, that albeit there be no impossibility but that we might, nevertheless we are not so easily able to do otherwise. In this consideration one

evil deed is made more pardonable than another. Finally, that which we do being evil, is notwithstanding by so much more pardonable, by how much the exigence of so doing, or the difficulty of doing otherwise is greater: unless this necessity or difficulty have originally risen from ourselves. It is no excuse therefore unto him, who being drunk, committeth incest, and allegeth that his wits were not his own, inasmuch as himself might have chosen whether his wits should by that mean have been taken from him. Now rewards and punishments do always presuppose something willingly done well or ill, without which respect though we may sometimes receive good or harm, yet then the one is only a benefit, and not a reward, the other simply an hurt, not a punishment. From the sundry dispositions of man's will, which is the root of all his actions, there groweth variety in the sequel of rewards and punishments, which are by these and the like rules measured: *"Take away the will, and all acts are equal: That which we do not and would do, is commonly accepted as done.* By these and the like rules men's actions are determined of and judged, whether they be in their own nature rewardable [9.2] or punishable. Rewards and punishments are not received, but at the hands of such as being above us, have power to examine and judge our deeds. How men come to have this authority one over another in external actions, we shall more diligently examine in that which followeth. But for this present so much all do acknowledge, that since every man's heart and conscience doth in good or evil, even secretly committed and known to none but itself, either like or disallow itself, and accordingly either rejoice, very nature exulting (as it were) in certain hope of reward, or else grieve (as it were) in a sense of future punishment, neither of which can in this case be looked for from any other, saving only from him, who discerneth and judgeth the very secrets of all hearts: therefore he is the only rewarder and revenger of all such actions, although not of such actions only, but of all, whereby the law of nature is broken, whereof himself is author. For which cause, the Roman laws called the laws of the twelve tables, "requiring offices of inward affection, which the eye of man cannot reach unto, threaten the neglecters of them with none but divine punishment.

ᵐ Justinian, *Code*, 9.9.20 and 5.4.16.

ⁿ They shall approach the gods in purity, bringing piety. Whoever does otherwise, God himself will be the avenger [Cicero, *On Laws*; *L*, pp. 392–393].

How reason doth lead men unto the making of human laws whereby politic societies are governed, and to agreement about laws, whereby the fellowship or communion of independent societies standeth.

10. That which hitherto we have set down, is (I hope) sufficient [10.1] to show their brutishness, which imagine that religion and virtue are only as men will account of them, that we might make as much account, if we would, of the contrary, without any harm unto ourselves, and that in nature they are as indifferent one as the other. We see then how nature itself teacheth laws and statutes to live by. The laws which have been hitherto mentioned, °do bind men absolutely, even as they are men, although they have never any settled fellowship, never any solemn agreement amongst themselves what to do, or not to do. But forasmuch as we are not by ourselves sufficient to furnish ourselves with competent store of things needful for such a life as our nature doth desire, a life fit for the dignity of man: therefore to supply those defects and imperfections, which are in us living, single, and solely by ourselves, we are naturally induced to seek communion and fellowship with others. This was the cause of men's uniting themselves at the first in politic societies, which societies could not be without government, nor government without a distinct kind of law from that which hath been already declared. Two foundations there are which bear up public societies, the one, a natural inclination, whereby all men desire sociable life and fellowship, the other an order expressly or secretly agreed upon, touching the manner of their union in living together. The latter is that which we call the law of a commonweal, the very soul of a politic body, the parts whereof are by law animated, held together, and set on work in such actions as the common good requireth. Laws politic, ordained for external order and regiment amongst men, are never framed as they should be, unless presuming the will of man to be inwardly obstinate, rebellious, and averse from all obedience unto the sacred laws of his nature; in a word, unless presuming man to be in regard of his depraved mind little better than a wild beast, they do accordingly provide notwithstanding so

---

° *For there is what all men divine to be just and unjust in general by nature, even with no community or agreement with one another.* Aristotle, *Rhetoric*, Bk 1 [1373b].

to frame his outward actions, that they be no hindrance unto the common good for which societies are instituted: unless they do this, they are not perfect. It resteth therefore that we consider how nature findeth out such laws of government as serve to direct even nature [10.2] depraved to a right end. All men desire to lead in this world an happy life. That life is led most happily, wherein all virtue is exercised without impediment or let. The Apostle *ᵖin exhorting men to contentment, although they have in this world no more than very bare food and raiment, giveth us thereby to understand, that those are even the lowest of things necessary, that if we should be stripped of all those things without which we might possibly be, yet these must be left, that destitution in these is such an impediment, as till it be removed, suffereth not the mind of man to admit any other care. For this cause *ᵠfirst God assigned *Adam* maintenance of life, and *ʳthen appointed him a law to observe. For this cause after men began to grow to a number: the first thing we read they gave themselves unto, *ˢwas the tilling of the earth, and the feeding of cattle. Having by this mean whereon to live, the principal actions of their life afterward are *ᵗnoted by the exercise of their religion. True it is *ᵘthat the kingdom of God must be the first thing in our purposes and desires. But inasmuch as righteous life presupposeth life, inasmuch as to live virtuously it is impossible except we live, therefore the first impediment, which naturally we endeavour to remove, is penury and want of things without which we cannot live. Unto life many implements are necessary; more, if we seek (as all men naturally do) such a life as hath in it joy, comfort, delight and pleasure. To this end we see *ᵛhow quickly sundry arts Mechanical were found out in the very prime of the world. As things of greatest necessity are always first provided for, so things of greatest dignity are most accounted of by all such as judge rightly. Although therefore riches be a thing which every man wisheth, yet no man of judgement can esteem it better to be rich, than wise, virtuous and religious. If we be both or either of these, it is not because we are so born. For into the world we come as empty of the one as of the other, as naked in mind as we are in body. Both which necessities of man had at the first no other helps and supplies, than only domestical; such as that which the prophet implieth, saying,

ᵖ 1 Tim. 6:8.   ᵠ Gen. 1:29.   ʳ Gen. 2:17.   ˢ Gen. 4:2.
ᵗGen. 4:26.   ᵘ Matt. 6:33.   ᵛ Gen. 4:20–22.

^wCan a mother forget her child? such as that which the Apostle mentioneth, saying, *^xHe that careth not for his own is worse than an Infidel:* such as that concerning *Abraham, ^yAbraham will command his sons and his household after him that they keep the way of the Lord.* But [10.3] neither that which we learn of ourselves, nor that which others teach us can prevail, where wickedness and malice have taken deep root. If therefore when there was but as yet one only family in the world, no means of instruction human or divine could prevent ^zeffusion of blood: how could it be chosen but that ^awhen families were multiplied and increased upon earth, after separation each providing for itself, envy, strife, contention and violence must grow amongst them? for hath not nature furnished man with wit and valour, as it were with armour, which may be used as well unto extreme evil as good? yea, were they not used by the rest of the world unto evil; unto the contrary only by *Seth, Enoch*, and those few the rest in that line? We all make complaint of the iniquity of our times: not unjustly; for the days are evil. But compare them with those times, wherein there were no civil societies, with those times wherein there was as yet no manner of public regiment established, with ^bthose times wherein there were not above 8 persons righteous living upon the face of the earth: and we have surely good cause to think that God hath blessed us exceedingly, and hath made us behold most happy days. To take away all such mutual [10.4] grievances, injuries, and wrongs, there was no way, but only by growing unto composition and agreement amongst themselves, by ordaining some kind of government public, and by yielding themselves subject thereunto, that unto whom they granted authority to rule and govern, by them the peace, tranquillity, and happy estate of the rest might be procured. Men always knew that when force and injury was offered, they might be defenders of themselves; they knew that howsoever men may seek their own commodity, yet if this were done with injury unto others, it was not to be suffered, but by all men and by all good means to be withstood; finally they knew that no man might in reason take upon him to determine his own right, and according to his own determination proceed in maintenance thereof, inasmuch as every man is towards himself and them whom he greatly affecteth partial; and therefore that strifes

^w Isa. 49:15.   ^x 1 Tim. 5:8.   ^y Gen. 18:19.
^z Gen. 4:8.   ^a Gen. 6:5. Gen. 5.   ^b 2 Pet. 2:5.

and troubles would be endless, except they gave their common consent all to be ordered by some whom they should agree upon: without which consent, there were no reason, that one man should take upon him to be Lord or Judge over another; because although there be according to the opinion of some very great and judicious men *c*a kind of natural right in the noble, wise, and virtuous, to govern them which are of servile disposition; nevertheless for manifestation of this their right, and men's more peaceable contentment on both sides, the assent of them who are to be governed, seemeth necessary. To fathers within their private families nature hath given a supreme power, for which cause we see throughout the world even from the first foundation thereof, all men have ever been taken as lords and lawful kings in their own houses. Howbeit over a whole grand multitude having no such dependency upon anyone, and consisting of so many families, as every politic society in the world doth, impossible it is that any should have complete lawful power but by consent of men, or immediate appointment of God; because not having the natural superiority of fathers, their power must needs be either usurped, and then unlawful; or if lawful, then either granted or consented unto by them over whom they exercise the same, or else given extraordinarily from God, unto whom all the world is subject. It is no improbable opinion therefore which the Arch-philosopher was of, *d*that as the chiefest person in every household was always as it were a king, so when numbers of households joined themselves in civil society together, kings were the first kind of governors amongst them. Which is also as it seemeth the reason why the name of *Father* continued still in them, who of fathers were made rulers; as also the ancient custom of governors to do as *Melchizedek*, and being kings to exercise the office of priests, which fathers did at the first, grew perhaps by the same occasion. Howbeit not this the only kind of regiment that hath been received in the world. The inconveniences of one kind have caused sundry other to be devised. So that in a word all public regiment of what kind soever seemeth evidently to have risen from deliberate advice, consultation, and composition between men, judging it convenient and behoveful; there being no impossibility in nature considered by itself, but that men might have lived without any public regiment. Howbeit, the

c Aristotle, *Politics*, Bks 1 and 4 [1255a and 1295b].
d Aristotle, *Politics*, Bk 1, ch. 2 [1252a]. See also Plato in Bk 3 of the *Laws* [680a–681c].

corruption of our nature being presupposed, we may not deny but that the law of nature doth now require of necessity some kind of regiment, so that to bring things unto the first course they were in, and utterly to take away all kind of public government in the world, were apparently to overturn the whole world. The case of [10.5] man's nature standing therefore as it doth, some kind of regiment the law of nature doth require; yet the kinds thereof being many, nature tieth not to any one, but leaveth the choice as a thing arbitrary. At the first when some certain kind of regiment was once approved, it may be that nothing was then further thought upon for the manner of governing, but all permitted unto their wisdom and discretion which were to rule, *till by experience they found this for all parts very inconvenient, so as the thing which they had devised for a remedy, did indeed but increase the sore which it should have cured. They saw that to live by one man's will, became the cause of all men's misery. This constrained them to come unto laws, wherein all men might see their duties beforehand, and know the penalties of transgressing them. *If things be simply good or evil, and withal universally so acknowledged, there needs no new law to be made for such things. The first kind therefore of things appointed by laws human, containeth whatsoever being in itself naturally good or evil, is notwithstanding more secret than that it can be discerned by every man's present conceipt, without some deeper discourse and judgement. In which discourse, because there is difficulty and possibility may ways to err, unless such things were set down by laws, many would be ignorant of their duties which now are not, and *many that know what they should do, would nevertheless dissemble it, and to excuse themselves pretend ignorance and simplicity which now they cannot. And because the greatest part of men are [10.6] such as prefer their own private good before all things, even that good which is sensual before whatsoever is most divine, and for

---

e *When the multitude were at first oppressed by those who had greater wealth, they fled to some one who was outstanding in virtue, who, when he prohibited wrongs against the weaker, managed by establishing equity to hold the higher with the lower in equal right. When less than this happened, laws were invented.* Cicero, *On Duties*, Bk 2 [ch. 12; *L*, pp. 208–211].

f *To honour parents and do good for friends and return favours to benefactors, these and suchlike are not enjoined on us by written laws but are observed by unwritten custom and common law.* Aristotle, *Rhetoric to Alexander* [ch. 1; 1421b].

g *For such is the force of pleasure that it can prolong ignorance to give itself occasion and pervert conscience to hide itself.* Tertullian, *On Spectacles* [ch. 1].

that the labour of doing good together with the pleasure arising from the contrary doth make men for the most part slower to the one and proner to the other, than that duty prescribed them by law can prevail sufficiently with them: therefore unto laws that men do make for the benefit of men it hath seemed always needful to add rewards which may more allure unto good than any hardness deterreth from it, and punishments which may more deter from evil than any sweetness thereto allureth. Wherein as the generality is natural, *Virtue rewardable and vice punishable:* so the particular determination of the reward or punishment belongeth unto them by whom laws are made. Theft is naturally punishable, but the kind of punishment is positive, and such lawful as men shall think with [10.7] discretion convenient by law to appoint. In laws that which is natural bindeth universally, that which is positive not so. To let go those kind of positive laws which men impose upon themselves as by vow unto God, contract with men, or such-like, somewhat it will make unto our purpose a little more fully to consider what things are incident into the making of the positive laws for the government of them that live united in public society. Laws do not only teach what is good but they enjoin it, they have in them a certain constraining force. And to constrain men unto anything inconvenient doth seem unreasonable. Most requisite therefore it is that to devise laws which all men shall be forced to obey none but wise men be admitted. Laws are matters of principal consequence; men of common capacity and but ordinary judgement are not able (for how should they?) to discern what things are fittest for each kind and state of regiment. We cannot be ignorant how much our obedience unto laws dependeth upon this point. Let a man though never so justly oppose himself unto them that are disordered in their ways, and what one amongst them commonly doth not stomach at such contradiction, storm at reproof, and hate such as would reform them? Notwithstanding even they which brook it worst that men should tell them of their duties, when they are told the same by a law, think very well and reasonably of it. For why? They presume that the law doth speak with all indifferency, that the law hath no side respect to their persons, that the law is as it were an oracle proceeded from wisdom and understand- [10.8] ing. Howbeit laws do not take their constraining force from the quality of such as devise them, but from that power which doth give them the strength of laws. That which we spake before concern-

ing the power of government must here be applied unto the power
of making laws whereby to govern, which power God hath over
all, and by the natural law whereunto he hath made all subject,
the lawful power of making laws to command whole politic societies
of men belongeth so properly unto the same entire societies, that
for any Prince or potentate of what kind soever upon earth to exercise
the same of himself and not either by express commission immediately and personally received from God, or else by authority derived
at the first from their consent upon whose persons they impose
laws, it is no better than mere tyranny. Laws they are not therefore
which public approbation hath not made so. But approbation not
only they give who personally declare their assent by voice sign
or act, but also when others do it in their names by right originally
at the least derived from them. As in parliaments, councils, and
the like assemblies, although we be not personally ourselves present,
notwithstanding our assent is by reason of others agents there in
our behalf. And what we do by others, no reason but that it should
stand as our deed, no less effectually to bind us than if ourselves
had done it in person. In many things assent is given, they that
give it not imagining they do so, because the manner of their assenting is not apparent. As for example, when an absolute Monarch
commandeth his subjects that which seemeth good in his own discretion, hath not his edict the force of a law, whether they approve
or dislike it? Again that which hath been received long since
and is by custom now established, we keep as a law which we may
not transgress; yet what consent was ever thereunto sought or
required at our hands? Of this point therefore we are to note, that
since men naturally have no full and perfect power to command
whole politic multitudes of men; therefore utterly without our consent we could in such sort be at no man's commandment living.
And to be commanded we do consent, when that society whereof
we are part hath at any time before consented, without revoking
the same after by the like universal agreement. Wherefore as any
man's deed past is good as long as himself continueth: so the act
of a public society of men done five hundred years since standeth
as theirs, who presently are of the same societies, because corporations are immortal: we were then alive in our predecessors, and
they in their successors do live still. Laws therefore human of what
kind soever are available by consent. If here it be demanded how [10.9]

it cometh to pass that this being common unto all laws which are made, there should be found even in good laws so great variety as there is: we must note the reason hereof to be, the sundry particular ends whereunto the different disposition of that subject or matter, for which laws are provided, causeth them to have especial respect in making laws. [h]A law there is mentioned amongst the Grecians whereof *Pittacus* is reported to have been author: And by that law it was agreed, that he which being overcome with drink did then strike any man, should suffer punishment double as much as if he had done the same being sober. No man could ever have thought this reasonable that had intended thereby only to punish the injury committed, according to the gravity of the fact. For who knoweth not, that harm advisedly done is naturally less pardonable, and therefore worthy of the sharper punishment? But forasmuch as none did so usually this way offend as men in that case, which they wittingly fell into, even because they would be so much the more freely outrageous: it was for their public good where such disorder was grown to frame a positive law for remedy thereof accordingly. To this appertain those known laws of making laws, as that lawmakers must have an eye to the place where, and to the men amongst whom; that one kind of laws cannot serve for all kinds of regiment; that where the multitude beareth sway, laws that shall tend unto preservation of that state must make common smaller offices to go by lot, for fear of strife and division likely to arise; by reason that ordinary qualities sufficing for discharge of such offices they could not but by many be desired and so with danger contended for, and not missed without grudge and discontentment, whereas at an uncertain lot none can find themselves grieved on whomsoever it lighteth; contrariwise the greatest, whereof but few are capable, to pass by popular election, that neither the people may envy such as have those honours, inasmuch as themselves bestow them; and that the chiefest may be kindled with desire to exercise all parts of rare and beneficial virtue, knowing they shall not lose their labour by growing in fame and estimation amongst the people: if the helm of chief government be in the hands of a few of the wealthiest, that then laws providing for continuance thereof must make the punishment of contumely and wrong offered unto any of the common

[h] Aristotle, *Politics*, Bk 2, last chapter [1274b].

sort sharp and grievous, that so the evil may be prevented whereby the rich are most likely to bring themselves into hatred with the people, who are not wont to take so great offence when they are excluded from honours and offices, as when their persons are contumeliously trodden upon. In other kinds of regiment the like is observed concerning the difference of positive laws which to be everywhere the same is impossible and against their nature. Now [10.10] as the learned in the laws of this land observe, ⁱthat our statutes sometimes are only the affirmation or ratification of that which by common law was held before: so here it is not to be omitted that generally all laws human, which are made for the ordering of politic societies, be either such as established some duty whereunto all men by the law of reason did before stand bound; or else such as make that a duty now which before was none. The one sort we may for distinction's sake call *mixedly*, and the other *merely* human. That which plain or necessary reason bindeth men unto may be in sundry considerations expedient to be ratified by human law: for example, if confusion of blood in marriage, the liberty of having many wives at once, or any other the like corrupt and unreasonable custom doth happen to have prevailed far and to have gotten the upper hand of right reason with the greatest part, so that no way is left to rectify such foul disorder without prescribing by law the same things which reason necessarily *doth* enforce but is not *perceived* that so it doth, or if many be grown unto that, which the apostle did lament in some, concerning whom he writeth saying, that ^j*Even what things they naturally know, in those very things as beasts void of reason they corrupted themselves;* or if there be no such special accident, yet forasmuch as ^kthe common sort are led by the sway of their sensual desires, and therefore do more shun sin for the sensible evils which follow it amongst men, than for any kind of sentence which reason doth pronounce against it: this very thing is cause sufficient why duties belonging unto each kind of virtue, albeit the law of reason teach them, should notwithstanding be prescribed even by human law. Which law in this case we term *mixed*, because the matter whereunto it bindeth, is the same which reason necessarily doth require at our hands, and from the law

---

ⁱ Staundford, preface to *the pleas of the Crown* [*STC* 23217].　　^j Jude, verse 10.
^k *The many obey necessity rather than reason and punishments rather than what is noble.*
Aristotle, *Nicomachean Ethics*, Bk 10, ch. 10 [1180a].

of reason it differeth in the manner of binding only. For whereas men before stood bound in conscience to do as the law of reason teacheth, they are now by virtue of human law become constrainable, and if they outwardly transgress, punishable. As for laws which are *merely* human, the matter of them is anything which reason doth but probably teach to be fit and convenient, so that till such time as law hath passed amongst men about it, of itself it bindeth no man. One example whereof may be this. Lands are by human law in some places after the owner's decease divided unto all his children, in some all descendeth to the eldest son. If the law of reason did necessarily require but the one of these two to be done they which by law have received the other should be subject to that heavy sentence, which denounceth, *'against all that decree wicked, unjust, and unreasonable things, woe.* Whereas now whichsoever be received there is no law of reason transgressed, because there is probable reason why either of them may be expedient, and for either of them more than probable reason there is not to be [10.11] found. Laws whether mixedly or merely human are made by politic societies: some, only as those societies are civilly united; some, as they are spiritually joined and make such a body as we call the Church. Of laws human in this latter kind we are to speak in the third book following. Let it therefore suffice thus far to have touched the force wherewith almighty God hath graciously endowed our nature, and thereby enabled the same to find out both those laws which all men generally are forever bound to observe, and also such as are most fit for their behoof, who lead their lives in any [10.12] ordered state of government. Now besides that law which simply concerneth men as men, and that which belongeth unto them as they are men linked with others in some form of politic society; there is a third kind of law which toucheth all such several bodies politic, so far forth as one of them hath public commerce with another. And this third is the *Law of nations.* Between men and beasts there is no possibility of sociable communion, because the wellspring of that communion is a natural delight which man hath to transfuse from himself into others, and to receive from others into himself especially those things wherein the excellency of his kind doth most consist. The chiefest instrument of human com-

' Isa. 10:1.

munion therefore is speech, *ᵐbecause thereby we impart mutually one to another the conceipts of our reasonable understanding.* And for that cause seeing beasts are not hereof capable, forasmuch as with them we can use no such conference, they being in degree, although above other creatures on earth to whom nature hath denied sense, yet lower than to be sociable companions of man to whom nature hath given reason; it is of Adam said that amongst the beasts *ⁿHe found not for himself any meet companion.* Civil society doth more content the nature of man than any private kind of solitary living, because in society this good of mutual participation is so much larger than otherwise. Herewith notwithstanding we are not satisfied, but we covet (if it might be) to have a kind of society and fellowship even with all mankind. Which thing Socrates intending to signify *ᵒprofessed himself a Citizen, not of this or that commonwealth, but of the world.* And an effect of that very natural desire in us, (a manifest token that we wish after a sort an universal fellowship with all men) appeareth by the wonderful delight men have, some to visit foreign countries, some to discover nations not heard of in former ages, we all to know the affairs and dealings of other people, yea to be in league of amity with them: and this not only for traffic's sake, or to the end that when many are confederated each may make other the more strong, but for such cause also as moved the *ᵖ*Queen of Sheba to visit Solomon; and in a word because nature doth presume that how many men there are in the world, so many Gods as it were there are, or at leastwise such they should be towards men. Touching laws which are to serve men in this [10.13] behalf, even as those laws of reason which (man retaining his original integrity) had been sufficient to direct each particular person in all his affairs and duties, are not sufficient but require the access of other laws, now that man and his offspring are grown thus corrupt and sinful; again as those laws of polity and regiment, which would have served men living in public society together with that harmless disposition which then they should have had, are not able now to serve when men's iniquity is so hardly restrained within any tolerable bounds: in like manner the national laws of mutual commerce

---

ᵐ Aristotle, *Politics*, Bk I, ch. 2 [1253a].   *ⁿ* Gen. 2:20.
ᵒ Cicero, *Tusculan Disputations*, Bk 5 [ch. 37; *L*, pp. 532–535] and Bk I of *On Laws* [ch. 12; *L*, pp. 332–335].
ᵖ I Kings 10:1. 2 Chron. 9:1. Matt. 12:42. Luke 11:31.

between societies of that former and better quality might have been other than now, when nations are so prone to offer violence injury and wrong. Hereupon hath grown in every of these three kinds that distinction between *Primary* and *Secondary* laws; the one grounded upon sincere, the other built upon depraved nature. Primary laws of nations are such as concern embassage, such as belong to the courteous entertainment of foreigners and strangers, such as serve for commodious traffic and the like. Secondary laws in the same kind are such as this present unquiet world is most familiarly acquainted with, I mean laws of arms, which yet are much better known than kept. But what matter the law of nations doth contain I omit to search. The strength and virtue of that law is such that no particular nation can lawfully prejudice the same by any their several laws and ordinances, more than a man by his private resolutions the law of the whole commonwealth or state wherein he liveth. For as civil law being the act of a whole body politic doth therefore overrule each several part of the same body: so there is no reason that any one commonwealth of itself should to the prejudice of another annihilate that whereupon the whole world hath agreed. For which cause the Lacedemonians forbidding all access of strangers into their coasts are in that respect both by *[q]*Josephus and Theodoret deservedly blamed, as being enemies to that hospitality which for common humanity's sake all the nations [10.14] on earth should embrace. Now as there is great cause of communion, and consequently of laws for the maintenance of communion, amongst nations: So amongst nations Christian the like in regard even of Christianity hath been always judged needful. And in this kind of correspondence amongst nations the force of general councils doth stand. For as one and the same law divine, whereof in the next place we are to speak, is unto all Christian churches a rule for the chiefest things, by means whereof they all in that respect make one Church, as having all but *[r]One Lord, one faith, and one baptism:* So the urgent necessity of mutual communion for preservation of our unity in these things, as also for order in some other things convenient to be everywhere uniformly kept, maketh it requisite that the Church of God here on earth have her laws of spiritual

---

[q] Josephus, Bk 2 *Against Apion* [ch. 36; *L*, pp. 396–397]. Theodoret, Bk 9 of the *Cure of the Affections of the Greeks* [*PG*, 83:1039–1040].
[r] Ephes. 4:5.

commerce between Christian nations, laws by virtue whereof all Churches may enjoy freely the use of those reverend religious and sacred consultations which are termed councils general. A thing whereof God's own blessed spirit was the author, ⁵a thing practised by the holy Apostles themselves, a thing always afterwards kept and observed throughout the world, a thing never otherwise than most highly esteemed of, till pride ambition and tyranny began by factious and vile endeavours to abuse that divine invention unto the furtherance of wicked purposes. But as the just authority of civil courts and Parliaments is not therefore to be abolished, because sometime there is cunning used to frame them according to the private intents of men over-potent in the commonwealth: So the grievous abuse which hath been of councils should rather cause men to study how so gracious a thing may again be reduced to that first perfection, than in regard of stains and blemishes since growing be held forever in extreme disgrace. To speak of this matter as the cause requireth would require very long discourse. All I will presently say is this. Whether it be for the finding out of anything whereunto divine law bindeth us, but yet in such sort that men are not thereof on all sides resolved; or for the setting down of some uniform judgement to stand touching such things, as being neither way matters of necessity, are notwithstanding offensive and scandalous when there is open opposition about them; be it for the ending of strifes touching matters of Christian belief, wherein the one part may seem to have probable cause of dissenting from the other; or be it concerning matters of polity, order, and regiment in the Church; I nothing doubt but that Christian men should much better frame themselves to ʼthose heavenly precepts, which our Lord and Saviour with so great instancy gave us concerning peace and unity, if we did all concur in desire to have the use of ancient councils again renewed, rather than these proceedings continued which either make all contentions endless, or bring them to one only determination and that of all other the worst, which is by sword. It followeth therefore [10.15] that a new foundation being laid we now adjoin hereunto that which cometh in the next place to be spoken of, namely, wherefore God hath himself by scripture made known such laws as serve for direction of men.

⁵ Acts 15:28.   ʼ John 14:27.

Wherefore God hath by scripture
further made known such supernatural laws
as do serve for men's direction.

[II.I] II. All things (God only excepted) besides the nature which they
have in themselves receive externally some perfection from other
things, as hath been showed. Insomuch as there is in the whole
world no one thing great or small but either in respect of knowledge
or of use it may unto our perfection add somewhat. And whatsoever
such perfection there is which our nature may acquire, the same
we properly term our good; our sovereign *good* or *blessedness* that
wherein the highest degree of all our perfection consisteth, that
which being once attained unto there can rest nothing further to
be desired, and therefore with it our souls are fully content and
satisfied, in that they have they rejoice and thirst for no more. Wherefore of good things desired some are such that for themselves we
covet them not, but only because they serve as instruments unto
that for which we are to seek, of this sort are riches: another kind
there is which although we desire for itself, as health and virtue
and knowledge, nevertheless they are not the last mark whereat
we aim but have their further end whereunto they are referred,
so as in them we are not satisfied as having attained the utmost
we may, but our desires do still proceed. These things are linked
and as it were chained one to another, we labour to eat, and we
eat to live, and we live to do good, and the good which we do
is as seed sown "with reference unto a future harvest: But we must
come at the length to some pause. For if everything were to be
desired for some other without any stint, there could be no certain
end proposed unto our actions, we should go on we know not
whither, yea, whatsoever we do were in vain, or rather nothing
at all were possible to be done. For as to take away the first efficient
of our being were to annihilate utterly our persons, so we cannot
remove the last final cause of our working, but we shall cause whatsoever we work to cease. Therefore something there must be desired
for itself simply and for no other. That is simply for itself desirable,
unto the nature whereof it is opposite and repugnant to be desired
with relation unto any other. The ox and the ass desire their food,

---

" Gal. 6:8. *He that soweth to the spirit shall of the spirit reap life everlasting.*

neither propose they unto themselves any end wherefore, so that of them this is desired for itself, but why? By reason of their imperfection which cannot otherwise desire it; whereas that which is desired simply for itself, the excellency thereof is such as permitteth it not in any sort to be referred to a further end. Now that which man [II.2] doth desire with reference to a further end, the same he desireth in such measure as is unto that end convenient: but what he coveteth as good in itself, towards that his desire is ever infinite. So that unless the last good of all, which is desired altogether for itself, be also infinite: we do evil in making it our end even as they who placed their felicity in wealth or honour or pleasure or anything here attained, because in desiring anything as our final perfection which is not so, we do amiss. *v*Nothing may be infinitely desired but that good which indeed is infinite, for the better the more desirable, that therefore most desirable wherein there is infinity of goodness, so that if anything desirable may be infinite, that must needs be the highest of all things that are desired. No good is infinite but only God: therefore he our felicity and bliss. Moreover desire tendeth unto union with that it desireth. If then in him we be blessed, it is by force of participation and conjunction with him. Again, it is not the possession of any good thing can make them happy which have it, unless they enjoy the thing wherewith they are possessed. Then are we happy therefore when fully we enjoy God, as an object wherein the powers of our souls are satisfied even with everlasting delight: so that although we be men, yet by being unto God united we live as it were the life of God. Happiness therefore [II.3] is that estate whereby we attain, so far as possibly may be attained, the full possession of that which simply for itself is to be desired, and containeth in it after an eminent sort the contentation of our desires, the highest degree of all our perfection. Of such perfection capable we are not in this life. For while we are in the world, subject we are unto sundry *w*imperfections, griefs of body, defects of mind,

---

v See Aristotle, *Nicomachean Ethics*, Bk 10, ch. 10 [1177b] and *Metaphysics*, Bk 12, ch. 6 and ch. 4 and ch. 30 [1072a, 1070a, 1075b].

w *In men, Asclepius, there is only the name of good, not at all the thing itself. That which is not excessively evil is good. The good here is what has the least amount of evil. It is therefore impossible for the good here to be pure from evil. And I give thanks to God, who puts in my mind the knowledge of the good – that it is impossible for it to be in the world. For the world is the fullness of evil, but God of the good or the good of God.* Mercurius Trismegistus [ed. 1924, 1:166–169].

yea the best things we do are painful, and the exercise of them grievous being continued, without intermission, so as in those very actions, whereby we are especially perfected in this life, we are not able to persist: forced we are with very weariness and that often to interrupt them: which tediousness cannot fall into those operations that are in the state of bliss, when our union with God is complete. Complete union with him must be according unto every power and faculty of our minds apt to receive so glorious an object. Capable we are of God both by understanding and will, by understanding as he is that sovereign truth, which comprehendeth the rich treasures of all wisdom; by will, as he is that sea of goodness, whereof whoso tasteth shall thirst no more. As the will doth now work upon that object by desire, which is as it were a motion towards the end as yet unobtained, so likewise upon the same hereafter received it shall work also by love. *Appetitus inhiantis fit amor fruentis*, saith Saint Augustine. *The longing disposition of them that thirst is changed into the sweet affection of them that taste and are replenished.* Whereas we now love the thing that is good, but good especially in respect of benefit unto us, we shall then love the thing that is good, only or principally for the goodness of beauty in itself. The soul being in this sort as it is active, perfected by love of that infinite good, shall, as it is receptive, be also perfected with those supernatural passions of joy peace and delight. *All this endless and everlasting. Which perpetuity, in regard whereof our blessedness is termed *a crown which withereth not*, doth neither depend upon the nature of the thing itself, nor proceed from any natural necessity that our souls should so exercise themselves forever in beholding and loving God, but from the will of God, which doth both freely perfect our nature in so high a degree and continue it so perfected. Under man no creature in the world is capable of felicity and bliss; first, because their chiefest perfection consisteth in that which is best for them, but not in that which is simply best, as ours doth; secondly, because whatsoever external perfection they tend unto, it is not better than themselves, as ours is. How just occasion have we therefore even in this respect with the Prophet to admire the goodness of

---

x Augustine, *On the Trinity*, Bk 9, last chapter.
y Matt. 25. *The just shall go into life everlasting.* Matt. 22. *They shall be as the Angels of God.*
z 2 Tim. 4:8. 1 Pet. 1:4.

God; [a]Lord what is man that thou shouldest exalt him above the works of thy hands, so far as to make thyself the inheritance of his rest and the substance of his felicity? Now if men had not naturally [II.4] this desire to be happy, how were it possible that all men should have it? All men have. Therefore this desire in man is natural. It is not in our power not to do the same: how should it then be in our power to do it coldly or remissly? So that our desire being natural is also in that degree of earnestness whereunto nothing can be added. And is it probable that God should frame the hearts of all men so desirous of that which no man may obtain? [b]It is an axiom of nature that natural desire cannot utterly be frustrate. This desire of ours being natural should be frustrate, if that which may satisfy the same were a thing impossible for man to aspire unto. Man doth seek a triple perfection, first, a sensual, consisting in those things which very life itself requireth either as necessary supplements, or as beauties and ornaments thereof; then an intellectual, consisting in those things which none underneath man is either capable of or acquainted with; lastly a spiritual and divine, consisting in those things whereunto we tend by supernatural means here, but cannot here attain unto them. They that make the first of these three the scope of their whole life, are said by the Apostle [c]to have no God, but only their belly, to be earthly minded men. Unto the second they bend themselves, who seek especially to excel in all such knowledge and virtue as doth most commend men. To this branch belongeth the law of moral and civil perfection. That there is somewhat higher than either of these two no other proof doth need, than the very process of man's desire, which being natural should be frustrate if there were not some further thing wherein it might rest at the length contented, which in the former it cannot do. For man doth not seem to rest satisfied either with fruition of that wherewith his life is preserved, or with performance of such actions as advance him most deservedly in estimation; but doth further covet, yea often times manifestly pursue with great sedulity and earnestness that which cannot stand him in any stead for vital use; that which exceedeth the reach of sense; yea, somewhat above

[a] Ps. 8.
[b] Thomas Aquinas, Prologue 2, *Commentary on Aristotle's Metaphysics* [commenting on the first sentence of the work].
[c] Philip. 3:19.

capacity of reason, somewhat divine and heavenly, which with hidden exultation it rather surmiseth than conceiveth; somewhat it seeketh and what that is directly it knoweth not, yet very intentive desire thereof doth so incite it, that all other known delights and pleasures are laid aside, they give place to the search of this but only suspected desire. If the soul of man did serve only to give him being in this life, then things appertaining unto this life would content him, as we see they do other creatures: which creatures enjoying what they live by, seek no further, but in this contentation do show a kind of acknowledgement, that there is no higher good which doth any way belong unto them. With us it is otherwise. For although the beauties, riches, honours, sciences, virtues, and perfections of all men living were in the present possession of one: yet somewhat beyond and above all this there would still be sought and earnestly thirsted for. So that nature even in this life doth plainly claim and call for a more divine perfection, than either of these two that have [II.5] been mentioned. This last and highest estate of perfection whereof we speak is received of men in the nature of a ^dreward. Rewards do always presuppose such duties performed as are rewardable. Our natural means therefore unto blessedness are our works: nor is it possible that nature should ever find any other way to salvation than only this. But examine the works which we do and since the first foundation of the world what one can say, My ways are pure? Seeing then all flesh is guilty of that for which God hath threatened eternally to punish, what possibility is there this way to be saved? There resteth therefore either no way unto salvation, or if any, then surely a way which is supernatural, a way which could never have entered into the heart of man as much as once to conceive or imagine, if God himself had not revealed it extraordinarily. For which cause we term it the mystery or secret way of salvation. And therefore Saint Ambrose in this matter appealeth justly from man to God, *^eCæli mysterium doceat me Deus qui condidit, non homo qui seipsum ignoravit. Let God himself that made me, let not man that knows not himself be my instructor concerning the mystical way to heaven.* *^fWhen men of excellent wit* (saith Lactantius) *had wholly betaken themselves*

---

^d Matt. 5:12. *Rejoice and be glad, for great is your Reward in heaven.* Augustine, *On Christian Teaching*, ch. 6 [Bk I, ch. 32]. *The highest reward is that we should enjoy Him.*

^e Ambrose *against Symmachus* [*PL*, 16:1015].

^f Lactantius, *The Divine Institutes*, Bk I, ch. I.

unto study, after farewell bidden unto all kind as well of private as public action, they spared no labour that might be spent in the search of truth, holding it a thing of much more price to seek and to find out the reason of all affairs as well divine as human, than to stick fast in the toil of piling up riches and gathering together heaps of honours. Howbeit they both did fail of their purpose, and got not as much as to quit their charges; because truth which is the secret of the most high God, whose proper handiwork all things are, cannot be compassed with that wit and those senses which are our own. For God and man should be very near neighbours, if man's cogitations were able to take a survey of the counsels and appointments of that majesty everlasting. Which being utterly impossible, that the eye of man by itself should look into the bosom of divine reason, God did not suffer him being desirous of the light of wisdom, to stray any longer up and down, and with bootless expense of travail to wander in darkness that had no passage to get out by. His eyes at the length God did open, and bestow upon him the knowledge of the truth by way of Donative, to the end that man might both be clearly convicted of folly, and being through error out of the way, have the path that leadeth unto immortality laid plain before him. Thus far *Lactantius Firmianus* to show that God himself is the teacher of the truth, whereby is made known the supernatural way of salvation and law for them to live in that shall be saved. In the natural path of everlasting life the first beginning is that ability of doing good, which God in the day of man's creation endowed him with; from hence obedience unto the will of his creator, absolute righteousness and integrity in all his actions; and last of all the justice of God rewarding the worthiness of his deserts with the crown of eternal glory. Had Adam continued in his first estate, this had been the way of life unto him and all his posterity. Wherein I confess notwithstanding with the ᵍwittiest of the School divines, that if we speak of strict justice God could no way have been bound to requite man's labours in so large and ample manner as human felicity doth import: inasmuch as the dignity of this exceedeth so far the other's value. But be it that God of his great liberality had determined in lieu of man's endeavours to bestow the same, by the rule of that justice which best beseemeth him, namely the justice of one that requiteth nothing mincingly, but all with pressed and heaped and even over-enlarged measure:

ᵍ John Duns Scotus, *Questions on the Four Books of Sentences of Peter Lombard*, Bk 4, distinction 49, question 6.

yet could it never hereupon necessarily be gathered that such justice should add to the nature of that reward the property of everlasting continuance; since possession of bliss, though it should be but for a moment, were an abundant retribution. But we are not now to enter into this consideration how gracious and bountiful our good God might still appear in so rewarding the sons of men, albeit they should exactly perform whatsoever duty their nature bindeth them unto. Howsoever God did propose this reward, we that were to be rewarded must have done that which is required at our hands; we failing in the one, it were in nature an impossibility that the other should be looked for. The light of nature is never able to find out any way of obtaining the reward of bliss, but by performing [II.6] exactly the duties and works of righteousness. From salvation therefore and life all flesh being excluded this way, behold how the wisdom of God hath revealed a way mystical and supernatural, a way directing unto the same end of life by a course which groundeth itself upon the guiltiness of sin, and through sin desert of condemnation and death. For in this way the first thing is the tender compassion of God respecting us drowned and swallowed up in misery; the next is redemption out of the same by the precious death and merit of a mighty Saviour, which hath witnessed of himself saying *hI am the way*, the way that leadeth us from misery into bliss. This supernatural way had God in himself prepared before all worlds. The way of supernatural duty which to us he hath prescribed, our Saviour in the Gospel of Saint John doth note, terming it by an excellency the work of God: *iThis is the work of God that ye believe in him whom he hath sent*. Not that God doth require nothing unto happiness at the hands of men saving only a naked belief (for hope and charity we may not exclude) but that without belief all other things are as nothing, and it the ground of those other divine virtues. Concerning faith the principal object whereof is that eternal verity which hath discovered the treasures of hidden wisdom in Christ; concerning hope the highest object whereof is that everlasting goodness which in Christ doth quicken the dead; concerning charity the final object whereof is that incomprehensible beauty which shineth in the countenance of Christ the son of the living God; concerning these virtues, the first of which beginning here with

h John 14:6.   *i* John 6:29.

a weak apprehension of things not seen, endeth with the intuitive vision of God in the world to come; the second beginning here with a trembling expectation of things far removed and as yet but only heard of, endeth with real and actual fruition of that which no tongue can express; the third beginning here with a weak inclination of heart towards him unto whom we are not able to approach, endeth with endless union, the mystery whereof is higher than the reach of the thoughts of men; concerning that faith hope and charity without which there can be no salvation; was there ever any mention made saving only in that law which God himself hath from heaven revealed? There is not in the world a syllable muttered with certain truth concerning any of these three, more than hath been supernaturally received from the mouth of the eternal God. Laws therefore concerning these things are supernatural, both in respect of the manner of delivering them which is divine, and also in regard of the things delivered which are such as have not in nature any cause from which they flow, but were by the voluntary appointment of God ordained besides the course of nature to rectify nature's obliquity withal.

The cause why so many natural or rational laws are set down in holy scripture.

12. When supernatural duties are necessarily exacted, natural are [12.1] not rejected as needless. The law of God therefore is though principally delivered for instruction in the one, yet fraught with precepts of the other also. The scripture is fraught even with laws of nature. Insomuch that [j]Gratian defining natural right (whereby is meant the right which exacteth those general duties, that concern men naturally even as they are men) termeth natural right that which the books of the law and the Gospel do contain. Neither is it vain that the scripture aboundeth with so great store of laws in this kind. For they are either such as we of ourselves could not easily have found out, and then the benefit is not small to have them readily set down to our hands, or if they be so clear and manifest that no man endowed with reason can lightly be ignorant of them, yet

[j] *Natural right is what is contained in the law and the Gospel.* Gratian, *Decretum*, 1.1, preface.

the spirit as it were borrowing them from the school of nature as serving to prove things less manifest, and to induce a persuasion of somewhat which were in itself more hard and dark, unless it should in such sort be cleared, the very applying of them unto cases particular is not without most singular use and profit many ways for men's instruction. Besides, be they plain of themselves or obscure, the evidence of God's own testimony added unto the natural assent of reason concerning the certainty of them, doth not a little

[12.2] comfort and confirm the same. Wherefore inasmuch as our actions are conversant about things beset with many circumstances, which cause men of sundry wits to be also of sundry judgements concerning that which ought to be done: requisite it cannot but seem the rule of divine law should herein help our imbecility, that we might the more infallibly understand what is good and what evil. The first principles of the law of nature are easy, hard it were to find men ignorant of them: but concerning the duty which nature's law doth require at the hands of men in a number of things particular, so *k*far hath the natural understanding even of sundry whole nations been darkened, that they have not discerned no not gross iniquity to be sin. Again, being so prone as we are to fawn upon ourselves, and to be ignorant as much as may be of our own deformities, without the feeling sense whereof we are most wretched, even so much the more, because not knowing them we cannot as much as desire to have them taken away: how should our festered sores be cured, but that God hath delivered a law as sharp as the two-edged

---

k Josephus, Bk 2 *Against Apion* [ch. 37; *L*, pp. 402–403]. *Are not the Lacedemonians to be reprehended for their inhospitality and their neglect of the marriage covenant? And the Elienses and Thebans, indeed, for practising sexual union of men with men, an act which is obviously shameless and against nature, but which they thought right and useful? And since they performed these things, they threw even their own laws into confusion.* See Thomas, *Summa Theologiae*, 1a2ae, q. 94, arts. 4–6. *The law of nature was so corrupt among the Germans that they did not consider robbery a sin.* Augustine or whoever is the author of the book of *Questions on the Old and New Testaments* [*PL*, 35:2219]. *Who is ignorant of what is fitting for a good life, or who does not know that what one does not will to happen to himself he should not at all do to others? But where natural law has disappeared, vanishing because of overwhelming custom, then it is necessary that it be manifest in the Scriptures, so that all men may hear the judgement of God and so that it be not completely obliterated. But since all men were cut off from the great authority of the natural law, idolatry was pursued, there was no fear of God in the land, fornication was practised, and there was avid lust for the neighbour's possession. Therefore, the law has been given so that those things which were known might have authority, and so that those things which had begun to disappear might become manifest.*

sword, piercing the very closest and most unsearchable corners of the heart which the law of nature can hardly, human laws by no means possible reach unto? Hereby we know even secret concupiscence to be sin, and are made fearful to offend though it be but in a wandering cogitation. Finally of those things which are for direction of all the parts of our life needful, and not impossible to be discerned by the light of nature itself, are there not many which few men's natural capacity, and some which no man's hath been able to find out? They are, saith Saint Augustine, but a few and they endowed with great ripeness of wit and judgement, free from all such affairs as might trouble their meditations, instructed in the sharpest and the subtlest points of learning, who have, and that very hardly, been able to find out but only the immortality of the soul. The resurrection of the flesh what man did ever at any time dream of, having not heard it otherwise than from the school of nature? Whereby it appeareth how much we are bound to yield unto our creator the father of all mercy eternal thanks, for that he hath delivered his law unto the world, a law wherein so many things are laid open clear and manifest; as a light which otherwise would have been buried in darkness, not without the hazard, or rather not with the hazard, but with the certain loss of infinite thousands of souls most undoubtedly now saved. We [12.3] see therefore that our sovereign good is desired naturally; that God the author of that natural desire had appointed natural means whereby to fulfill it; that man having utterly disabled his nature unto those means hath had other revealed from God, and hath received from heaven a law to teach him how that which is desired naturally must now supernaturally be attained; finally we see that because those latter exclude not the former quite and clean as unnecessary, therefore together with such supernatural duties as could not possibly have been otherwise known to the world, the same law that teacheth them, teacheth also with them such natural duties as could not by light of nature easily have been known.

The benefit of having divine laws written.

13. In the first age of the world God gave laws unto our fathers, [13.1] and by reason of the number of their days their memories served

instead of books; whereof the manifold imperfections and defects being known to God, he mercifully relieved the same by often putting them in mind of that whereof it behoved them to be specially mindful. In which respect we see how many times one thing hath been iterated unto sundry even of the best and wisest amongst them. After that the lives of men were shortened, means more durable to preserve the laws of God from oblivion and corruption grew in use, not without precise direction from God himself. First therefore of Moses it is said, that he *¹wrote all the words of God;* not by his own private motion and device: for God taketh this act to himself, *ᵐI have written.* Furthermore were not the Prophets following commanded also to do the like? Unto the holy Evangelist Saint John how often express charge is given, *ⁿScribe, write these things?* Concerning the rest of our Lord's disciples the words of St. Augustine are, *ᵒQuicquid ille de suis factis et dictis nos legere voluit hoc scribendum illis tanquam suis* [13.2] *manibus imperavit.* Now although we do not deny it to be a matter merely accidental unto the law of God to be written; although writing be not that which addeth authority and strength thereunto; finally though his laws do require at our hands the same obedience howsoever they be delivered; his providence notwithstanding which hath made principal choice of this way to deliver them, who seeth not what cause we have to admire and magnify? The singular benefit that hath grown unto the world by receiving the laws of God, even by his own appointment committed unto writing, we are not able to esteem as the value thereof deserveth. When the question therefore is, whether we be now to seek for any revealed law of God otherwhere than only in the sacred scripture, whether we do now stand bound in the sight of God to yield to traditions urged by the Church of *Rome* the same obedience and reverence we do to his written law, honoring equally and adoring both as Divine: our answer is, no. They that so earnestly plead for the authority of Tradition, as if nothing were more safely conveyed than that which spreadeth itself by report, and descendeth by relation of former generations unto the ages that succeed, are not all of them (surely a miracle it were if they should be) so simple, as thus to persuade themselves; howso-

---

¹ Exod. 24:4.   *ᵐ* Hos. 8:12.   *ⁿ* Rev. 1:11 and 14:13.
ᵒ [*For whatever God has wished us to read about his deeds and sayings, this he has commanded them to write down as if by his own hands.*] Augustine, *On the Agreement of the Evangelists,* Bk 1, last chapter [*PL*, 34:1070].

ever if the simple were so persuaded, they could be content perhaps
very well to enjoy the benefit, as they account it, of that common
error. What hazard the truth is in when it passeth through the hands
of report, how maimed and deformed it becometh; they are not,
they cannot possibly be ignorant. Let them that are indeed of this
mind consider but only that little of things Divine, which the
*P*Heathen have in such sort received. How miserable had the state
of the Church of God been long ere this, if wanting the sacred
scripture we had no record of his laws, but only the memory of
man receiving the same by report and relation from his predecessors?
By scripture it hath in the wisdom of God seemed meet to deliver [13.3]
unto the world much but personally expedient to be practised of
certain men; many deep and profound points of doctrine, as being
the main original ground whereupon the precepts of duty depend;
many prophecies the clear performance whereof might confirm the
world in belief of things unseen; many histories to serve as looking
glasses to behold the mercy, the truth, the righteousness of God
towards all that faithfully serve, obey and honour him; yea, many
entire meditations of piety to be as patterns and precedents in cases
of like nature; many things needful for explication, many for appli-
cation unto particular occasions, such as the providence of God
from time to time hath taken to have the several books of his holy
ordinance written. Be it then that together with the principal necessary laws of God there are sundry other things written, whereof
we might happily be ignorant, and yet be saved. What? shall we
hereupon think them needless? shall we esteem them as riotous
branches wherewith we sometimes behold most pleasant vines over-
grown? Surely no more than we judge our hands, or our eyes superfluous, or what part soever, which if our bodies did want, we might
notwithstanding any such defect retain still the complete being of
men. As therefore a complete man is neither destitute of any part
necessary, and hath some parts whereof though the want could not
deprive him of his essence, yet to have them standeth him in singular
stead in respect of the special uses for which they serve: in like

P I mean those historical matters concerning the ancient state of the first world, the
deluge, the sons of Noah, the children of Israel's deliverance out of Egypt, the life
and doings of Moses their Captain, with such like: the certain truth whereof delivered
in holy scripture, is of the Heathen which had them only by report, so intermingled
with fabulous vanities, that the most which remaineth in them to be seen, is the
show of dark and obscure steps, where some part of the truth hath gone.

sort all those writings which contain in them the law of God, all
those venerable books of scripture, all those sacred tomes and
volumes of holy writ, they are with such absolute perfection framed,
that in them there neither wanteth anything, the lack whereof might
deprive us of life; nor anything in such wise aboundeth, that as
being superfluous, unfruitful, and altogether needless, we should
think it no loss or danger at all if we did want it.

The sufficiency of scripture unto the end for which it was instituted.

[14.1] 14. Although the scripture of God therefore be stored with infinite
variety of matter in all kinds, although it abound with all sorts of
laws, yet the principal intent of scripture is to deliver the laws of
duties supernatural. Oftentimes it hath been in very solemn manner
disputed, *q*whether all things necessary unto salvation be necessarily
set down in the holy scriptures or no. If we define that necessary
unto salvation, whereby the way to salvation is in any sort made
more plain, apparent, and easy to be known; then is there no part
of true philosophy, no art of account, no kind of science rightly
so called, but the scripture must contain it. If only those things
be necessary, as surely none else are, without the knowledge and
practice whereof it is not the will and pleasure of God to make
any ordinary grant of salvation, it may be notwithstanding, and oftentimes hath been demanded, how the books of holy scripture contain
in them all necessary things, when of things necessary the very
chiefest is to know what books we are bound to esteem holy, which
point is confessed impossible for the scripture itself to teach. Whereunto we may answer with truth, that there is not in the world any
Art or Science, which proposing unto itself an end (as every one
doth some end or other) hath been therefore thought defective,
if it have not delivered simply whatsoever is needful to the same
end: but all kinds of knowledge have their certain bounds and limits;
each of them presupposeth many necessary things learned in other
sciences and known beforehand. He that should take upon him

---

q *Whether the supernatural knowledge necessary to the wayfarer is sufficiently conveyed in
holy scripture.* This question proposed by Scotus, is affirmatively concluded. *Questions
on the Four Books of Sentences of Peter Lombard*, prologue, part 2.

to teach men how to be eloquent in pleading causes, must needs deliver unto them whatsoever precepts are requisite unto that end, otherwise he doth not the thing which he taketh upon him. Seeing then no man can plead eloquently, unless he be able first to speak, it followeth that ability of speech is in this case a thing most necessary. Notwithstanding every man would think it ridiculous, that he which undertaketh by writing to instruct an Orator, should therefore deliver all the precepts of Grammar, because his profession is to deliver precepts necessary unto eloquent speech, yet so, that they which are to receive them be taught beforehand, so much of that which is thereunto necessary as comprehendeth the skill of speaking. In like sort, albeit scripture do profess to contain in it all things which are necessary unto salvation; yet the meaning cannot be simply of all things that are necessary, but all things that are necessary in some certain kind or form; as all things that are necessary, and either could not at all, or could not easily be known by the light of natural discourse; all things which are necessary to be known that we may be saved, but known with presupposal of knowledge concerning certain principles whereof it receiveth us already persuaded, and then instructeth us in all the residue that are necessary. In the number of these principles one is the sacred authority of scripture. Being therefore persuaded by other means that these scriptures are the oracles of God, themselves do then teach us the rest, and lay before us all the duties which God requireth at our hands as necessary unto salvation. Further, there hath been [14.2] some doubt likewise, whether *containing in scripture* do import express setting down in plain terms, or else *comprehending* in such sort that by reason we may from thence conclude all things which are necessary. Against the former of these two constructions, instance hath sundry ways been given. For our belief in the Trinity, the Coeternity of the Son of God with his Father, the proceeding of the Spirit from the Father and the Son, the duty of baptizing infants, these with such other principal points, the necessity whereof is by none denied, are notwithstanding in scripture nowhere to be found by express literal mention, only deduced they are out of scripture by collection. This kind of comprehension in scripture being therefore received, still there is doubt how far we are to proceed by collection before the full and complete measure of things necessary be made up. For let us not think that as long as the world doth endure, the wit of man shall be able to sound the bottom of that which may be concluded out of the scripture, especially if things contained by collection do so far extend, as to draw in whatsoever may be at any time out of scripture but probably and conjecturally surmised. But let necessary collection be made requisite, and we may boldly deny that of all those things which at this day are with so great necessity urged upon this Church under the name of reformed Church discipline, there is any one which their books hitherto have made manifest to be contained in the scripture. Let them if they can allege but one properly belonging to their cause, and not common to them and us, and show the deduction thereof out of scripture [14.3] to be necessary. It hath been already showed how all things necessary unto salvation in such sort as before we have maintained, must needs be possible for men to know, and that many things are in such sort necessary, the knowledge whereof is by the light of nature impossible to be attained. Whereupon it followeth that either all flesh is excluded from possibility of salvation, which to think were most barbarous, or else that God hath by supernatural means revealed the way of life so far forth as doth suffice. For this cause God hath so many times and ways spoken to the sons of men. Neither hath he by speech only, but by writing also instructed and taught his Church. The cause of writing hath been to the end that things by him revealed unto the world might have the longer continuance, and the greater certainty of assurance, by how much that which standeth on record hath in both those respects preeminence above that which passeth from hand to hand, and hath no pens but the tongue, no books but the ears of men to record it. The several books of scripture having had each some several occasion and parti-cular purpose which caused them to be written, the contents thereof are according to the exigence of that special end whereunto they are intended. Hereupon it groweth that every book of holy scripture doth take out of all kinds of truth, [r]natural, [s]historical, [t]foreign, [u]supernatural, so much as the matter handled requireth. Now foras-much as there hath been reason alleged sufficient to conclude, that all things necessary unto salvation must be made known, and that God himself hath therefore revealed his will, because otherwise men could not have known so much as is necessary, his surceasing

[r] Ephes. 5:29.   [s] 2 Tim. 3:8.   [t] Tit. 1:12.   [u] 2 Pet. 2:4.

to speak to the world since the publishing of the Gospel of Jesus Christ, and the delivery of the same in writing, is unto us a manifest token that the way of salvation is now sufficiently opened, and that we need no other means for our full instruction, than God hath already furnished us withal. The main drift of the whole new Testa- [14.4] ment is that which Saint *John* setteth down as the purpose of his own history, *°These things are written, that ye might believe that Jesus is Christ the Son of God, and that in believing ye might have life through his name.* The drift of the old that which the Apostle mentioneth to *Timothy*, *™The holy Scriptures are able to make thee wise unto salvation.* So that the general end both of old and new is one, the difference between them consisting in this, that the old did make wise by teaching salvation through Christ that should come, the new by teaching that Christ the Saviour is come, and that Jesus whom the Jews did crucify, and whom God did raise again from the dead is he. When the Apostle therefore affirmeth unto *Timothy*, that the old was able to make him wise to salvation, it was not his meaning that the old alone can do this unto us which live since the publication of the new. For he speaketh with presupposal of the doctrine of Christ known also unto *Timothy*, and therefore first it is said, *°Continue thou in those things which thou hast learned and art persuaded, knowing of whom thou hast been taught them.* Again those scriptures he granteth were able to make him wise to salvation; but he added, *°through the faith which is in Christ.* Wherefore without the doctrine of the new Testament teaching that Christ hath wrought the redemption of the world, which redemption the old did foreshow he should work, it is not the former alone which can on our behalf perform so much as the Apostle doth avouch, who presupposeth this when he magnifieth that so highly. And as his words concerning the books of ancient scripture do not take place but with presupposal of the Gospel of Christ embraced: so our own words also when we extol the complete sufficiency of the whole entire body of the scripture, must in like sort be understood with this caution, that the benefit of nature's light be not thought excluded as unnecessary, because the necessity of a diviner light is magnified. There is in scripture therefore no defect, but that any man what place or calling soever he hold in the Church of God, may have thereby the light of his

---

° John 20:31.   ™ 2 Tim. 3:15.   ° 2 Tim. 3:14.   ° Verse 15.

natural understanding so perfected, that the one being relieved by the other, there can want no part of needful instruction unto any good work which God himself requireth, be it natural or supernatural, belonging simply unto men as men, or unto men as they are united in whatsoever kind of society. It sufficeth therefore that nature and scripture do serve in such full sort, that they both jointly and not severally either of them be so complete, that unto everlasting felicity we need not the knowledge of anything more than these two, may easily furnish our minds with on all sides, and therefore they which add traditions as a part of supernatural necessary truth, have not the truth, but are in error. For they only plead, that whatsoever God revealeth as necessary for all Christian men to do or believe, the same we ought to embrace, whether we have received it by writing or otherwise, which no man denieth, when that which they should confirm, who claim so great reverence unto traditions, is, that the same traditions are necessarily to be acknowledged divine and holy. For we do not reject them only because they are not in the Scripture, but because they are neither in Scripture, nor can otherwise sufficiently by any reason be proved to be of God. That which is of God, and may be evidently proved to be so, we deny not but it hath in his kind, although unwritten, yet the selfsame force and authority with the written laws of God. It is by ours acknowledged *that the Apostles did in every Church institute and ordain some rites and customs serving for the seemliness of Church regiment, which rites and customs they have not committed unto writing.* Those rites and customs being known to be Apostolical, and having the nature of things changeable, were no less to be accounted of in the Church than other things of the like degree, that is to say, capable in like sort of alteration, although set down in the Apostles' writings. For both being known to be Apostolical, it is not the manner of delivering them unto the Church, but the author from whom they proceed which doth give them their force and credit.

*Whitaker against Bellarmine, question 6, ch. 6.

Of laws positive contained in scripture, the mutability of certain of them, and the general use of scripture.

15. Laws being imposed either by each man upon himself, or by [15.1] a public society upon the particulars thereof, or by all the nations of men upon every several society, or by the Lord himself upon any or every of these, there is not amongst these four kinds any one but containeth sundry both natural and positive laws. Impossible it is but that they should fall into a number of gross errors, who only take such laws for positive, as have been made or invented of men, and holding this position hold also, that all positive and none but positive laws are mutable. Laws natural do always bind, laws positive not so, but only after they have been expressly and wittingly imposed. Laws positive there are in every of those kinds before mentioned. As in the first kind the promises which we have passed unto men, and the vows we have made unto God, for these are laws which we tie ourselves unto, and till we have so tied ourselves they bind us not. Laws positive in the second kind are such as the civil constitutions peculiar unto each particular commonweal. In the third kind the law of Heraldry in war is positive, and in the last all the judicials which God gave unto the people of *Israel* to observe. And although no laws but positive be mutable, yet all are not mutable which be positive. Positive laws are either permanent or else changeable, according as the matter itself is concerning which they were first made. Whether God or man be the maker of them, alteration they so far forth admit, as the matter doth exact. Laws [15.2] that concern supernatural duties, are all positive, and either concern men supernaturally as men, or else as parts of a supernatural society, which society we call the Church. To concern men as men supernaturally is to concern them as duties which belong of necessity to all, and yet could not have been known by any to belong unto them, unless God had opened them himself, inasmuch as they do not depend upon any natural ground at all out of which they may be deduced, but are appointed of God to supply the defect of those natural ways of salvation, by which we are not now able to attain thereunto. The Church being a supernatural society, doth differ from natural societies in this, that the persons unto whom we associate ourselves, in the one are men simply considered as men, but

they to whom we be joined in the other, are God, Angels, and holy men. Again the Church being both a society and a society supernatural, although as it is a society it have the self-same original grounds which other politic societies have, namely, the natural inclination which all men have unto sociable life, and consent to some certain bond of association, which bond is the law that appointeth what kind of order they shall be associated in: yet unto the Church as it is a society supernatural this is peculiar, that part of the bond of their association which belong to the Church of God, must be a law supernatural, which God himself hath revealed concerning that kind of worship which his people shall do unto him. The substance of the service of God therefore, so far forth as it hath in it anything more than the law of reason doth teach, *may not be invented of men, as it is amongst the Heathens, but must be received from God himself, as always it hath been in the Church, saving [15.3] only when the Church hath been forgetful of her duty. Wherefore to end with a general rule concerning all the laws which God hath tied men unto: those laws divine that belong whether naturally or supernaturally either to men as men, or to men as they live in politic society, or to men as they are of that politic society which is the Church, without any further respect had unto any such variable accident as the state of men and of societies of men and of the Church itself in this world is subject unto, all laws that so belong unto men, they belong for ever, yea, although they be positive laws, unless being positive God himself which made them alter them. The reason is, because the subject or matter of laws in general is thus far forth constant: which matter is that for the ordering whereof laws were instituted, and being instituted are not changeable without cause, neither can they have cause of change, when that which gave them their first institution, remaineth forever one and the same. On the other side laws that were made for men or societies or Churches, in regard of their being such as they do not always continue, but may perhaps be clean otherwise a while after, and so may require to be otherwise ordered than before: the laws of God himself which are of this nature, no man endowed with common sense will ever deny to be of a different constitution from the former, in respect of the one's constancy, and the mutability of the other.

---

a Isa. 29:13. *Their fear towards me was taught by the precept of men.*

And this doth seem to have been the very cause why Saint *John* doth so peculiarly term the doctrine that teacheth salvation by Jesus Christ, [b]*Evangelium æternum, an eternal Gospel,* because there can be no reason wherefore the publishing thereof should be taken away, and any other instead of it proclaimed, as long as the world doth continue; whereas the whole law of rites and Ceremonies, although delivered with so great solemnity, is notwithstanding clean abrogated, inasmuch as it had but temporary cause of God's ordaining it. But that we may at the length conclude this first general introduction unto the nature and original birth as of all other laws, so likewise of those which the sacred Scripture containeth, concerning the author whereof, even infidels have confessed, [c]that he can neither err nor deceive; albeit about things easy and manifest unto all men by common sense there needeth no higher consultation, because as a man whose wisdom is in weighty affairs admired, would take it in some disdain to have his counsel solemnly asked about a toy, so the meanness of some things is such that to search the Scripture of God for the ordering of them were to derogate from the reverend authority and dignity of the Scripture, no less than they do by whom Scriptures are in ordinary talk very idly applied unto vain and childish trifles: yet better it were to be superstitious, than profane; to take from thence our direction even in all things great or small, than to wade through matters of principal weight and moment, without ever caring what the law of God hath, either for or against our designs. Concerning the custom of the very Paynims, thus much *Strabo* witnesseth, [d]*Men that are civil do lead their lives after one common law appointing them what to do. For that otherwise a multitude should with harmony amongst themselves, concur in the doing of one thing (for this is civilly to live) or that they should in any sort manage community of life, it is not possible. Now laws or statutes are of two sorts. For they are either received from Gods, or else from men. And our ancient predecessors did surely most honour and reverence that which was from the Gods; for which cause consultation with Oracles was a thing very usual and frequent in their times.* Did they make so much account of the

[15.4]

---

[b] Rev. 14:6.

[c] *Then God is altogether simple and true in deed and word and neither changes himself nor deceives others by visions or words or the sending of signs in waking or in dreams.* Plato, *Republic,* Bk 2 at the end [382e].

[d] Strabo, *Geography,* Bk 16 [*L,* 7:286–287].

voice of their Gods, which in truth were no Gods: and shall we neglect the precious benefit of conference with those Oracles of the true and living God, whereof so great store is left to the Church, and whereunto there is so free, so plain, and so easy access for all men? *By thy Commandments* (this was *David's* confession unto God) *thou hast made me wiser than mine enemies.* Again, *I have had more understanding than all my teachers, because thy testimonies are my meditations.* What pains would not they have bestowed in the study of these books, who travelled sea and land to gain the treasure of some few days talk with men, whose wisdom the world did make any reckoning of? *f*That little which some of the Heathens did chance to hear, concerning such matter as the sacred Scripture plentifully containeth, they did in wonderful sort affect; their speeches as oft as they make mention thereof are strange, and such as themselves could not utter as they did other things, but still acknowledged that their wits which did everywhere else conquer hardness, were with profoundness here overmatched. Wherefore seeing that God hath endowed us with sense to the end that we might perceive such things as this present life doth need, and with reason lest that which sense cannot reach unto, being both now and also in regard of a future estate hereafter necessary to be known, should lie obscure; finally with the heavenly support of *g*prophetical revelation, which doth open those hidden mysteries that reason could never have been able to find out, or to have known the necessity of them unto our everlasting good: use we the precious gifts of God unto his glory and honour that gave them, seeking by all means to know what the will or our God is, what righteous before him, in his sight what holy, perfect, and good, that we may truly and faithfully do it.

A conclusion showing how all this belongeth to the cause in question

[16.1] 16. Thus far therefore we have endeavoured in part to open, of what nature and force laws are, according unto their several kinds;

e Ps. 119:98.

f See the *Songs of Orpheus.*

g *For prophecy finds its way to those things which reason fails to reach.* Philo, *On Moses* [L, 6:452–453].

the law which God with himself hath eternally set down to follow in his own works; the law which he hath made for his creatures to keep, the law of natural and necessary agents; the law which Angels in heaven obey; the law whereunto by the light of reason men find themselves bound in that they are men; the law which they make by composition for multitudes and politic societies of men to be guided by; the law which belongeth unto each nation; the law that concerneth the fellowship of all; and lastly the law which God himself hath supernaturally revealed. It might peradventure have been more popular and more plausible to vulgar ears, if this first discourse had been spent in extolling the force of laws, in showing the great necessity of them when they are good, and in aggravating their offence by whom public laws are injuriously traduced. But forasmuch as with such kind of matter the passions of men are rather stirred one way or other, than their knowledge any way set forward unto the trial of that whereof there is doubt made; I have therefore turned aside from that beaten path and chosen though a less easy, yet a more profitable way in regard of the end we propose. Lest therefore any man should marvel whereunto all these things tend, the drift and purpose of all is this, even to show in what manner [h]as every good and perfect gift, so this very gift of good and perfect laws is derived from the father of lights; to teach men a reason why just and reasonable laws are of so great force, of so great use in the world; and to inform their minds with some method of reducing the laws whereof there is present controversy unto their first original causes, that so it may be in every particular ordinance thereby the better discerned, whether the same be reasonable just and righteous or no. Is there anything which can either be thoroughly understood, or soundly judged of, till the very first causes and principles from which originally it springeth be made manifest? If all parts of knowledge have been thought by wise men to be then [i]most orderly delivered and proceeded in, when they are drawn to their first original; seeing that our whole question concerneth the quality of Ecclesiastical laws, let it not seem a labour superfluous that in the entrance thereunto all these several kinds of laws have been considered, inasmuch as they all concur as principles, they all have their forcible operations therein, although

---

[h] James 1:17.   [i] Aristotle, *Physics*, Bk 1, ch. 1 [184a].

not all in like apparent and manifest manner. By means whereof it cometh to pass that the force which they have is not observed [16.2] of many. Easier a great deal it is for men by law to be taught what they ought to do, than instructed how to judge as they should do of law; the one being a thing which belongeth generally unto all, the other such as none but the wiser and more judicious sort can perform. Yea, the wisest are always touching this point the readiest to acknowledge, *j*that soundly to judge of a law is the weightiest thing which any man can take upon him. But if we will give judgement of the laws under which we live, first let that law eternal be always before our eyes, as being of principal force and moment to breed in religious minds a dutiful estimation of all laws, the use and benefit whereof we see; because there can be no doubt but that laws apparently good, are (as it were) things copied out of the very tables of that high everlasting law, even as the book of that law hath said concerning itself, *k*By me *Kings reign, and* by me *Princes decree justice.* Not as if men did behold that book, and accordingly frame their laws, but because it worketh in them, because it discovereth and (as it were) readeth itself to the world by them when the laws which they make are righteous. Furthermore although we perceive not the goodness of laws made, nevertheless since things in themselves may have that which we peradventure discern not; should not this breed a fear in our hearts, how we speak or judge in the worse part concerning that, the unadvised disgrace whereof may be no mean dishonour to him, towards whom we profess all submission and awe? Surely there must be very manifest iniquity in laws, against which we shall be able to justify our contumelious invectives. The chiefest root whereof, when we use them without cause, is ignorance how laws inferior are derived from [16.3] that supreme or highest law. The first that receive impression from thence are natural agents. The law of whose operations might be happily thought less pertinent, when the question is about laws for human actions, but that in those very actions which most spiritually and supernaturally concern men, the rules and axioms of natural operations have their force. What can be more immediate to our salvation than our persuasion concerning the love of Christ towards

---

j Aristotle, *Ethics*, 10 [1181a]. *To judge rightly is the greatest thing.* He means judgement about the quality of laws.
k Prov. 8:15.

his Church? What greater assurance of love towards his Church, than the knowledge of that mystical union whereby the Church is become as near unto Christ, as any one part of his flesh is unto other? That the Church being in such sort his, he must needs protect it, what proof more strong, than if a manifest law so require, which law it is not possible for Christ to violate? And what other law doth the Apostle for this allege, but such as is both common unto Christ with us, and unto us with other things natural, *¹No man hateth his own flesh, but doth love and cherish it?* The axioms of that law therefore, whereby natural agents are guided, have their use in the moral, yea, even in the spiritual actions of men, and consequently in all laws belonging unto men howsoever. Neither are the Angels them- [16.4] selves, so far severed from us in their kind and manner of working, but that, between the law of their heavenly operations and the actions of men in this our state of mortality, such correspondence there is, as maketh it expedient to know in some sort the one, for the other's more perfect direction. Would Angels acknowledge them- selves *ᵐ*fellow servants with the sons of men, but that both having one Lord, there must be some kind of law which is one and the same to both, whereunto their obedience being perfecter, is to our weaker both a pattern and a spur? Or would the Apostles speaking of that which belongeth unto Saints, *ⁿ*as they are linked together in the bond of spiritual society, so often make mention how Angels therewith are delighted, if in things publicly done by the Church we are not somewhat to respect what the Angels of heaven do? Yea, so far hath the Apostle St. Paul proceeded, as to signify, *ᵒ*that even about the outward orders of the Church which serve but for comeli- ness, some regard is to be had of Angels, who best like us, when we are most like unto them in all parts of decent demeanour. So that the law of Angels we cannot judge altogether impertinent unto the affairs of the Church of God. Our largeness of speech how [16.5] men do find out what things reason bindeth them of necessity to observe, and what it guideth them to choose in things which are left as arbitrary; the care we have had to declare the different nature of laws which severally concern all men, from such as belong unto men either civilly or spiritually associated, such as pertain to

---

ˡ Ephes. 5:29.   *ᵐ* Rev. 19:10.
ⁿ 1 Pet. 1:12. Ephes. 3:10. 1 Tim. 5:21.   *ᵒ* 1 Cor. 11:10.

the fellowship which nations, or which Christian nations have
amongst themselves, and in the last place such as concerning every
or any of these, God himself hath revealed by his holy word; all
serveth but to make manifest that as the actions of men are of sundry
distinct kinds, so the laws thereof must accordingly be distinguished.
There are in men operations some natural, some rational, some
supernatural, some politic, some finally Ecclesiastical. Which if we
measure not each by his own proper law, whereas the things themselves are so different; there will be in our understanding and judgement of them confusion. As that first error showeth whereon our
opposites in this cause have grounded themselves. For as they rightly
maintain, that God must be glorified in all things, and that the
actions of men cannot tend unto his glory, unless they be framed
after his law: So it is their error to think that the only law which
God hath appointed unto men in that behalf is the sacred Scripture.
By that which we work naturally, as when we breathe, sleep, move,
*p*we set forth the glory of God as natural agents do, albeit we have
no express purpose to make that our end, nor any advised determination therein to follow a law, but do that we do, (for the most
part) not as much as thinking thereon. In reasonable and moral
actions another law taketh place, *q*a law by the observation whereof
we glorify God in such sort, as no creature else under man is able
to do, because other creatures have not judgement to examine the
quality of that which is done by them, and therefore in that they
do, they neither can accuse nor approve themselves. *r*Men do both,
as the Apostle teacheth, yea, those men which have no written law
of God to show what is good or evil, carry written in their hearts
the universal law of mankind, the law of reason, whereby they judge
as by a rule which God hath given unto all men for that purpose.
The law of reason doth somewhat direct men how to honour God
as their Creator, but how to glorify God in such sort as is required,
to the end he may be an everlasting Saviour, this we are taught
by divine law, which law both ascertaineth the truth and supplieth
unto us the want of that other law. So that in moral actions, divine
law helpeth exceedingly the law of reason to guide man's life, but
in supernatural it alone guideth. Proceed we further, let us place
man in some public society with others, whether Civil or Spiritual:

p Ps. 148:7, 8, 9.   *q* Rom. 1:21.   *r* Rom. 2:15.

and in this case there is no remedy but we must add yet a further law. For although even here likewise the laws of nature and reason be of necessary use, yet somewhat over and besides them is necessary, namely human and positive law, together with that law which is of commerce between grand societies, the law of nations and of nations Christian. For which cause the law of God hath likewise said, *Let every soul be subject to the higher powers.* The public power of all societies is above every soul contained in the same societies. And the principal use of that power is to give laws unto all that are under it, which laws in such case we must obey, unless there be reason showed which may necessarily enforce that the law of reason or of God, doth enjoin the contrary. Because except our own private, and but probable resolutions be by the law of public determinations overruled, we take away all possibility of sociable life in the world. A plainer example whereof than ourselves we cannot have. How cometh it to pass that we are at this present day so rent with mutual contentions, and that the Church is so much troubled about the polity of the Church? No doubt if men had been willing to learn how many laws their actions in this life are subject unto, and what the true force of each law is, all these controversies might have died the very day they were first brought forth. It is both com- [16.6] monly said, and truly, that the best men otherwise are not always the best in regard of society. The reason whereof is for that the law of men's actions is one, if they be respected only as men; and another, when they are considered as parts of a politic body. 'Many men there are, than whom nothing is more commendable when they are singled. And yet in society with others none less fit to answer the duties which are looked for at their hands. Yea, I am persuaded, that of them with whom in this cause we strive, there are whose betters amongst men would be hardly found, if they did not live amongst men, but in some wilderness by themselves. The cause of which, their disposition so unframeable unto societies where-in they live is, for that they discern not aright what place and force these several kinds of laws ought to have in all their actions. Is there question either concerning the regiment of the Church in general, or about conformity between one Church and another,

---

⁵ Rom. 13:1.
ᵗ *For many are able to practise virtue in their private affairs but cannot do so towards others.* Aristotle, *Ethics*, Bk 5, ch. 3 [1129b].

or of ceremonies, offices, powers, jurisdictions in our own Church? Of all these things they judge by that rule which they frame to themselves with some show of probability, and what seemeth in that sort convenient, the same they think themselves bound to practise; the same by all means they labour mightily to uphold, whatsoever any law of man to the contrary hath determined they weigh it not. Thus by following the law of private reason, where the law of public [16.7] should take place, they breed disturbance. For the better inuring therefore of men's minds with the true distinction of laws and of their several force, according to the different kind and quality of our actions, it shall not peradventure be amiss to show in some one example how they all take place. To seek no further, let but that be considered than which there is not anything more familiar unto us, our food. "What things are food, and what are not we judge naturally by sense, neither need we any other law to be our director in that behalf than the self-same which is common unto us with beasts. But when we come to consider of food, *as of a benefit which God of his bounteous goodness hath provided for all things living, the law of reason doth here require the duty of thankfulness at our hands, towards him at whose hands we have it. And lest appetite in the use of food, should lead us beyond that which is meet, we owe in this case obedience to that law of reason, which teacheth mediocrity in meats and drinks. The same things divine law teacheth also, as at large we have showed it doth all parts of moral duty, whereunto we all of necessity stand bound in regard of the life to come. But of certain kinds of food the Jew sometime had, and we ourselves likewise have a mystical, religious, and supernatural use, they of their Paschal lamb and oblations, we of our bread and wine in the Eucharist; which use none but divine law could institute. Now as we live in civil society, the state of the commonwealth wherein we live, both may and doth require certain laws concerning food; which laws, saving only that we are members of the commonwealth where they are of force, we should not need to respect as rules of action, whereas now in their place and kind they must be respected and obeyed. Yea, the self-same matter is also a subject wherein sometime Ecclesiastical laws have place, so that, unless we will be authors of confusion in the Church,

u Job 34:3.   *v* Ps. 145:15–16.

our private discretion, which otherwise might guide us a contrary way, must here submit itself to be that way guided, which the public judgement of the Church hath thought better. In which case that of *Zonaras* concerning fasts may be remembered. *ʷFastings are good, but let good things be done in good and convenient manner. He that transgresseth in his fasting the orders of the holy fathers*, the positive laws of the Church of Christ, must be plainly told, *that good things do lose the grace of their goodness, when in good sort they are not performed.* And as here men's private fancies must give place to the higher judgement of that Church which is in authority a mother over them: so the very actions of whole Churches have in regard of commerce and fellowship with other Churches been subject to laws concerning food, the contrary unto which laws had else been thought more convenient for them to observe, as by ˣthat order of abstinence from strangled and blood may appear; an order grounded upon that fellowship which the Churches of the Gentiles had with the Jews. Thus we see how even one and the self-same thing is under divers considerations conveyed through many laws, and that to measure by any one kind of law all the actions of men were to confound the admirable order, wherein God hath disposed all laws, each as in nature, so in degree distinct from other. Wherefore that here [16.8] we may briefly end, of law there can be no less acknowledged, than that her seat is the bosom of God, her voice the harmony of the world, all things in heaven and earth do her homage, the very least as feeling her care, and the greatest as not exempted from her power, but Angels and men and creatures of what condition soever, though each in different sort and manner, yet all with uniform consent, admiring her as the mother of their peace and joy.

ʷ Zonaras on Apostolic canon 66 [*PG*, 137:172].   ˣ Acts 15:20.

THE EIGHTH BOOK

Their Seventh Assertion,
That unto no Civil Prince or Governor there may be given such power of Ecclesiastical Dominion as by the Laws of this Land belongeth unto the Supreme Regent thereof.

An admonition concerning men's judgements about the question of regal power.

[1.1] 1. We come now to the last thing, whereof there is controversy moved, namely the *power* of *Supreme Jurisdiction*, which for distinction sake, we call the power of *Ecclesiastical Dominion*.

It was not thought fit in the *Jews' Commonwealth* that the exercise of *Supremacy Ecclesiastical* should be denied unto him, to whom the exercise of *Chiefly Civil* did appertain, and therefore their kings were invested with both. This power they gave unto *Simon*, *"when they consented that he should be their *Prince*, not only to set men over the works and over the Country, and over the weapons and over the fortresses, but also to provide for *the holy things*, and that he should be obeyed of every man and that all the writings in the *Country* should be made in his *name, and that it should not be lawful for any of the people or Priests to withstand his words or to call any Congregation in the Country without him.* And if it be happily surmised that thus much was given unto *Simon* as being both *Prince* and *High Priest*, which otherwise (being only their *Civil Governor*) he could not lawfully have enjoyed, we must note that all this is no more than the ancient *Kings* of that people had being *Kings and not Priests*. By this power *David, Asa, Jehosaphat, Hezekiah, Josiah* and the rest made those laws and orders, which the Sacred History speaketh of concerning matter of mere religion, the affairs of the

^a *1 Macc. 14:41–42.*

Temple and *Service* of God. Finally had it not been by the virtue of this power, how should it possibly have come to pass that the piety or impiety of the *King* did always accordingly change the public face of religion, which thing the *Priests* by themselves never did, neither could at any time hinder from being done? Had the *Priests* alone been possessed with all power in *Spiritual* affairs how should any law concerning matter of religion have been made, but only by them? In them it had been and not in the *King*, to change the face of religion at any time. The altering of religion, the making of *Ecclesiastical* laws with other the like actions belonging unto the power of dominion are still termed the deeds of the *King*, to show that in him was placed *Supremacy* of power even in this kind over all, and that unto their *High Priests* the same was never committed, saving only at such times as their *Priests* were also *Kings* or *Princes* over them.

According to the pattern of which example the like power in [1.2] causes *Ecclesiastical* is by the laws of this Realm annexed unto the *Crown*. And there are which imagine, that kings being mere lay persons, do by this means exceed the lawful bounds of their calling. Which thing to the end that they may persuade, they first make a necessary separation perpetual and personal between the *Church* and *Commonwealth*. Secondly they so tie all kind of power *Ecclesiastical* unto the *Church* as if it were in every degree their only right, which are by proper spiritual function termed *Church-Governors* and might not to *Christian Princes* any wise appertain. To lurk under shifting ambiguities and equivocations of words in matters of principal weight is childish. A *Church* and a *Commonwealth* we grant are things in nature the one distinguished from the other, a *Commonwealth* is one way, and a *Church* another way defined. In their opinion the *Church* and the *Commonwealth* are corporations not distinguished only in nature and definition, but in subsistence perpetually severed, so that they that are of the one can neither appoint, nor execute in whole nor in part the duties which belong unto them, which are of the other, without open breach of the law of *God*, which hath divided them, and doth require that being so divided they should distinctly and severally work as depending both upon *God* and not hanging one upon the other's approbation for that which either hath to do.

We say that the care of religion being common unto all *Societies*

politic, such *Societies* as do embrace the true religion, have the name
of the *Church* given unto every of them for distinction from the
rest. So that every body politic hath some religion, but the *Church*
that religion, which is only true. Truth of religion is that proper
difference, whereby a *Church* is distinguished from other politic
societies of men. We here mean true religion in gross, and not
according to every particular for they which in some particular
points of religion do swerve from the truth, may nevertheless most
truly, if we compare them to men of an heathenish religion, be
said to hold and profess that religion which is true. For which
cause there being of old so many politic *Societies* established
throughout the world only the *Commonwealth* of *Israel* which had
the truth of religion, was in that respect the *Church* of *God.* And
the *Church* of *Jesus Christ* is every such politic society of men as
doth in religion hold that truth which is proper to *Christianity.* As
a politic *Society* it doth maintain religion; as a *Church* that religion
which *God* hath revealed by *Jesus Christ.* With us therefore the
name of a *Church* importeth only a *Society* of men first united
into some public form of regiment and secondly distinguished
from other *Societies*, by the exercise of *Christian* religion. With
them on the other side the name of the *Church* in this present
question importeth not only a multitude of men, so united and so
distinguished, but also further the same divided necessarily and
perpetually from the body of the *Commonwealth.* So that even in
such a politic *Society*, as consisteth of none but *Christians*, yet the
Church of *Christ* and the *Commonwealth* are two corporations inde-
pendently each subsisting by itself. We hold that seeing there is
not any man of the *Church* of *England*, but the same man is also
a member of the *Commonwealth*, nor any man a member of the *Commonwealth* which is not also of the *Church* of *England*, therefore
as in a figure *triangular* the base doth differ from the sides thereof,
and yet one and the selfsame line, is both a base and also a side;
a side simply, a base if it chance to be the bottom and underlie
the rest: So albeit properties and actions of one kind do cause the
name of a Commonwealth, qualities and functions of another sort
the name of a *Church* to be given unto a multitude, yet one and
the selfsame multitude may in such sort be both and is so with
us, that no person appertaining to the one can be denied to be
also of the other. Contrariwise (unless they against us should hold

that the *Church* and the *Commonwealth* are two both distinct and separate societies, of which two the one comprehendeth always persons not belonging to the other) that which they do, they could not conclude out of the difference between the *Church* and the *Commonwealth*; namely, that *Bishops* may not meddle with the affairs of the commonwealth because they are governors of another corporation, which is the *Church*, nor *Kings*, with making laws for the *Church* because they have government not of this corporation, but of another divided from it, the *Commonwealth*, and the walls of separation between these two must forever be upheld. They hold the necessity of personal separation which clean excludeth the power of one man's dealing in both, we of natural which doth not hinder, but that one and the same person may in both bear a principal sway.

The causes of common received error in this point seem to have [1.3] been especially two: One, that they who embrace true religion living in such Commonwealths as are opposite thereunto and in other public affairs retaining civil Communion, with such are constrained for the exercise of their religion to have a several Communion with those who are of the same religion with them. This was the state of the *Jewish Church* both in *Egypt* and *Babylon*, the state of *Christian Churches* a long time after *Christ*. And in this case because the proper affairs and actions of the *Church*, as it is the *Church*, have no dependency upon the laws or upon the Governors of the Civil state, an opinion hath thereby grown, that even so it should be always. This was it which deceived *Allen* in his writing of his *Apology*. *The Apostles* (saith he) *did govern the Church in Rome when Nero did bear rule, even as at this day in all the Turk's Dominions the Church hath a spiritual Regiment without dependence and so ought she to have, live she amongst Heathens or with Christians.*

Another occasion of which misconceipt is, that things appertaining [1.4] unto religion are both distinguished from other affairs and have always had in the *Church* special persons chosen to be exercised about them. By which distinction of spiritual affairs and persons therein employed from temporal, the error of personal separation always necessary between the *Church* and the *Commonwealth* hath strengthened itself; for of every politic society that being true which Aristotle hath, namely, *[b]That the scope thereof is not simply to live,*

[b] Aristotle, *Politics*, p. 102 [1291a].

nor the duty so much to provide for life as for means of living well, and that even as the soul is the worthier part of man, so human societies are much more to care for that which tendeth properly unto the soul's estate than for such temporal things as this life doth stand in need of. Other proof there needs none to show that as by all men *'the kingdom of God is first to be sought for*: So in all commonwealths things spiritual ought above temporal to be provided for. *^dAnd of things spiritual the chiefest is *Religion*. For this cause persons and things employed peculiarly about the affairs of religion are by an excellency termed *Spiritual*. *^eThe *Heathen* themselves had their *Spiritual Laws*, causes and offices always severed from their *temporal*. Neither did this make two independent states amongst them. *God* by revealing true religion doth make them that receive it his *Church*. Unto the *Jews* he so revealed the truth of religion, that he gave them in special consideration laws not only for the administration of things spiritual, but also temporal. The Lord himself appointing both the one and the other in that *Commonwealth*, did not thereby distract it into several independent *Communities*, but instituted several functions of one and the same *Community*. Some reason therefore must be alleged, why it should be otherwise in the *Church* of *Christ*.

Three kind of proofs for confirmation of the aforesaid separation between the Church and Commonwealth. The first taken from difference of affairs and offices in each.

I shall not need to spend any great store of words in answering that which is brought out of holy *Scripture* to show that secular and Ecclesiastical affairs and offices are distinguished, neither that which hath been borrowed from antiquity using by phrase of speech to oppose the *Commonwealth* to the *Church* of *Christ*; neither yet the reasons, which are wont to be brought forth as witnesses that the *Church* and *Commonwealth* are always distinct. For whether *a Church* and *a Commonwealth* do differ is not the question we strive

*^c Matt. 6:33.   ^d Aristotle, *Politics*, p. 196 [1328b].*
*^e Aristotle, *Politics*, p. 123, I. 10 [1299a]; p. 181, I. 28 [1322b]. Livy, *Roman Histories*, Bk
I [*L*, 1:70–72].*

for, but our controversy is concerning the kind of distinction, whereby they are severed the one from the other; whether, as under *Heathen
Kings* the church did deal with her own affairs within herself, without
depending at all upon any in civil authority, and the *Commonwealth*
in hers altogether without the privity of the *Church*, so it ought
to continue still even in such *Commonwealths* as have now publicly
embraced the truth of *Christian religion*, whether they ought to be
evermore two societies in such sort several and distinct.

I ask therefore what society that was, that was in *Rome*, whereunto
the *Apostle* did give the name of the *Church* of *Rome* in his time?
If they answer as needs they must that the *Church* of *Rome* in those
days was that whole society of men which in *Rome* professed the
name of *Christ* and not that religion which the laws of the *Commonwealth* did then authorize, we say as much and therefore grant that
the *Commonwealth* of *Rome* was one society and the *Church* of *Rome*
another, in such sort as there was between them no mutual dependency. But when whole *Rome* became *Christian*, when they all
embraced the Gospel, and made laws in the defence thereof, if
it be held that the *Church* and the *Commonwealth* of *Rome* did then
remain as before, there is no way how this could be possible save
only one, and that is, They must restrain the name of the *Church*
in a *Christian Commonwealth* to the *Clergy*, excluding all the residue
of believers both *Prince* and *People*. For if all that believe, be contained in the name of the *Church*, how should the *Church* remain
by personal subsistency divided from the *Commonwealth* when the
whole *Commonwealth* doth believe? The *Church* and the *Commonwealth* therefore are in this case personally one society, which society
being termed a *Commonwealth* as it liveth under whatsoever form
of secular law and regiment, a *Church* as it hath the *Spiritual* law
of *Jesus Christ*, forasmuch as these two laws contain so many and
so different offices, there must of necessity be appointed in it some
to one charge and some to another, yet without dividing the whole
and making it two several impaled societies.

The difference therefore either of ᶠaffairs of offices Ecclesiastical
from secular is no argument that the *Church* and the *Commonwealth*
are always separate and independent the one from the other, which
thing even *Allen* himself considering somewhat better doth in this

---

ᶠ 2 Chron. 19:8, 11. Heb. 5:1. 1 Thess. 5:12. T.C., Bk 3, p. 151.

point a little correct his former judgement before mentioned, and confesseth in his defence of English Catholics that *The power political hath her Princes, Laws, Tribunals: The Spiritual her Prelates, Canons, Councils, Judgements, and those (when the Princes are Pagans) wholly separate, but in Christian Commonwealths joined though not confounded.* Howbeit afterwards his former sting appeareth again. For in a *Christian Commonwealth* he holdeth that the *Church* ought not to depend at all upon the authority of any civil person whatsoever, as in *England* he saith it doth.

Proofs of separation between the Church and Commonwealth taken from the speeches of the Fathers opposing the one to the other.

[1.5] It will be objected ᵍthat the *Fathers* do oftentimes mention the *Commonwealth* and the *Church* of God by way of opposition. Can the same thing be opposite unto itself? If one and the same society be both, what sense can there be in that speech which saith ʰ*They suffer and flourish together?* What sense in that which maketh ⁱ*one thing adjudged to the Church, another to the Commonwealth?* Finally in that which ʲputteth a difference between the causes of the *Province and of the Church?* Doth it not hereby appear, that the *Church* and the *Commonwealth* are things evermore personally separate? No, it doth not hereby appear that there is perpetually any such separation. We may speak of them as two, we may sever the rights and causes of the one well enough from the other in regard of that difference which we grant there is between them, albeit we make no personal difference. For the truth is that the *Church* and the *Commonwealth* are names which import things really different. But those things are accidents and such accidents as may and should always lovingly dwell together in one subject. Wherefore the real difference between the accidents signified by those names doth not prove different subjects for them always to reside in: for albeit the subjects wherein they are resident be sometime different, as when the people of God have their being among infidels, yet the nature of them is not such, but that their subject may be one, and therefore it is but a changeable

ᵍ T.C., Bk 3, p. 151.
ʰ Socrates, *Ecclesiastical History*, Bk 5, preface. Sozomen, *Ecclesiastical History*, Bk 3, ch. 26 [Bk 8, ch. 25].
ⁱ Eusebius, *Life of Constantine*, Bk 3 [ch. 65].
ʲ Augustine, Epistle 167 [*PL*, 33:310; *FOTC*, 18:35–36].

accident in those accidents, when the subjects they are in be diverse. There can be no error in our conceipt concerning this point, if we remember still what accident that is, for which a *Society* hath the name of a *Commonwealth*, and what accident that, which doth cause it to be termed a *Church*.

A *Commonwealth* we name it simply in regard of some regiment or policy under which men live, a *Church* for the truth of that religion which they profess. Now names betokening accidents unabstracted, do betoken not only those accidents but also together with them, the subjects whereunto they cleave. As when we name a *Schoolmaster* and a *Physician*, these names do not only betoken two accidents, teaching and curing, but also some person or persons in whom these accidents are. For there is no impediment but both may be one man, as well as they are for the most part diverse. The *Commonwealth* and the *Church* therefore being such names, they do not only betoken those accidents of civil government and Christian religion which we have mentioned, but also together with them such multitudes as are the subjects of those accidents. Again, their nature being such, that they may well enough dwell together in one subject, it followeth that their names though always implying that difference of accidents which hath been set down, yet do not always imply different subjects also. When we oppose the *Church* therefore and the *Commonwealth* in a *Christian Society*, we mean by the *Commonwealth* that society with relation unto all the public affairs thereof, only the matter of true religion excepted. By the *Church*, the same society with only reference unto the matter of true religion without any other affairs besides. When that society which is both a *Church* and a *Commonwealth* doth flourish in those things which belong unto it as a *Commonwealth*, we then say the *Commonwealth* doth flourish; when in those things which concern it as a *Church*, the *Church* doth flourish; when in both, then the *Church* and *Commonwealth* flourish together.

The *Prophet Isaiah*, to note corruptions in the *Commonwealth* complaineth [k]*that where judgement and justice had lodged now were murderers. Princes were become companions of thieves, everyone loved gifts and rewards, but the fatherless was not judged, neither did the widow's cause come before them.* To show abuses in the *Church*, *Malachi* doth make

[k] Isa. 1:21.

his complaint, *¹Ye offer unclean bread upon mine altar; if ye offer the blind for Sacrifice it is not evil as you think; if the lame and the sick, nothing is amiss.* The treasures which *ᵐDavid* did bestow upon the *Temple* do argue the *Love* which he bore to the *Church*. The pains that *ⁿNehemiah* took for building the walls of the *City* are tokens of his care for the *Commonwealth*. Causes of the *Commonwealth* or Province are such as *Gallio* was content to be judge of. *ᵒIf it were a matter of wrong or an evil deed, O ye Jews, I would according to reason maintain you.* Causes of the *Church*, are such as *Gallio* there rejecteth; *If it be a question of your law look you unto it: I will be no judge of those things.* In respect of these differences therefore the *Church* and the *Commonwealth* may in speech be compared or opposed aptly enough the one to the other, yet this is no argument that they are two independent societies.

Proofs of perpetual separation and independency between the Commonwealth and the Church taken from the effects of punishments inflicted and released by the one or the other.

[1.6] Some other reasons there are, which seem a little more nearly to make for the purpose, as long as they are but heard and not sifted. *ᵖ*For what though a man being severed by excommunication from the *Church*, be not thereby deprived of freedom in the *City*, nor being there discommoned is thereby forthwith excommunicated and excluded from the *Church*? What though the *Church* be bound to receive them upon repentance, whom the *Commonwealth* may refuse again to admit, if it chance the same men to be shut out of both? That division of the *Church* and *Commonwealth* which they contend for will very hardly hereupon follow. For we must note that members of a *Christian Commonwealth* have a triple state, a *natural* a *civil* and a *spiritual*. No man's *natural* estate is cut off otherwise than by that capital execution, after which he that is gone from the body of the *Commonwealth* doth not I think remain still in the body of the visible *Church*. And concerning man's *civil* state, the same is subject partly to inferior abatements of liberty and partly unto diminution in the very highest degree, such as banishment is; which since it casteth out quite and clean from the body of the common-

---

ˡ Mal. 1:7.   *ᵐ* 1 Chron. 29:3.   *ⁿ* Neh. 2:17.
ᵒ Acts 18:14.   *ᵖ* T.C., Bk 3, p. 152.

wealth must needs also consequently cast the banished party even out of the very *Church* he was of before, because that *Church* and the *Commonwealth* he was of were both one and the same society, so that whatsoever doth separate utterly a man's person from the one it separateth also from the other.

As for such abatements of *Civil* state as take away only some privilege dignity or other benefit which a man enjoyeth in the *Commonwealth*, they reach only unto our dealing with public affairs from which what should let, but that men may be excluded and thereunto restored again without diminishing or augmenting the number of persons in whom either *Church* or *Commonwealth* consisteth. He that by way of punishment loseth his voice in a public election of Magistrates ceaseth not thereby to be a *Citizen*. A man disfranchized, may notwithstanding enjoy as a *Subject* the *Common* benefit of protection under Laws and Magistrates, so that these inferior diminutions which touch men civilly, but neither do clean extinguish their estate as they belong to the *Commonwealth* nor impair a whit their condition as they are of the *Church* of *God*, these I say clearly do prove a difference of the affairs of the one from the other but such a difference as maketh nothing for their surmise of distracted societies.

And concerning *Excommunication* it cutteth off indeed from the *Church*, and yet not from the *Commonwealth*: Howbeit so that the party excommunicate is not thereby severed from one body which subsisteth in itself and retained of another in like sort subsisting. But he that before had fellowship with that society, whereof he was a member as well touching things spiritual as Civil, is now by force of excommunication although not severed from the same body in Civil affairs nevertheless for the time cut off from it as touching *Communion* in those things, which belong to the said body as it is the *Church*.

A man which having been both excommunicated by the *Church* and deprived of civil dignity in the Commonwealth is upon his repentance necessarily readunited into the one but not of necessity into the other. What then? That which he is adunited unto is a *Communion* in things divine, whereof *Saints* are partakers, that from which he is withheld is the benefit of some human privilege or right which other *Citizens* happily enjoy. But are not those *Saints* and *Citizens* one and the same people? Are they not one and the same society? Doth it hereby appear that the *Church* which receiveth an Excommunicate man, can have no dependency of any person which is of chief authority and power, in those things of the *Common-* [1.7] *wealth* whereunto the same party is not admitted? Wherefore to end this point I conclude first that under dominions of *Infidels* the *Church* of *Christ* and their Commonwealth were two societies independent. Secondly, that in those *Commonwealths* where the *Bishop* of *Rome* beareth sway one society is both the *Church* and the *Commonwealth.* But the *Bishop* of *Rome* doth divide the body into two diverse bodies and doth not suffer the *Church* to depend upon the power of any *Civil Prince* or *Potentate.* Thirdly, that within this *Realm* of *England* the case is neither as in the one nor as in the other of the former two. But from the state of Pagans we differ in that with us one society is both the *Church* and *Commonwealth* which with them it was not, as also from the state of those nations which subject themselves to the *Bishop* of *Rome* in that our church hath dependency upon the chief in our Commonwealth which it hath not under him. In a word our estate is according to the pattern of God's own ancient elect people, which people was not part of them the *Commonwealth* and part of them the *Church* of *God*, but the selfsame people whole and entire, were both under one chief Governor, on whose supreme authority they did depend.

[1.8; K2.1]   Now the drift of all that hath been alleged to prove perpetual separation and independency between the *Church* and the *Common-wealth* is that this being held necessary it might consequently be thought, that in a *Christian Kingdom* he whose power is greatest over the *Commonwealth* may not lawfully have supremacy of power also over the *Church* as it is a *Church*, that is to say so far as to order and dispose of spiritual affairs, as the highest uncommanded Commander in them. Whereupon it is grown a question, whether power Ecclesiastical over the *Church*, power of dominion in such degree as the laws of this land do grant unto the sovereign Governor thereof, may by the said supreme head and Governor lawfully be enjoyed and held. For resolution wherein, we are first to define what the power of dominion is, then to show by what right, after what sort, in what measure, with what conveniency, according unto whose example *Christian Kings* may have it. And when these generalities are opened, to examine afterwards how lawful that is which we in regard of dominion do attribute unto our own, namely the title of *Headship* over the *Church* so far as the bounds of this Kingdom do reach; Secondly, the prerogative of calling and dissolving greater assemblies about spiritual affairs public; Thirdly, the right of assenting unto all those orders, concerning religion, which must after be in force as laws; Fourthly, the advancement of Principal *Church-Governors* to their rooms of prelacy; Fifthly, judicial authority higher than others are capable of; and Sixthly, exemption from being punishable with* such kind of censures as the platform of reformation doth teach that they ought to be subject unto.

What their power of Dominion is.

2. Without order there is no living in public society, because the [2.1; K2.2] want thereof is the mother of confusion, whereupon division of necessity followeth, *q*and out of division inevitable destruction. *'*The *Apostle* therefore giving instruction to public societies requireth that all things be orderly done. Order can have no place in things unless it be settled amongst the persons that shall by office be conversant about them. And if things or persons be ordered, this doth imply that they are distinguished by degrees. For order is a gradual disposition. The whole world consisting of parts so many so different is by this only thing upheld, he which framed them hath set them in order. Yea the very deity itself both keepeth and requireth forever this to be kept as a law, that wheresoever there is a coagmentation of many, the lowest be knit to the highest by that which being interjacent may cause each to cleave unto other and so all to continue one. This order of things and persons in public societies is the work of polity and the proper instrument thereof in every degree is *power*, power being that ability which we have of ourselves or receive from others for performance of any action. If the action which we are to perform be conversant about matter of mere religion, the power of performing it is then spiritual. And if that power be such as hath not any other to overrule it, we term it dominion or power supreme, so far as the bounds thereof do extend. When there- [K2.3] fore Christian Kings are said to have spiritual dominion or supreme power in Ecclesiastical affairs and causes, the meaning is, that within

q Luke 11.   *'* 1 Cor. 14:40.

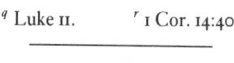

* *F:* which

their own precincts and territories they have authority and power to command even in matters of *Christian Religion,* and that there is no higher, nor greater, that can in those causes over-command them, where they are placed to reign as *Kings.* But withal we must likewise note, that their power is termed *supremacy* as being the highest not simply without exception of anything. For what man is there so brainsick as not to except in such speeches *God* himself, the king of all the kings of the earth? Besides, where the law doth give *Dominion,* who doubteth but that the king who receiveth it must hold it of and under the law according to that old Axiom *Attribuat Rex Legi quod Lex attribuit ei potestatem et Dominium.* And again *Rex non debet esse sub homine, sed sub Deo et Lege.* Thirdly whereas it is not altogether without reason that kings are judged to have by virtue of their dominion although greater power than any, yet not than all the states of those societies conjoined, wherein such sovereign rule is given them, there is not hereunto anything contrary by us affirmed, no not when we grant supreme authority unto *Kings,* because *supremacy* is no otherwise intended or meant, than to exclude partly foreign powers, and partly the power, which belongeth in several unto others contained as parts, within that politic body over which those *Kings* have supremacy. Where the *King* hath power of Dominion or supreme power, there no foreign state or *Potentate,* no state or *potentate* Domestical whether it consist of one or of many can possibly have in the same affairs and causes authority higher than the *King.* Power of spiritual dominion therefore is in causes Ecclesiastical that ruling authority, which neither any foreign state nor yet any part of that politic body at home wherein the same is established, can lawfully overrule.

By what ¹right, after what ²sort, in what ³measure, with what ⁴conveniency, and according to what ⁵example Christian Kings may have it. In a word, their manner of holding Dominion.

¹*By what right namely such as though men do give God doth ratify.*

[3.1; K2.4] 3. Unto which supreme power in Kings two kinds of adversaries there are that have opposed themselves: One sort defending that supreme power in causes *Ecclesiastical* throughout the world appertaineth of divine right to the *Bishop* of *Rome*, another sort that the said power belongeth in every *national Church* unto the Clergy thereof assembled. We which defend as well against the one as the other, that *Kings* within their own precincts may have it, must show by what right it may come unto them.

First unto me it seemeth almost out of doubt and controversy [K2.5] that every independent multitude before any certain form of regiment established hath under *God's* supreme authority full dominion over itself, even as a man not tied with the bond of subjection as yet unto any other hath over himself the like power. God creating mankind did endow it naturally with full power to guide itself in what kinds of societies soever it should choose to live. A man which is born *Lord* of himself may be made another's servant, and that power which naturally whole societies have may be derived into many few or one under whom the rest shall then live in subjection. Some multitudes are brought in subjection by force, as they who being subdued are fain to submit their necks, unto what yoke it pleaseth their Conquerors to lay upon them, which *Conquerors* by just and lawful wars do hold their power over such multitudes as a thing descending unto them, divine providence itself so disposing. For it is God, who giveth victory in the day of war and unto whom *Dominion* in this sort is derived, the same they enjoy according unto that law of nations, which law authorizeth Conquerors to reign as absolute *Lords* over them whom they vanquish. Sometimes it pleaseth God himself by special appointment to choose out and nominate such as to whom *Dominion* shall be given, which thing he did often in the *Commonwealth* of *Israel*: They who in this sort receive power have it immediately from God by mere divine right, they by human on whom the same is bestowed according unto men's discretion when they are left free by God to make choice of their own governor. By which of these means soever it happen, that *Kings* or governors be advanced unto their seats, ⁵we must acknowledge both their lawful choice to be approved of God, and themselves for *God's Lieutenants* and confess their power his.

As for supreme power in Ecclesiastical affairs, the word of God doth nowhere appoint, that all kings should have it, neither that any should not have it. For which cause it seemeth to stand altogether

⁵ *The crown is a power delegated by God.* Dan. 2:21, Dan. 4. Isa. 45. Rom. 13.

by human right 'that unto *Christian Kings* there is such dominion
[K2.6] given. Again on whom the same is bestowed, even at men's discretion, they likewise do hold it by divine right, if God in his own
revealed word have appointed such power to be, although himself
extraordinarily bestow it not but leave the appointment of the persons
unto men. Yea albeit God do neither appoint the thing, nor assign
the person, nevertheless when men have established both, who doth
doubt but that sundry duties and offices depending thereupon are
prescribed in the *Word* of *God*, and consequently by that very right,
to be exacted?

For example's sake, the power which the *Roman Emperors* had
over foreign Provinces was not a thing which the law of God did
ever institute, neither was *Tiberius Cæsar* by special commission from
heaven therewith invested. And yet the payment of tribute unto *Cæsar*
being made *Emperor* is the plain law of *Jesus Christ.* Unto *Kings*
by human right honour by very divine right is due. Man's ordinances
are many times presupposed as grounds in the statutes of God.
And therefore of what kind soever the means be, whereby Governors
are lawfully advanced unto their seats as we by the law of God
stand bound meekly to acknowledge them for *God's Lieutenants* and
to confess their power his, so they by the same law are both authorized
and required to use that power as far as it may be in any sort available
to his honour. The law appointeth no man to be an husband, but
if a man have betaken himself into that condition, it giveth him
then authority over his own wife. That the *Christian* world should
be ordered by kingly regiment the law of *God* doth not anywhere
command. And yet the law of God doth give them right which
once are exalted to that estate, to exact at the hands of their Subjects
general obedience in whatsoever affairs their power may serve to
command. So God doth ratify the works of that Sovereign authority
which *Kings* have received by men.

²*After what sort.*

[3.2; K2.7] This is therefore the right whereby *Kings* do hold their power. But
yet in what sort the same doth rest and abide in them, it somewhat

---

¹ *A King* (says Sthenidas of Locrus in *On Kingship*) *in regard of the tabernacle of his
body is like to other men; as made of the same matter, but fashioned by the best workman,
who artificially framed him, using himself for the pattern* [ed. 1822, pp. 28–29; ed. 1958, 2:272].

further behoveth to search. Wherein that we be not enforced to make overlarge discourses about the different conditions of sovereign or supreme power, that which we speak of Kings shall be with respect to the state and according to the nature of this Kingdom, where the people are in no subjection but such as willingly themselves have condescended unto for their own most behoof and security. In Kingdoms therefore of this quality the highest Governor hath indeed universal dominion, but with dependence upon that whole entire body over the several parts whereof he hath dominion so that it standeth for an axiom in this case, *The King is major singulis universis minor.* The *King's* dependency we do not construe as some [K2.8] have done, who are of opinion that no man's birth can make him a king, but every particular person advanced unto such authority hath at his entrance into his reign, the same bestowed upon him as an estate in condition by the voluntary deed of the people, in whom it doth lie to put by anyone and to prefer some other before him better liked of or judged fitter for the place, and that the party so rejected hath herein no injury, no not although this be done in a place where the crown doth go κατὰ γένος by succession and to a person, which being capable hath apparently if blood be respected the nearest right. They plainly affirm "that in all well appointed *Kingdoms* the custom evermore hath been and is, that children succeed not their deceased parents, till the people after a sort have created them anew, neither that they grow to their Fathers as natural and proper heirs but are then to be reckoned for *Kings*, when at the hands of such as represent the people's *Majesty* they have by a scepter and diadem received as it were the investiture of *Kingly* power. Their very words are ᵛthat where such power is settled into a family or kindred, the stock itself is thereby chosen, but not the twig that springeth of it. The next of the stock unto him which reigneth are not through nearness of blood made *Kings* but rather set forth to stand for the *Kingdom*. ᵂWhere regal dominion is hereditary, it is notwithstanding (if ye look to the persons themselves which have it) altogether elective. To this purpose are ˣalleged heaps of scriptures concerning the solemn coronation or inauguration of *Saul*, of *David*, of *Solomon*, of others by the *Nobles Ancients* and *People* of the Commonwealth of *Israel* as if these solemnities

---

ᵘ *A Defence Against Tyrants*, p. 83.   ᵛ*A Defence*, p. 85.   ᵂ p. 81.   ˣ p. 78.

were a kind of deed, whereby the right of dominion is given. Which strange untrue and unnatural conceits set abroad by seedsmen of rebellion, only to animate unquiet spirits, and to feed them with a possibility of aspiring unto thrones and scepters if they can win the hearts of the people, what hereditary title soever any other before them may have, I say, these unjust and insolent positions I would not mention were it not thereby to make the countenance of truth more orient. For unless we will openly proclaim defiance unto all law, equity and reason, we must (there is no remedy) acknowledge that in *Kingdoms* hereditary birth giveth right unto sovereign dominion and the death of the predecessor putteth the successor by blood in seisin*; those public solemnities before mentioned do but either serve for an open testification of the inheritor's right or belong to the form of inducting him into possession of that thing he hath right unto. And therefore in case it doth happen that without right of blood a man in such wise be possessed, all those new elections, and investings are utterly void; they make him no indefeasible estate, the inheritor by blood may dispossess him as an usurper.

[K2.9]   The case thus standing albeit we judge it a thing most true, that *Kings* even Inheritors do hold their right to the power of dominion with dependency upon the whole entire body politic over which they rule as *Kings* yet so it may not be understood as if such dependency did grow, for that every supreme governor doth personally take from thence his power by way of gift bestowed of their own free accord upon him at the time of his entrance into the said place of sovereign government; but the cause of dependency is in that first original conveyance, when power was derived by the whole unto one to pass from him into them, whom out of him nature by lawful birth should produce and no natural or legal inability make incapable. ʸNeither can any man with reason think but that the first institution of *Kings* is a sufficient consideration, wherefore their power should always depend on that from which it did then flow. Original influence of power from the body into the *King* is [K2.10] cause of the *King's* dependency in power upon the body. By dependency we mean subordination and subjection. A manifest token of which dependency may be this. As there is no more certain argument

---

ʸ See Cicero, *On Duties* [ch. 12; *L*, pp. 208–211].

F: scism

that *Lands* are held under any as *Lord*, than if we see that such Lands in defect of heirs do fall by escheat unto him: in like manner it doth rightly follow that seeing dominion, when there is none to inherit, it returneth unto the body, therefore they which before were inheritors thereof did hold it with dependency upon the body; so that by comparing the body with the head as touching power, it seemeth always to reside in both, fundamentally or radically in the one, in the other derivatively, in the one the habit, in the other the act of power.

May then a body politic at all times withdraw in whole or in part that influence of dominion which passeth from it, if inconvenience doth grow thereby? It must be presumed that supreme governors will not in such case oppose themselves and be stiff in detaining that, the use whereof is with public detriment. But surely without their consent I see not how the body should be able by any just means to help itself, saving when *Dominion* doth escheat. Such things therefore must be thought upon beforehand, that power may be limited ere it be granted, which is the next thing we are to consider.

[3]*In what measure.*

In power of dominion all kings have not an equal latitude. *Kings* [3.3; K2.*11*] by conquest make their own charter, so that how large their power either civil or spiritual is, we cannot with any certainty define further, than only to set them in general the law of God and nature for bounds. *Kings* by God's own special appointment have also that largeness of power, which he doth assign or permit with approbation. Touching *Kings* which were first instituted by agreement and composition made with them over whom they reign how far their power may lawfully extend, the articles of compact between them must show, not the articles only of compact at the first beginning which for the most part are either clean worn out of knowledge, or else known unto very few, but whatsoever hath been after in free and voluntary manner condescended unto whether by express consent, whereof positive laws are witnesses, or else by silent allowance famously notified through custom reaching beyond the memory of man. By which means of after agreement it cometh many times to pass in kingdoms, that they whose ancient predecessors were by violence and force made subject do grow even by little and little into that most sweet form of kingly government which *Philosophers* define to be ^zregency, willingly sustained and endowed with chiefty [K2.12] of power in the greatest things. Many of the ancient in their writings do speak ^aof kings, with such high and ample terms, as if universality of power even in regard of things and not of persons only did appertain to the very being of a *King*. The reason is because their speech concerning *Kings* they frame according to the state of those *Monarchs*, to whom unlimited authority was given. Which some not observing, imagine that all *Kings* even in that they are *Kings*, ought to have whatsoever power they find any Sovereign ruler lawfully to have enjoyed. But that most judicious *Philosopher*, whose eye scarce any thing did scape which was to be found in the bosom of nature, he considering how far the power of one Sovereign ruler may be different from another's regal authority, noteth in *Spartan Kings* ^bthat of all others lawfully reigning, they had the most restrained power. A king which hath not supreme power in the greatest things is rather entitled a *King* than invested with real sovereignty. We can not properly term him a king, of whom it may not be said at the leastwise as touching certain the very chiefest affairs of state ^cαὐτῷ μὲν ἄρχειν ἄρχεσθαι δὲ ὑπ' οὐδενός, his right in them is to have rule, not subject to any other predominant.

I am not of opinion, that simply always in *Kings* the most, but the best limited power is best, both for them and for the people; the most limited is that which may deal in fewest things, the best that which in dealing is tied unto the soundest perfectest and most indifferent rule; which rule is the law. I mean not only the law of nature and of *God* but very national or municipal law consonant thereunto. Happier that people, whose law is their *King* in the greatest things than that whose *King* is himself their law. Where the *King* doth guide the state and the law the *King*, that commonwealth is like an harp or melodious instrument, the strings whereof are tuned and handled all by one hand, following as laws the rules and canons

---

^z Aristotle, *Politics*, Bk 3 [1284b–1285b].

^a Ecphantus, *On Kingship* [ed. 1822, p. 32; ed. 1958, 2:276]. *He that ruleth according to virtue is called a king, and hath such friendship and community toward those that be under him, as God hath toward the world and those things that be in it.*

^b Aristotle, *Politics*, Bk 3, ch. 14 [1284b–1285b].

^c Pythagoras in Ecphantus, *On Kingship* [ed. 1822, pp. 36–37; ed. 1958, 2:279].

of Musical science. Most divinely therefore *Archytas* maketh unto public felicity these four steps, every later whereof doth spring from the former as from a mother cause, ^dὉ μὲν Βασιλεὺς νόμιμος, ὁ δὲ ἄρχων ἀκόλουθος, ὁ δὲ ἀρχόμενος ἐλεύθερος, ἁ δ' ὅλα κοινωνία εὐδαίμων, adding on the contrary side, that where this order is not it cometh by transgression thereof to pass that the *King* grows a *Tyrant*, he that ruleth under him abhorreth to be guided and commanded by him, the people subject unto both have freedom under neither and the whole community is wretched. In which [K2.13] respect I cannot choose but commend highly their wisdom by whom the foundations of this Commonwealth have been laid, wherein though no manner person or cause be unsubject to the *King's* power, yet so is the power of the *King* over all and in all limited that unto all his proceedings the law itself is a rule. The axioms of our regal government are these, *Lex facit Regem.* The *King's* grant of any favour made contrary to law is void. *Rex nihil potest, nisi quod jure potest.* Our *Kings* therefore when they take possession of the room they are called into, have it pointed out before their eyes, even by the very solemnities and rites of their inauguration to what affairs by the said law their supreme authority and power reacheth. Crowned we see they are, and inthronized and annointed. The *Crown* a sign of military, the *Throne* of sedentary or judicial, the *Oil* of religious or sacred power. It is not on any side denied that *Kings* may have [K2.14] such authority in secular affairs. The question then is what power they lawfully may have and exercise in causes of *God.* ^eA Prince, a Magistrate or Community (saith *Dr. Stapleton*) may have power to lay corporal punishments on them which are teachers of perverse things, power to make laws for the peace of the *Church*, power to proclaim, to defend, and even by revenge to preserve from violation dogmata, very articles of religion themselves. Others in affection no less devoted unto the *Papacy* do likewise yield ^fthat the *Civil Magistrate* may by his edicts and laws keep all Ecclesiastical persons within the bounds of their duties and constrain them to observe the *Canons* of the *Church* to follow the rules of ancient discipline,

---

^d *The king ruling by Law, the magistrate following, the subject free and the whole society happy* [ed. 1958, 2:82].
^e Stapleton, *A Demonstration of the Doctrinal Principles of the Faith*, Bk 5, ch. 17.
^f Choppin, *On Sacred Public Polity*, Preface.

^gthat if *Joash* were commended for his care and provision concerning so small a part of religion as the *Church* treasury it must needs be both unto *Christian Kings* themselves greater honour and to *Christianity* a larger benefit, when the custody of religion whole and of the worship of God in general is their charge.

If therefore all these things mentioned be most properly the affairs of God, and *Ecclesiastical* causes, if the actions specified be works of power and if that power be such as *Kings* may use of themselves, without the leave of any other power superior in the same things, it followeth necessarily that *Kings* may have supreme power not only in civil but also in *Ecclesiastical* affairs and consequently that they may withstand what *Bishop* or *Pope* soever shall under the pretended claim of higher spiritual authority oppose himself against their proceedings. But they which have made us the former grant will hereunto never condescend. What they yield that *Princes* may do it is with secret exception always understood, if the *Bishop* of *Rome* give leave, if he interpose no prohibition. Wherefore somewhat it is in show, in truth nothing which they grant. Our own reformers do the very like. When they make their discourses in general concerning the authority which *Magistrates* may have a man would think them far from withdrawing any jot of that which with reason may be thought due. ^h*The Prince and Civil Magistrate* (saith one of them) *hath to see that the Laws of God touching his worship and touching all matters and orders of the Church be executed and duly observed and to see that every Ecclesiastical person do that office whereunto he is appointed and to punish those which fail in their office accordingly.* Another acknowledgeth ⁱthat the Magistrate may lawfully uphold all truth by his sword, punish all persons, enforce all to do their duties unto *God* and men, maintain by his laws every point of *God's* word, punish all vice in all men, see into all causes, visit the *Ecclesiastical* state and correct the abuses thereof, finally so look to his subjects that under him they may lead their lives in all godliness and honesty. A third more frankly professeth ^jthat in case their *Church* discipline were established, so little it shorteneth the arms of sovereign dominion in causes *Ecclesiastical* that her *Gracious Majesty* for anything which they teach or hold to the contrary may no less than now

^g 2 Kings 12:4. 2 Chron. 24:8.   ^h T.C., Bk 1, p. 192 [*W*, 3:295–301].
ⁱ Fenner's *defence of the godly Ministers* [*STC* 10771, sigs. D2^r–D3^r].
^j *Humble motion* [*STC* 7754], p. 63.

remain still over all persons in all things supreme governess, even with that full and royal authority, superiority, preeminence, supremacy and prerogative which the laws already established do give her and her *Majesty's Injunctions* and the *Articles* of the *Convocation* house and other writings *Apologetical* of her royal authority and supreme dignity do declare and explain. *Posidonius* was wont to say [K2.15] of the *Epicure* ᵏthat he thought there were no Gods, but that those things which he spake concerning the Gods were only given out for fear of growing odious amongst men, and therefore that in words he left Gods remaining, but in very deed overthrew them, inasmuch as he gave them no kind of motion, no kind of action. After the very selfsame manner when we come unto those particular effects and prerogatives of dominion, which the laws of this land do grant to the *Kings* thereof, it will appear how those men notwithstanding their large and liberal speeches abate such parcels out of the fore-alleged grand and flourishing sum that a man comparing the one with the other may half stand in doubt lest their opinions in very truth be against that authority which by their speeches they seem mightily to uphold, partly for the avoiding of public obloquy envy and hatred, partly to the intent they may both in the end by establishment of their discipline extinguish the force of supreme power which *Princes* have and yet in the meanwhile by giving forth these smooth discourses, obtain that their favourers may have somewhat to allege for them by way of *Apology*, and that in such words as sound towards all kind of fulness in power. But for myself I had rather construe such their contradictions in the better part, and impute their general acknowledgment of the lawfulness of *Kingly power* unto the force of truth presenting itself before them sometimes alone, their particular contrarieties oppositions denials unto that error, which having so fully possessed their minds casteth things inconvenient upon them. Of which things in their due place.

Touching that which is now in hand we are on all sides fully [K2.16] agreed (1) first that there is not any restraint or limitation of matter for regal authority and power to be conversant in, but of religion whole, and of whatsoever cause thereto appertaineth *Kings* may lawfully have charge, they lawfully may therein exercise dominion and use the temporal sword. (2) Secondly that some kinds of actions

ᵏ Cicero, Bk I, *On the Nature of the Gods* [*L*, pp. 118–120].

conversant about such affairs are denied unto *Kings*, as namely actions of the power of order and of that power of jurisdiction which is with it inseparably joined, power to administer the word and Sacraments, power to ordain, to judge as an Ordinary, to bind and loose, to excommunicate and such like. (3) Thirdly that even in these very actions which are proper unto *Dominion* there must be some certain rule whereunto *Kings* in all their proceedings ought to be strictly tied, which rule for proceedings in *Ecclesiastical* affairs and causes by regal power hath not hitherto been agreed upon with so uniform consent and certainty as might be wished. The different sentences of men herein I will not now go about to examine but it shall be enough to propose what rule doth seem in this case most reasonable.

[K2.17]   It hath been declared already in general how the best established dominion is, where the law doth most rule the *King*, the true effect whereof particularly is found as well in *Ecclesiastical* as in *Civil* affairs. In these the *King* through his supreme power may do sundry great things himself, both appertaining unto peace and war both at home by commandment, and by commerce with states abroad because so much the law doth permit. Some things on the other side the *King* alone hath no power to do without consent of the *Lords* and *Commons* assembled in *Parliament*. The *King* of himself cannot change the nature of pleas nor courts, no not so much as restore blood, because the law is a bar unto him, not any law divine or natural, for against neither it were though *Kings* of themselves might do both, but the positive laws of the realm have abridged therein and restrained the *King's* power. Which positive laws whether by custom or otherwise established, without repugnance unto the law of God and nature ought no less to be of force even in the spiritual affairs of the *Church*. Wherefore in regard of *Ecclesiastical* laws we willingly embrace that of *Ambrose* [1]*Imperator bonus intra Ecclesiam, non supra Ecclesiam est. Kings* have dominion to exercise in *Ecclesiastical* causes but according to the laws of the *Church*. Whether it be therefore the nature of *Courts* or the form of pleas, or the kind of governors or the order of proceedings in whatsoever spiritual businesses for the received laws and liberties of the *Church*, the *King* hath supreme authority and power but against them none.

---

[1] [*A good emperor is within the church, not over the church.*] Ambrose, Epist. 32, fol. 160 [*PL*, 16:1018].

What such positive laws have appointed to be done by others than the *King* or by others with the *King* and in what form they have appointed the doing of it, the same of necessity must be kept, neither is the *King's* sole authority to alter it. Yea even as it were a thing unreasonable, if in civil affairs the *King* (albeit the whole universal body did join with him) should do anything by their absolute supreme power for the ordering of their state at home in prejudice of any of those ancient laws of nations which are of force throughout the world because the necessary commerce of *Kingdoms* dependeth on them, so in principal matters belonging to *Christian* religion, a thing very scandalous and offensive it must needs be thought, if either *Kings* or laws should dispose of the affairs of God, without any respect had to that which of old hath been reverently thought of throughout the world, and wherein there is no law of God which forceth us to swerve from the way wherein so many and so holy ages have gone. Wherefore not without good consideration the very law itself hath provided that Judges Ecclesiastical appointed under the *King's* commission shall not adjudge for heresy anything but that which heretofore hath been so adjudged by the authority of the *Canonical* scriptures, or by the first four general Councils or by some other general Council wherein the same hath been declared heresy by the express words of the said *Canonical Scriptures* or *m*such as hereafter shall be termed heresy by the high Court of *Parliament* of this Realm with the assent of the *Clergy* in the *Convocation*. By which words of the law who doth not plainly see how in that one branch of proceeding by virtue of the *King's* supreme authority the credit which those four general Councils hath throughout all Churches evermore had was judged by the makers of the aforesaid Act a just cause wherefore they should be mentioned in that case as a requisite part of the rule wherewith dominion was to be limited. But of this we shall further consider when we come unto that which sovereign power may do in making *Ecclesiastical* laws.

4*With what conveniency.*

The cause of deriving supreme power from an whole entire multi- [3.4; K3.*18*]
tude unto some special part thereof is partly the necessity of
expedition in public affairs, partly the inconveniency of confusion

m Year I of Queen Elizabeth [*SR*, 4.1:354].

and trouble where a multitude of equals dealeth, and partly the dissipation which must needs ensue in companies, where every man wholly seeketh his own particular, as we all would do even with other men's hurt, and happily the very overthrow of ourselves in the end also, if for procurement of the common good of all men, by keeping every several man in order, some were not armed with authority over all and encouraged with prerogatives of honour to sustain the weighty burden of that charge. The good which is proper unto each man belongeth to the common good of all as a part of the whole's perfection. But yet these two are things different; for men by that which is proper are severed, united they are by that which is common. Wherefore besides that which moveth each man in particular to seek his private, there must of necessity in all public societies be also a general mover, directing unto the common good and framing every man's particular to it. The end whereunto all government was instituted was *bonum publicum*, the universal or common good. Our question is of dominion for that end and purpose derived into one. "Such as in one public state have agreed that the supreme charge of all things should be committed unto one, they I say considering what inconveniences may grow where states are subject unto sundry supreme authorities were for fear of those inconveniences withdrawn from liking to establish many οὐκ ἀγαθὸν πολυκοιρανίη: The multitude of supreme commanders is troublesome. *No man* (saith our *Saviour*) *can serve two Masters.* Surely two supreme Masters would make any one man's service somewhat uneasy in such cases as might fall out. Suppose that tomorrow the power which hath dominion in justice require thee at the *Court*, that which in war at the field, that which in religion at the *Temple*. All have equal authority over thee and impossible it is that thou shouldst be in such case obedient to all. By choosing any one whom thou wilt obey, certain thou art for thy disobedience to incur the displeasure of the other two.

[5]*According unto what example or pattern.*

[3.5; K3.1] But there is nothing for which some colourable reason or other may not be found. Are we able to show any commendable state of

---

" *The most prudent jurists have taught it to be necessary for the public welfare to be attended to by one person.* Justinian, *Digest*, 1.2.11.

government which by experience and practice hath felt the benefit of being in all causes subject unto the supreme authority of one? Against the polity of *Israel* I hope there will no man except, where *Moses* deriving so great a part of his burden in government unto others did notwithstanding retain to himself universal supremacy. *Jehosaphat* appointing one to be chief in the affairs of *God* and another in the *King's* affairs did this as having himself dominion over them in both. If therefore with approbation from heaven the *Kings* of God's own chosen people had in the affairs of *Jewish* religion supreme power, why not *Christian Kings* the like power also in *Christian* religion? Unless men will answer as some have done *"that touching the Jews first their religion was of far less perfection and dignity then ours is, ours being that truth whereof theirs was but a shadowish prefigurative resemblance. *"Secondly that all parts of their religion, their laws, their sacrifices, their rites and ceremonies being fully set down to their hands and needing no more but only to be put in execution, the *Kings* might well have highest authority to see that done, whereas with us there are a number of mysteries even in belief which were not so generally for them as for us necessary to be with sound express acknowledgement understood, a number of things belonging unto external regiment and our manner of serving God not set down by particular ordinances and delivered unto us in writing, for which cause the state of the *Church* doth now require that the spiritual authority of *Ecclesiastical* persons be large, absolute, and not subordinate to regal power. *"Thirdly, that whereas God armeth religion *Jewish* with temporal, *Christian* with a sword but of spiritual punishment, the one with power to imprison to scourge and to put to death, the other with bare authority to censure and excommunicate, there is no reason that the church which now hath no visible sword should in regiment be subject unto any other power than only unto theirs which have authority to bind and loose. *Fourthly that albeit while the Church was restrained unto one people it seemed not incommodious to grant their *Kings* the general chiefty of power. Yet now the Church having spread itself over

---

" The priesthood of the Jews was imperfect, because it only foreshadowed and prefigured a better one, and in its own time was to be changed for the better: so was the government of that priesthood imperfect, in that, namely, some part of it could also pertain, not inappropriately, to Kings. Stapleton, *A Demonstration of the Doctrinal Principles of the Faith*, Bk 5, ch. 22, p. 197.
*" Stapleton, *ibid.*   *" See Stapleton, *ibid.*   *" The same *ibid.*

all nations, great inconveniency might thereby grow if every *Christian King* in his several territory should have the like power. Of all these differences there is not one which doth prove it a thing repugnant unto the law either of God or nature that all supremacy of external power be in *Christian Kingdoms* granted unto the *Kings* thereof for preservation of quietness, unity, order and peace in such manner as hath been showed.

[K3.2]   The service which we do unto the true God who made heaven and earth is far different from that which Heathens have done unto their supposed Gods, though nothing else were respected but only the odds between their hope and ours. The offices of piety or true religion sincerely performed have the promises both of this life and of the life to come, the practices of superstition have neither. If notwithstanding the heathens reckoning upon no other reward for all which they did but only protection and favour in the temporal estate and condition of this present life, and perceiving how great good did hereby publicly grow as long as fear to displease (they knew not what) divine power was some kind of bridle unto them, did therefore provide that the highest degree of care for their religion should be the principal charge of such, as having otherwise also the greatest and chiefest power, were by so much the more fit to have custody thereof, shall* the like kind of provision be in us thought blameworthy?

A gross error it is to think that regal power ought to serve for the good of the body and not of the soul, for men's temporal peace and not their eternal safety; as if God had ordained *Kings* for no other end and purpose but only to fat up men like hogs and to see that they have their mash? Indeed to lead men unto salvation by the hand of secret, invisible and ghostly regiment or by the external administration of things belonging unto priestly order (such as the word and Sacraments are) this is denied unto *Christian Kings*, no cause in the world to think them uncapable of supreme authority in the outward government which disposeth the affairs of religion so far forth as the same are disposable by human authority and to think them uncapable thereof only for that, the said religion is everlastingly beneficial to them that faithfully continue in it. ⁵And

---

⁵ 2 Cor. 3:7–8.

---

* *F:* thereof. Shall

even as little cause there is, that being admitted thereunto amongst the *Jews*, they should amongst the *Christians* of necessity be delivered from ever exercising any such power for the dignity and perfection which is in our religion more than in theirs.

It may be a question, whether the affairs of *Christianity* require [K3.3] more wit, more study, more knowledge of divine things in him which shall order them, than the *Jewish* religion did. For although we deny not the form of external government together with all other rites and ceremonies to have been in more particular manner set down, yet withal it must be considered also that even this very thing did in some respects make the burden of their spiritual regiment the harder to be borne by reason of infinite doubts and difficulties which the very obscurity and darkness of their law did breed and which being not first decided the law could not possibly have due execution.

Besides inasmuch as their law did also dispose even of all kind of civil affairs, their Clergy being the Interpreters of the whole law sustained not only the same labour which *Divines* do amongst us, but even the burden of our Lawyers too. Nevertheless be it granted that more things do now require to be publicly deliberated and resolved upon with exacter judgement in matters divine than *Kings* for the most part have. Their personal inability to judge in such sort as Professors do, letteth not but that their *Regal* authority may have the selfsame degree or sway which the *Kings* of *Israel* had in the affairs of their religion to rule and command according to the manner of supreme governors.

As for the sword wherewith God armed his *Church* of old, if [K3.4] that were a reasonable cause why *Kings* might then have dominion, I see not but that it ministereth still as forcible an argument for the lawfulness and expediency of their continuance therein now. As we degrade and excommunicate, even so did the *Church* of the Jews both separate offenders from the *Temple* and depose the Clergy also from their rooms when cause required. The other sword of corporal punishment is not by *Christ's own appointment* in the hands of the *Church* of *Christ* as God did place it himself in the hands of the Jewish *Church*. For why? He knew that they whom he sent abroad to gather a people unto him only by persuasive means were to build up his *Church* even within the bosom of *Kingdoms*, the chiefest governors whereof would be open enemies unto it everywhere for the space of many years. Wherefore such commission for discipline he gave them as they might anywhere exercise in quiet and peaceable manner, the subjects of no Commonwealth being touched in goods or person by virtue of that spiritual regiment whereunto *Christian* religion embraced did make them subject.

Now when afterwards it came to pass that whole *Kingdoms* were made *Christian* I demand whether that authority which served before for the furtherance of religion, may not as effectually serve to the maintenance of *Christian* religion? *Christian* religion hath the sword of spiritual discipline. But doth that suffice? The Jewish which had it also did nevertheless stand in need to be aided with the power of the *Civil* sword. The help whereof, although when *Christian* religion cannot have it, must without it sustain itself as far as the other which it hath will serve, notwithstanding where both may be had, what forbiddeth the *Church* to enjoy the benefit of both? Will any man deny that the Church doth need the rod of corporal punishment to keep her children in obedience withal, such a law as *Macabeus* made amongst the *Scots*, that he which continued an excommunicate two years together and reconciled not himself to the *Church* should forfeit all his goods and possessions?

Again, the custom which many *Christian Churches* have to fly to the Civil Magistrate for coercion of those that will not otherwise be reformed, these things are proof sufficient that even in *Christian* religion the power wherewith *Ecclesiastical* persons were endowed at the first is unable to do of itself so much as when secular power doth strengthen it, and that not by way of ministry or service but of predominancy such as the *Kings* of *Israel* in their time exercised over the *Church* of God.

[K3.5]   Yea but the *Church* of God was then restrained more narrowly to one people and one *King*, which now being spread throughout all *Kingdoms*, it would be a cause of great dissimilitude in the exercise of *Christian* religion if every king should be over the affairs of the *Church* where he reigneth supreme ruler. Dissimilitude in great things is such a thing which draweth great inconvenience after it, a thing which *Christian* religion must always carefully prevent. And the way to prevent it is not as some do imagine the yielding up of supreme power over all *Churches* into one only Pastor's hands, but the framing of their government especially for matter of substance everywhere according to the rule of one only law to stand in no less force than the law of nations doth to be received in all kingdoms, all sovereign Rulers to be sworn no otherwise unto it than some are to maintain the liberties, laws, and received customs of the country where they reign. This shall cause uniformity even under several dominions without those woeful inconveniences where-unto the state of *Christendom* was subject heretofore through the tyranny and oppression of that one universal *Nimrod* who alone did all.

And till the *Christian* world be driven to enter into the peaceable and true consultation about some such kind of general law concerning those things of weight and moment wherein now we differ, if one Church hath not the same order which another hath, let every Church keep as near as may be the order it should have and commend the just defence thereof unto God, even as *Judah* did when it differed in the exercise of religion from that form which *Israel* followed.

Concerning therefore the matter whereof we have hitherto spoken, [K3.6] let it stand for our final conclusion that in a free *Christian* state or kingdom where one and the selfsame people are the *Church* and the *Commonwealth*, God through *Christ* directing that people, to see it for good and weighty considerations expedient that their Sovereign *Lord* and Governor in causes civil have also in *Ecclesiastical* affairs a supreme power, forasmuch as the light of reason doth lead them unto it, and against it, God's own revealed law hath nothing; surely they do not in submitting themselves thereunto any other than that which a wise and religious people ought to do. It was but a little overflowing of wit in *Thomas Aquinas* to so play upon the words of *'Moses* in the old, and of *"Peter* in the new *Testament* as though because the one did term the *Jews* a *priestly Kingdom*, the other as a *Kingly priesthood*, those two substantives *Kingdom* and *Priesthood* should import that *Judaism* did stand through the *King's* Superiority over *Priests, Christianity* through the *Priest's* supreme authority over *Kings*. Is it probable that *Moses* and *Peter* had herein so nice and curious conceipts? Or else more likely that both meant one and the same thing, namely that God doth glorify and sanctify his, even with full perfection in both, which thing *St. John* doth

---

' Exod. 19:6.   *"* 1 Pet. 2:9. Thomas on that place.

in plainer sort express saying that *Christ hath made us both Kings and Priests.*

Of their title of Headship which we give to the kings of England in relation unto the church.

[4.1] 4. These things being thus first considered, it will be the easier to judge concerning our own estate whether by force of *Ecclesiastical Dominion*, with us *Kings* have any other kind of prerogative, than they may lawfully hold and enjoy. It is as some do imagine too much that *Kings* of *England* should be termed Heads in relation to the *Church*. That which we understand by *Headship* is their only supreme power in *Ecclesiastical* affairs or causes. That which lawfully *Princes* are, what should make it unlawful for men by special styles or titles to signify? If the having of supreme power be allowed, why is the expressing thereof by the title of *Head* condemned? They seem in words, at the leastwise some of them, now at the length to acknowledge that *Kings* may have supreme government even over all both persons and causes. We in terming our Princes *Heads of the Church* do but testify that we acknowledge them such Governors.

[4.2] Against this peradventure it will be replied, *That howsoever we interpret ourselves it is not fit for a mortal man, and therefore not for a civil Magistrate to be entitled *Head of the Church*. Why so? First this title *Head of the Church* was given unto our Saviour *Christ* *to lift him above all powers rules and dominions, either in heaven or in earth. Where if this title belong also to the Civil Magistrate, then it is manifest that there is a power in earth whereunto our *Saviour Christ* is not in this point superior. Again if the Civil Magistrate may have this title, he may be also termed *the first begotten of all creatures, the first begotten of the dead, yea the Redeemer of his people.* For these are alike given him as dignities whereby he is lifted up above all creatures. Besides this the whole argument of the *Apostle* in both places doth lead to show that this title *Head of the Church* cannot be said of any creature. And further the very demonstrative *Article* amongst the *Hebrews* especially, whom *St. Paul* doth follow, serveth to tie that which is verified of one unto himself

---

v Rev. 1:6.   *w* T.C., Bk 2, p. 411.   *x* Ephes. 1:21. Col. 1:18.

alone. So that when the *Apostle* doth say that *Christ* is ἡ κεφαλὴ *The Head*, it is as much as if he should say *Christ* and no other is the head of the *Church*. Thus have we against the entitling of [4.3] the *Highest Magistrates, Head* with relation unto the *Church*, four several arguments gathered by strong surmise out of words marvelous unlikely to have been written for any such purpose as that whereunto they are now urged. To the *Ephesians* the *Apostle* writeth *ʸthat Christ, God hath seated on his own right hand in the heavenly places above all Regency and authority and power and Dominion and whatsoever name is named not in this world only but in that which shall be also. And hath under his feet set all things and hath given him Head above all things unto the Church, which is his body even the complement of him which accomplisheth all in all.* To the *Colossians* in like manner *ᶻthat He is the Head of the body of the Church, who is a first born Regency out of the dead to the end He might be made amongst them all such an one as hath the chiefty.* He meaneth amongst all them, whom before he mentioned, saying *In him all things that are were made, the things in the heavens and the things on the earth; the things that are visible and the things that are invisible, whether they be Thrones or Dominations or Regencies.*

Unto the forealleged arguments therefore we answer. First that it is not simply the *title* of *Head* which lifteth our *Saviour* above all powers, but the *title* of *Head* in such sort understood, as the *Apostle* himself meant it, so that the same being imparted in another sense unto others doth not any way make those others therein his equals inasmuch as diversity of things is usual to be understood, even when of words there is no diversity and it is only the adding of one and the selfsame thing unto diverse persons which doth argue equality in them. If I term *Christ* and *Cæsar Lords* yet this is no equalling of *Cæsar* with *Christ*, because it is not thereby intended. *ᵃTo term the Emperor Lord* (saith *Tertullian*) *I for mine own part will not refuse so that I be not required to term him Lord in the same sense that God is so termed.* Neither doth it follow which is objected in the second place that if the civil Magistrate may be entitled an *Head* he may be also as well termed, *The first begotten of all creatures, The first begotten of the dead* and *The Redeemer of his people.* For albeit the former dignity do lift him up no less than

---

ʸ Ephes. 1:20–23.   ᶻ Col. 1:18. Col. 1:16.   ᵃ *Apology* [ch. 35].

these, yet these terms are not applicable and apt to signify any other inferior dignity as the former term of *Head* was. The argument or matter which the *Apostle* followeth hath small evidence for proof that his meaning was to appropriate unto *Christ* the aforesaid title otherwise than only in such sense as doth make it being so understood too high to be given to any creature.

As for the force of the article whereby our *Lord* and *Saviour* is named *The Head* it serveth to tie that unto him by way of excellency which in a meaner degree is common to others; it doth not exclude any other utterly from being termed *Head*, but from being entitled as *Christ* is, *The Head* by way of the very highest degree of excellency. Not in the communication of names but in the confusion of things [4.4] is error. Howbeit if *Head* were a name which well could not be or never had been used to signify that which a Magistrate may be in relation unto some *Church*, but were by continual use of speech appropriated unto that only thing which it signifieth being applied unto *Jesus Christ*, then although we might carry in ourselves a right understanding yet ought we otherwise rather to speak unless we interpret our own meaning by some clause of plainer speech because we are else in manifest danger to be understood according to that construction and sense wherein such words are usually taken; but here the rarest construction and most removed from common sense is that which the word doth import being applied unto *Christ*. That which we signify by it in giving it unto the Magistrate is a great deal more familiar in the common conceipt of men. The word is so fit to signify [b]all kinds of superiority preeminence and chiefty, that no one thing is more ordinary than so to use it even in vulgar speech and in common understanding so to take it. If therefore a *Christian King* may have any preeminence or chiefty above all others in the *Church* (albeit it were less than *Theodore Beza* giveth who [c]placeth *Kings* amongst the principal members whereunto public function in the *Church* belongeth and denieth not but [d]that of them which have public function, the civil Magistrate's power hath all

---

[b] *Heads of poppies, chief men of the city.* Livy, *Roman Histories*, Bk 1 [*L*, 1:188]. *Rome the head of all Italy.* Dionysius of Halicarnassus, *Roman Antiquities*, Bk 2 [Bk 4, ch. 61; *L*, 2:463]. *Pekah* is termed the Head of *Samaria*, which was the state of his throne and kingdom. Isa. 7:9.

[c] *Confession*, ch. 5, art. 23 [*STC* 2007, pp. 181–182].

[d] *Confession*, ch. 5, art. 32 [*STC* 2007, pp. 199–200].

the rest at commandment in regard of that part of his office which is to procure, that peace and good order be especially kept in things concerning the first table), even hereupon to term him the *Head* of that *Church* which is his *Kingdom* should not seem so unfit a thing. Which title surely we would not communicate to any other, no not although it should at our hands be exacted with torments, but that our meaning herein is made known to the whole world, so that no man which will understand can easily be ignorant that we do not impart to *Kings* when we term them *Heads* the honour which properly is given to our *Lord* and *Saviour Christ*, when the blessed *Apostles* in *Scripture* do term him the *Head of the Church*.

Differences between Christ's Headship and that which we give to Kings.

The power which we signify by that name differeth in three things [4.5] plainly from that which *Christ* doth challenge. It differeth in order, measure and kind. In order, because God hath given him to his *Church* for the head ^{e}ὑπὲρ πάντα, above all ὑπεράνω πάσης τῆς ἀρχῆς, *Far above all principality and power and might and dominion and every name that is named not in this world only, but also in that which is to come*, whereas the power which others have is subordinated unto his.

Again as he differeth in order so in measure of power also, because God hath given unto him ^{f}*The ends of the earth for his possession, unto him Dominion from Sea to Sea, unto him all power in heaven and in earth*, unto him such sovereignty as doth not only reach over all places persons and things but doth rest in his one only person and is not by any succession continued; he reigneth as *Head* and *King* forever, nor is there any kind of law which tieth him but his own proper will and wisdom; his power is absolute, the same jointly over all which it is severally over each. Not so the power of any other *Headship*. How *Kings* are restrained and in what sort their authority is limited we have showed before, so that unto him is given by the title of *Headship* over the *Church* that largeness of power wherein neither man nor Angel can be matched or compared with him.

The last and the weightiest difference between him and them

^{e} Ephes. 1:21–22. ^{f} Ps. 2:8.

is in the very kind of their power. The *Head* being of all other parts of man's body *gthe most divine hath Dominion over all the rest.* It is the fountain of sense, of motion, the throne where the guide of the soul doth reign, the court from whence direction of all things human proceedeth. Why *Christ* is called *Head* of his *Church* these causes they themselves do yield. As the *Head* is the highest part of a man above which there is none, always joined with the body: So *Christ* is the highest in his *Church* inseparably knit with it. Again as the *Head* giveth sense and moving to all the body so he quickeneth and together with understanding of heavenly things giveth strength to walk therein. Seeing therefore that they cannot affirm *Christ* sensibly present, or always visibly joined unto his body the Church which is on earth, inasmuch as his corporal residence is in heaven: again seeing they do not affirm (it were intolerable if they should) that *Christ* doth personally administer the external regiment of outward actions in the *Church* but by the secret inward influence of his grace giveth spiritual life and the strength of ghostly motions thereunto, impossible it is that they should so close up their eyes as not to discern what odds there is between that kind of operation which we imply in the *Headship* of *Princes* and that which agreeth to our *Saviour's Dominion* over the *Church*. The *Headship* which we give unto *Kings* is altogether visibly exercised and ordereth only the external frame of the *Church's* affairs here amongst us, so that it plainly differeth from *Christ's* even in very nature and kind. To be in such sort united unto the *Church* as he is, to work as he worketh either on the whole *Church,* or on any particuler assembly or in any one man, doth neither agree nor hath possibility of agreeing unto any besides him.

Opposition against the first difference whereby Christ being Head simply Princes are said to be Heads under Christ.

[4.6] Against the first distinction or difference *h*it is objected that to entitle a magistrate *Head* of the *Church* although it be under *Christ* is most absurd. For *Christ* hath a two-fold superiority, a superiority over his *Church,* and a superiority over *Kingdoms.* *i*According to the one he hath a superior which is his Father, according to the other none

---

g Plato in *Timaeus* [44d].   *h* T.C., Bk 2, p. 411.   *i* T.C., Bk 2, p. 411.

but immediate authority with his Father. That is to say, Of the *Church* he is *Head* and governor only as the son of man, *Head* and governor over *Kingdoms* only as the son of God. In the *Church* as man he hath Officers under him, which Officers are *Ecclesiastical* persons. As for the Civil Magistrate his office belongeth unto *Kingdoms* and Commonwealths, neither is he therein an under or subordinate *Head* of *Christ* considering that his authority cometh from God simply and immediately even as our *Saviour Christ's* doth. Whereunto the sum of our answer is, First that as *Christ* being *Lord* or *Head* over all doth by virtue of that Sovereignty rule all, so he hath no more a superior in governing his *Church* than in exercising sovereign Dominion upon the rest of the world besides. Secondly, that all authority as well civil as Ecclesiastical is subordinate unto his: And thirdly that the *Civil Magistrate* being termed *Head* by reason of that authority in Ecclesiastical affairs which it hath been already declared that themselves do in word acknowledge to be lawful, it followeth that he is an *Head* even subordinated of and to *Christ*.

For more plain explication whereof, first unto God we acknowledge daily *ʲthat Kingdom power and glory are his,* *ᵏthat he is the immortal and the invisible King of ages as well the future which shall be as the present, which now is.* That which the Father doth work as *Lord* and *King* over all he worketh not without but by the son who through coeternal generation receiveth of the Father that power which the Father hath of himself. And for that cause our *Saviour's* words concerning his own Dominion are, *To me all power both in heaven and earth is given.* The Father by the son both did create and doth guide all. Wherefore *Christ* hath supreme dominion over the whole universal world. *Christ* is *God*, *Christ* is λόγος the consubstantial word of *God*; *Christ* is also that consubstantial word made man. As God he saith of himself, *ˡI am* Alpha *and* Omega, *the beginning and the end. He which was, which is and which is to come even the very omnipotent.* As the consubstantial word of God, he had with God before the beginning of the world that glory which as man he requesteth to have. *ᵐFather glorify thy Son now with that glory which with thee I enjoyed before the world was,* for there is no necessity that all things spoken of *Christ* should agree unto him either

---

ʲ Matt. 6:13.　ᵏ 1 Tim. 1:17.　ˡ Rev. 1:8.　ᵐ John 17:5.

as God or else as man, but some things as he is the consubstantial word of *God*, some things as he is that word incarnate. The works of supreme Dominion which have been since the first beginning wrought by the power of the Son of God are now most truly and properly the works of the Son of man. The *word* made *flesh* doth sit for ever and reign as Sovereign *Lord* over all. Dominion belongeth unto the *Kingly* office of *Christ* as propitiation and mediation unto his priestly, instruction unto his pastoral or prophetical office. His works of dominion are in sundry degrees or kinds according to the different condition of them which are subject unto it. He presently doth govern and hereafter shall judge the world entire and whole, therefore his regal power cannot be with truth restrained unto a portion of the world only. Notwithstanding forasmuch as all do not show and acknowledge with dutiful submission that obedience which they owe unto him, therefore such as do, their Lord he is termed by way of excellency no otherwise than the *Apostle* doth term God [n]*the Saviour generally of all but especially of the faithful.* These being brought to the obedience of Faith are everywhere spoken of as men translated into that *Kingdom* wherein whosoever is comprehended [o]*Christ is the author of eternal salvation unto them.* [p]They have a high kind of *ghostly fellowship with God and Christ and Saints*, or (as the *Apostle* in more ample manner speaketh, [q]*aggregated they are unto* Mount Sion *and to the city of the living God the celestial* Jerusalem *and to the company of innumerable Angels and to the congregation of the first born, which are written in heaven and to God the judge of all and to the spirits of just and perfect men and to* Jesus *the mediator of the new Testament.*) In a word they are of that mystical body which we term the *Church* of *Christ.* As for the rest we find them accounted *Aliens* from the Commonwealth of *Israel*, men that live in the *Kingdom* of darkness and that are in the present world without God. Our Saviour's dominion is therefore over these as over rebels, over them as dutiful subjects. Which things being in holy *Scripture* so plain I somewhat muse at those strange positions [r]*That Christ in the government of the Church and superiority over the officers of it hath himself a Superior which is his father; but in the government of Kingdoms and Commonwealths and in the superiority which he*

[n] 1 Tim. 4:10. [o] Heb. 5:9. [p] 1 John 1:3. [q] Heb. 12:22.
[r] Bk 2, p. 411, l. 14.

hath over Kings no superior. Again that *[s]The Civil Magistrate's authority cometh from God immediately as Christ's doth and is not subordinate unto Christ.* In what Evangelist, Apostle or Prophet is it found, that *Christ Supreme Governor of the Church* should be so unequal to himself as he is supreme Governor of *Kingdoms?* The works of his providence for preservation of mankind by upholding of Kingdoms not only obedient unto but even rebellious and obstinate against him are such as proceed from divine power; and are not the works of his providence for safety of God's elect, by gathering inspiring comforting, and every way preserving his Church, such as proceed from the same power likewise? *[t]Surely if Christ as God and man have ordained certain means for the gathering and keeping of his Church,* seeing this doth belong to the government of his *Church* it must in reason follow I think that as *God* and *man* he worketh in *Church* regiment, and consequently hath no more therein any superior than in the government of Commonwealths. Again to be *in the midst of his wheresoever they are assembled in his name and to be with them till the world's end,* are comforts which *Christ* doth perform to his Church as Lord and Governor, yea such as he cannot perform but by that very power, wherein he hath no superior. Wherefore unless it can be proved that all the works of our Saviour's government in the Church are done by the mere and only force of his human nature, there is no remedy but to acknowledge it a manifest error that *Christ* in the government of the world is equal unto the Father but not in the government of the *Church.* Indeed to the honour of this *Dominion* it cannot be said that God did exalt him otherwise than only according to that human nature wherein he was made low. For as the Son of God there could no advancement or exaltation grow unto him. And yet the dominion whereunto he was in his human nature lifted up is not without divine power exercised. It is by divine power that the Son of man, who sitteth in heaven doth work as *King* and *Lord* upon us which are on earth. The exercise of his Dominion over the *Church* militant cannot choose but cease when there is no longer any militant Church in the world. And therefore as Generals of Armies when they have finished their work are wont to yield up such Commissions as were given them for that purpose and to remain in the state of subjects and not of *Lords* as concerning

---

[s] Bk 2, p. 418, l. 10.   [t] Bk 2, p. 417, l. 12.

their former authority: even so when the end of all things is come the Son of man, who till then reigneth shall do the like as touching regiment, over the militant church on earth. So that between the son of man and his brethren over whom he now reigneth, in this their warfare there shall be then as touching the exercise of that regiment no such difference, they not warfaring under him any longer, but he together with them under God receiving the joys of everlasting triumph, that so God may be all in all, all misery in all the wicked through his justice, in all the righteous, through his love all felicity and bliss. In the meanwhile he reigneth over this world as *King* and doth those things wherein none is superior unto him whether we respect the works of his providence over kingdoms or of his regiment over the *Church*.

The cause of error in this point, doth seem to have been a misconceipt "that *Christ* as mediator being inferior unto his Father doth as Mediator all works of regiment over the *Church*, when in truth government doth belong to his *Kingly* office, *mediatorship* to his priestly. For as the *High Priest* both offered sacrifice for expiation of the people's sins and entered into the holy place there to make intercession for them, "so *Christ* having finished upon the *Cross* that part of his priestly office which wrought the propitiation for our sins did afterwards enter into very heaven and doth there as mediator of the new *Testament* appear in the sight of God for us. A like slip of judgement it is when they hold that civil authority is from God but not mediately through *Christ* nor with any subordination unto *Christ*. *"For there is no power* (saith the *Apostle*) *but from God, nor doth anything come from God, but by the hands of our* Lord Jesus Christ. *"They deny it not to be said of *Christ* in the old *Testament*. *"By me Kings reign and Princes decree justice; By me Princes rule, and the Nobles and all the judges of the earth.* In the new as much is taught that *"Christ is the Prince of the Kings of the earth.* Wherefore to the end it may more plainly appear how all authority of man is derived from God through *Christ* and must by *Christian* men be acknowledged to be no otherwise held than of and under him, we* are to note that because whatsoever hath necessary being

---

" Bk 2, p. 411, I. 16.   *v* Heb. 9:24. Heb. 7:25.   *w* Rom. 13:1.
x *Humble motion* [STC 7754], p. 63.   *y* Prov. 8:15–16.   *z* Rev. 1:5.

---

* *F:* him. We

166

the son of *God* doth cause it to be and those things without which the world cannot well continue have necessary being in the world, a thing of so great use as government amongst men and human dominion in government cannot choose but be originally from him and have reference also of subordination unto him.

Touching that authority which civil Magistrates have in Ecclesiastical affairs, it being from God by *Christ* as all other good things are, cannot choose but be held as a thing received at his hands. And because such power as is of necessary use for the ordering of religion wherein the essence and very being of the *Church* consisteth can no otherwise flow from him than according to that special care which he hath to guide and govern his own people, it followeth that the said authority is of and under him after a more peculiar manner namely in that he is *Head of the Church* and not in respect of his general regency over the world. *"All things* (saith the *Apostle* speaking unto the *Church*) *are yours, and ye are Christ's and Christ is God's.* Kings are *Christ's* as *Saints*, and *Kings* are *Christ's* as *Kings*, as *Saints* because they are of the *Church*, as *Kings* because they are in authority over the *Church* if not collectively yet divisively understood, that is over each particular person within that *Church* where they are *Kings*. Such authority reaching both unto all men's persons and unto all kinds of causes also, it is not denied but that they lawfully may have and exercise. Such authority it is for which and for no other in the world we term them *Heads*. Such authority they have under *Christ* because he in all things is *Lord* over all. And even of *Christ* it is that they have received such authority inasmuch as of him all lawful powers are. Therefore the Civil Magistrate is in regard of this power an under and subordinate *Head* of *Christ's* people.

Against the second difference whereby Christ is said to be universally Head, the King no further than within his own dominions.

It is but idle when they plead *[b]*that although for several companies [4.7] of men there may be several *Heads* or Governors differing in the measure of their authority from the chiefest who is *Head* of all: yet so it cannot be in the *Church* for that the reason why *Head*

---

[a] 1 Cor. 3:21–23.   [b] T.C., Bk 2, p. 413.

Magistrates appoint others for such several places is because they cannot be present everywhere to perform the office of an Head. But Christ is never from his body nor from any part of it and therefore needeth not to substitute any which may be Heads some over one Church and some over another. Indeed the consideration of man's imbecility which maketh many hands necessary where the burden is too great for one, moved *Jethro* to be a persuader of *Moses* that a number of *Heads* or *Rulers* might be instituted for discharge of that duty by parts which in whole he saw was troublesome. Now although there be not in *Christ* any such defect or weakness yet other causes there may be diverse more than we are able to search into, wherefore it might seem to him expedient to divide his *Kingdom* into many portions and to place many *Heads* over it that the power which each of them hath in particular with restraint might illustrate the greatness of his unlimited authority. Besides howsoever *Christ* be spiritually always united unto every part of his body which is the *Church*: nevertheless we do all know and they themselves who allege this will (I doubt not) confess also that from every *Church* here visible, *Christ* touching visible and corporal presence is removed as far as heaven from earth is distant. Visible government is a thing necessary for the *Church*. And it doth not appear how the exercise of visible government over such multitudes everywhere dispersed throughout the world should consist without sundry visible governors whose power being the greatest in that kind so far as it reacheth they are in consideration thereof termed so far *Heads*, wherefore notwithstanding that perpetual conjunction by virtue whereof our Saviour remaineth always spiritually united unto the parts of his mystical body; *Heads* endowed with supreme power extending unto a certain compass are for the exercise of visible regiment not unnecessary.

Some other reasons there are belonging unto this branch which seem to have been objected rather for the exercise of men's wits in dissolving Sophisms than that the authors of them could think in likelihood thereby to strengthen their cause. For example, *'If the Magistrate be Head of the Church within his own Dominion, then is he none of the Church. For all that Church maketh the body of Christ, and every one of the Church fulfilleth the place of one member of the*

<hr>

ᶜ T.C., Bk 2. p. 419.

body. *By making the Magistrate therefore Head we do exclude him from being a member subject to the Head and so leave him no place in the Church.* By which reason the name of a body politic is supposed to be always taken of the inferior sort alone excluding the principal guides and governors contrary to all men's custom of speech. The error riseth by misconstruing of some Scripture sentences where *Christ* as the head and the *Church* as the body are compared or opposed the one to the other, and because in such comparisons and oppositions the body is taken for those only parts which are subject to the head, they imagine that whoso is head of any *Church*, he is even thereby excluded from being a part of that *Church*. That the Magistrate can be none of the Church if so be we make Him the Head of the Church in his own Dominions, a chief and principal part therefore no part, this is surely a strange conclusion. A *Church* doth indeed make the body of *Christ* being wholly taken together. And every one in the same *Church* fulfilleth the place of a member in the body but not the place of an inferior member, he which hath supreme authority and power over all the rest. Wherefore by making the *Magistrate Head* in his own *Dominions* we exclude him from being a member subject unto any other person which may visibly there rule in place of an *Head* or *Governor* over him, but so far are we off from leaving him by this means no place in the *Church*, that we grant him the chiefest place. Indeed the *Heads* of those visible bodies which are many can be but parts inferior in that spiritual body which is but one, yea they may from this be excluded clean who notwithstanding ought to be honoured as possessing in the other the highest rooms. But for the Magistrate to be termed one way within his own dominions an Head doth not bar him from being either way a part or member of the Church of God.

As little to the purpose are those other cavils. *A Church which hath the Magistrate for Head is a perfect man without Christ. So that the knitting of our Saviour thereunto should be an addition of that which is too much.* Again, *If the Church be the body of Christ and of the Civil Magistrate it shall have two Heads, which being monstrous is to the great dishonour of Christ and his Church.* Thirdly, *If the Church be*

---

d As Henry VIII, 6.9 [Henry VIII, 26.1 (*SR*, 3:492)? This reference is not in the passage from Cartwright being quoted, nor does it appear in all mss. of *Laws* VIII].

e T.C., Bk 2, p. 412.

planted in a popular estate then forasmuch as all govern in Common and all have authority, all shall be Heads there and no body at all. Which is another monster. It might be feared, what this birth of so many monsters might portend but that we know how things natural enough in themselves may seem monstrous through misconceit, which error of mind is indeed a monster, and so the skillful in nature's mysteries have used to term it. The womb of monsters, if any be, is that troubled understanding wherein because things lie confusedly mixed together what they are it appears not. A *Church* perfect without *Christ* I know not which way a man should imagine, unless there may be either *Christianity* without *Christ* or else a *Church* without *Christianity*. If *Magistrates* be *Heads* of the *Church* they are of necessity *Christians*, if *Christians*, then is their head *Christ.* The adding of *Christ* the universal *Head* over all unto the Magistrate's particular *Headship* is no more superfluous in any *Church* than in other *Societies* it is to be both severally each subject unto some *Head* and to have also an *Head General* for them all to be subject unto. For so in armies and in civil corporations we see it fareth. A body *Politic* in such respects is not like to a natural body; in this more Heads than one are superfluous, in that not. It is neither monstrous nor as much as uncomely for a *Church* to have different *Heads*; for if *Christian Churches* be in number many and every of them a body perfect by itself *Christ* being *Lord* and *Head* over all, why should we judge it a thing more monstrous for one body to have two *Heads* than one *Head* so many bodies? *Him God* hath made the supreme *Head* of the whole *Church*, the *Head* not only of that mystical body which the eye of man is not able to discern, but even of every *Christian politic Society* of every visible *Church* in the world. And whereas lastly it is thought so strange that in Popular States a multitude should to itself be both body and *Head*, all this wonderment doth grow from a little oversight in deeming that the subject wherein *Headship* is to reside should be evermore some one person. Which thing is not necessary. For in a collective body that hath not derived as yet the principality of power into some one or few the whole of necessity must be *Head* over each part. Otherwise it could not possibly have power to make any one certain person *Head* inasmuch as the very power of making an *Head* belongeth unto *Headship*. These supposed Monsters therefore we see are no such Giants that there should need any *Hercules* to tame them.

Opposition against the difference in kind.

The last difference which we have made between the title of *Head* [4.8; κ4.9] when we gave it unto *Christ* and when we gave it to other Governors is that the kind of Dominion which it importeth is not the same in both. *Christ* is *Head* as being the fountain of life and ghostly nutriment, the wellspring of spiritual blessings poured into the body of the *Church*, these *Heads* as being his principal instruments for the *Church's* outward government: he *Head*, as founder of the house, they as his chiefest overseers. Against this there is exception especially taken, and our Purveyors are herein said to have their provision from the Popish shambles. For by *Pighius* and *Harding* to prove that *Christ* alone is not *Head* of the *Church* this distinction they say is brought that according to the inward influence of Grace *Christ* only is *Head* but according to outward Government the being of *Head* is a thing common with him to others. To raise up falsehoods of old condemned and to bring that for confirmation of anything doubtful which hath already been sufficiently proved an error and is worthily so taken this would justly deserve censuring. But shall manifest truth be therefore reproached because men in some things convicted of manifest untruth have at any time taught or alleged it? If too much eagerness against their Adversaries had not made them forget themselves, they might remember where being charged as maintainers of those very things for which others before them have been condemned of heresy yet lest the name of any such heretic holding the same which they do should make them odious, they stick not frankly to profess that they are not afraid to consent in some points with *Jews* and *Turks*. ʄWhich defence for all that were a very weak Buckler for such as should consent with *Jews* and *Turks* in that which they have been abhorred and hated for of the *Church*.

But as for this distinction of headship spiritual and mystical in *Jesus Christ*, Ministerial and outward in others besides *Christ* what cause is there to dislike either *Harding* or *Pighius* or any other besides for it? That which they have been reproved for is not because they did herein utter an untruth but such a truth as was not sufficient to bear up the cause which they did thereby seek to maintain. By this distinction they have both truly and sufficiently proved that

ʄ T.C., Bk 3, p. 168.

171

the name of *Head* importing power of dominion over the *Church* might be given unto others besides *Christ* without prejudice unto any part of his honour. That which they should have made manifest was that the name of *Head* importing the power of *Universal* dominion over the whole *Church* of *Christ* militant doth and that by divine right appertain unto the *Pope* of *Rome*. They did prove it lawful to grant unto others besides *Christ* the power of *Headship* in a different kind from his. But they should have proved it lawful to challenge as they did to the *Bishop* of *Rome* a power universal in that different kind. Their fault was therefore in exacting wrongfully so great power as they challenged in that kind and not in making two kinds of power unless some reason can be showed for which this distinction [4.9; K4.10] of power should be thought erroneous and false. A little they stir although in vain to prove that we cannot with truth make any such distinction of power whereof the one kind should agree unto *Christ* only and the other to be further communicated. Thus therefore they argue, *gIf there be no head but Christ in respect of the spiritual government, there is no head but He in respect of the Word Sacraments and Discipline administered by those whom he hath appointed, forasmuch as that is also his spiritual government.* Their meaning is, that whereas we make two kinds of power of which two the one being Spiritual is proper unto *Christ*, the other men are capable of because it is visible and external, we do amiss altogether they think in so distinguishing, forasmuch as the visible and external power of regiment over the *Church* is only in relation unto the *Word* the *Sacraments* and *Discipline* administered by such as *Christ* hath appointed thereunto, and the exercise of this power is also his spiritual government. Therefore we do but vainly imagine a visible and external power in the *Church* differing from his spiritual power. Such disputes as this do somewhat resemble the wonted practising of wellwillers upon their friends in the pangs of death, whose manner is even then to put smoke in their nostrils and so to fetch them again although they know it a matter impossible to keep them living. The kind affection, which the favourers of this labouring cause bear towards it, will not suffer them to see it die although by what means they should be able to make it live they do not see. But they may see that these wrestlings will not help. Can they be ignorant how little

---

g T.C., Bk 2, p. 415.

it booteth to overcast so clear a light with some mist of ambiguity in the name of spiritual regiment? To make things therefore so plain that henceforth a Child's capacity may serve rightly to conceive our meaning, we make the *Spiritual* regiment of *Christ* to be generally that whereby his *Church* is ruled and governed in things spiritual. Of this general we make two distinct kinds, the one invisibly exercised by *Christ* himself in his own person, the other outwardly administered by them whom *Christ* doth allow to be the *Rulers* and guiders of his *Church*.

Touching the former of these two kinds, we teach that *Christ* in regard thereof is peculiarly termed the *Head* of the *Church* of *God*, neither can any other Creature in that sense and meaning be termed *Head* besides him, because it importeth the conduct and government of our Souls, by the hand of that blessed *Spirit*, wherewith we are sealed and marked, as being peculiarly *His*. *Him* only therefore we do acknowledge to be that *Lord* which dwelleth liveth and reigneth in our hearts; *him* only to be that *Head* which giveth salvation and life unto his body; *him* only to be that fountain, from whence the influence of heavenly grace distilleth and is derived into all parts whether the Word or Sacraments or Discipline or whatsoever be the mean whereby it floweth. As for the power of administering those things in the *Church* of *Christ* which power we call the power of order, it is indeed both spiritual and *His; Spiritual*, because such duties properly concern the *Spirit*, *His* because by him it was instituted, howbeit neither *Spiritual* as that which is inwardly and invisibly exercised nor *His*, as that which *He* himself in person doth exercise. Again that power of dominion which is indeed the point of this *Controversy* and doth also belong to the second kind of *Spiritual regiment*, namely unto that regiment which is external and visible, this likewise being *Spiritual* in regard of the matter about which it dealeth and being *His* inasmuch as *He* approveth whatsoever is done by it, must notwithstanding be distinguished also from that power whereby he himself in person administereth the former kind of his own spiritual regiment because he himself in person doth not administer this. We do not therefore vainly imagine but truly and rightly discern a power external and visible in the *Church* exercised by men and severed in nature from that *spiritual* power of Christ's own regiment, which power is termed *spiritual* because it worketh secretly inwardly and invisibly: *His*, because none doth or can it personally exercise either besides or together with him. So that *Him* only we may name our *Head* in regard of this and yet in regard of that other power differing from this, term others also besides him *Heads* without any contradiction [4.10; K4.11] at all. Which thing may very well serve for answer unto that also which they further allege against the aforesaid distinction, [h]*namely that even in the outward society and assemblies of the Church where one or two are gathered in his name either for hearing of the word or for prayer or any other Church exercise, our Saviour Christ being in the midst of them as Mediator must needs be there as Head and if he be there not idle but doing the office of the Head fully, it followeth that even in the outward society and meetings of the Church no mere man can be called the Head of it seeing that our Saviour Christ doing the whole office of the Head himself alone leaveth nothing to men by doing whereof they may obtain that title.* Which objection I take as being made for nothing but only to maintain argument. For they are not so far gone as to argue thus in sooth and right good earnest. [i]*God standeth* (saith the *Psalmist*) *in the midst of Gods.* If *God* be there present he must undoubtedly be present as a God. If he be there not idle but doing the office of a God fully, it followeth that God himself alone doing the whole office of a God leaveth nothing in such assemblies unto any other by doing whereof they may obtain so high a name. The *Psalmist* therefore hath spoken amiss and doth ill to call Judges Gods: Not so. For as God hath his office differing from theirs and doth fully discharge it even in the very midst of them so they are not thereby excluded from all kind of duty for which that name should be given unto them also; but in that duty for which it was given them, they are encouraged religiously and carefully to order themselves. After the selfsame manner *Our Lord* and *Saviour* being in the midst of his *Church* as *Head* is our *Comfort*, and not the abridgement of any one duty, for performance whereof [4.11; K4.12] others are termed *Heads* in another kind than *He* is. If there be of the ancient fathers which say [j]*There is but one Head of the Church, Christ, and that the Minister which baptizeth cannot be the Head of Him which is baptized, because Christ is the Head of the whole Church*

---

[h] T.C., Bk 2, p. 415.   [i] Ps. 82:1.
[j] T.C., Bk 2, p. 413. Cyprian, *On the Simplicity of Prelates* [*ACW*, 25:48, 54–55, 45–46]. Augustine, *Against the Letter of Petilian*, Bk 1, ch. 5 [*CSEL*, 52:6–7] and Bk 3, ch. 42 [*CSEL*, 52:203–204].

and that Paul could not be the head of the Churches which he planted because Christ is Head of the whole body: they understand the name of *Head* in such sort as we grant that it is not applicable to any other, no not in relation to the least part of the whole *Church.* He which baptizeth, baptizeth into *Christ,* he which converteth, converteth unto *Christ,* he which ruleth, ruleth for *Christ.* The whole *Church* can have but one to be *Head* as *Lord* and owner of all. Wherefore if *Christ* be *Head* in that kind it followeth that no other can be so else, either to the whole or to any part.

. . . .

For the title or style itself, although the laws of this Land have [4.12; K4.8] annexed it to the Crown, yet so far we would not strive, if so be men were nice and scrupulous in this behalf only because they do wish that for reverence unto *Christ Jesus* the *Civil Magistrate* did rather use some other form of speech wherewith to express that Sovereign authority which he lawfully hath over all, both persons and causes of the *Church.* But I see that hitherto they which condemn utterly the name so applied do it because they mislike that any such power should be given unto civil Governors. The greatest exception that *Sir Thomas More* took against that *Title,* who suffered death for denial of it, was for that ᵏ*it maketh a lay or secular person the Head of the State spiritual or Ecclesiastical.* As though God himself did not name even *Saul* the *Head* of all the tribes of *Israel* and consequently of that Tribe also amongst the rest, whereunto the state Spiritual or Ecclesiastical belonged. When the Authors of the *Centuries* reprove it in *Kings* and civil Governors, the reason is ˡ*Istis non competit iste Primatus,* such kind of power is too high for them, they fit it not. ᵐIn excuse of *Mr. Calvin,* by whom this *Realm* is condemned of blasphemy for entitling *Henry VIII Supreme Head of this Church under Christ,* a charitable conjecture is made that he spake by misinformation and thought we had meant thereby far otherwise than we do. Howbeit as he professeth utter dislike of that name, so whether the name be used or no, the very power

---

ᵏ G. Courin, *Epistle on the Death of T. More and the Bishop of Rochester,* p. 517.
ˡ [*Magdeburg Centuries,*] *Century* 7, Preface.   ᵐ Calvin on Amos 7:13.

itself which we give unto civil Magistrates he much complaineth of and testifieth *that their power over all things was it which had ever wounded him deeply, that unadvised persons had made them too spiritual, that through Germany this fault did reign, that in those very parts where Calvin himself was, it prevailed more than were to be wished, that Rulers by imagining themselves so Spiritual have taken away Ecclesiastical regiment, that they think they cannot reign unless they abolish all authority of the Church, and be themselves the chief judges as well in doctrine as in the whole spiritual regency.* So that in truth the question is whether the *Magistrate* by being head in such sense as we term him do use or exercise any part of that authority, not which belongeth unto *Christ*, but which other men ought to have.

Of their prerogative to call general assemblies about the affairs of the church.

[5.1]   5. The Consuls of Rome *Polybius* "affirmeth to have had a kind of regal authority in that they might call together the *Senate* and *People* whensoever it pleased them. Seeing therefore the affairs of the *Church* and *Christian* religion are public affairs, for the ordering whereof more solemn assemblies sometimes are of as great importance and use as they are for secular affairs it seemeth no less an act of supreme authority to call the one than the other. Wherefore amongst sundry other prerogatives of *Simon's Dominion* over the *Jews*, this is reckoned as not the least °that no man might gather any great assembly in the Land without him. For so the manner of *Jewish* regiment had always been, that whether the cause for which men assembled themselves in peaceable good and orderly course were ecclesiastical or civil, supreme authority should assemble them. *David* gathered all *Israel* together unto *Jerusalem*; ᵖwhen the *Ark* was to be removed, he assembled the sons of *Aaron* and the *Levites*. ᑫ*Solomon* did the like at such time as the *Temple* was to be dedicated. When the *Church* was to be reformed ʳ*Asa*

ⁿ Polybius [*Histories*], Bk 6 on the military and domestic discipline of the Romans [*L*, 3:296].
° 1 Macc. 14:44.   ᵖ 1 Chron. 15:3.   ᑫ 1 Kings 8:1.
ʳ 2 Chron. 15:9, 24:5, 30:1, 34:29

in his time did the same, the same upon like occasions done afterwards by *Joash Hezekiah Josiah* and others.

The ancient Imperial Law *forbiddeth such assemblies as the [5.2] Emperor's authority did not cause to be made. Before Emperors became *Christian* the *Church* had never any *Synod* General. Their greatest meetings consisted of *Bishops* and others, the gravest in each province. As for the civil Governor's authority it suffered them only as things not regarded or accounted of at such times as it did suffer them. So that what right a *Christian King* hath as touching assemblies of that kind we are not able to judge till we come unto later times when religion had won the hearts of the highest powers. *Constantine* (as *Pighius* doth grant) was not only the first that ever did call any General Council together but even the first that devised the calling of them for consultation about the business of God. After he had once given the example *his *Successors* a long time followed the same, insomuch that *St. Jerome* to disprove the authority of a *Synod* which was pretended to be general, used this as a forcible argument, *Dic quis Imperator hanc Synodum jusserit convocari.* Their answer hereunto is no answer which say that Emperors did not this without conference had with *Bishops*. For to our purpose it is enough if the *Clergy* alone did it not otherwise than by the leave or appointment of their Sovereign *Lords* and *Kings*. Whereas therefore it is on the contrary side alleged that *Valentinian* the elder being requested by *Catholic Bishops* to grant that there might be a *Synod* for the ordering of matters called in question by the *Arians*, answered that he being one of the laity might not meddle with such affairs and therefore wished that the *Priests* and *Bishops* to whom the care of those things belonged should meet and consult thereof by themselves wheresoever they thought good. We must together with the Emperor's speech weigh the occasion and the drift thereof.

---

*See Justinian, *Digest*, 47.22.1. and *Code*, 1.3.15.

t Pighius, *Hierarchy*, Bk 6, ch. 1.

u The Council of Constantinople was called by Theodosius the Elder. Theodoret, *Ecclesiastical History*, Bk 1, ch. 9 [*N2*, 3:47]. The first of Ephesus convened at the motion of Thedosius the Younger. Evagrius, *Ecclesiastical History*, Bk 1, ch. [3]. Constantius called the Sardican. Theodoret, Bk 2, ch. 4 [*N2*, 3:69]. Chalcedon was sought from Marcian. Leo I, Epist. 43 [*FOTC*, 34:162].

v [*Say what emperor commanded this synod to be convoked.*] Bk 2 *Against Ruffinus* [ch. 19; *PL*, 23;443].

w Sozomen, Bk 6, ch. 7. Ambrose, Epist. 32 [*PL*, 16:1004; *FOTC*, 26:53]. *Although otherwise very distant, Nicephorus*, Bk 7, ch. 12 [*PG*, 146:592].

Valentinian and *Valens*, the one a *Catholic* the other an *Arian*, were Emperors together, *Valens* the governor of the East, *Valentinian* of the *West Empire*. *Valentinian* therefore taking his journey from the *East* part into the *West* and passing to that intent through *Thrace*, the *Bishops* there which held the soundness of *Christian* belief because they knew that *Valens* was their professed enemy, and therefore if the other were once departed out of those quarters the Catholic cause was like to find small favour, moved presently *Valentinian* about a *Council* to be assembled under the Countenance of his authority, who by likelihood considering what inconvenience might thereby grow inasmuch as it could not but be a mean to incense *Valens* the more against them refused himself to be author of or present at any such assembly. And of this his denial gave them a colourable reason, to wit that he was although an Emperor yet a secular person and therefore not able in matters of so great obscurities to sit as a competent judge. But if they which were *Bishops* and Learned men did think good to consult thereof together they might. Whereupon when they could not obtain that which they most desired, yet that which was granted them they took and forthwith had a *Council*. *Valentinian* went on towards *Rome*, they remaining in consultation till *Valens* which accompanied him returned back, so that now there was no remedy but either to incur a manifest contempt or else at the hands even of *Valens* himself to seek approbation of that they had done. To him therefore they became suitors. His answer was short, Either *Arianism* or else exile, which they would, whereupon their banishment ensued. Let reasonable men therefore now be judges how much this example of *Valentinian* doth make against the authority which we say that Sovereign *Rulers* may lawfully have as concerning *Synods* and meetings *Ecclesiastical*.

Wherefore the Clergy in such wise gathered together is an *Ecclesiastical Senate* which with us as in former times the chiefest *Prelate* at his discretion did use to assemble, so afterwards in such considerations as have been before specified it seemeth more meet to annex the said prerogative unto the *Crown*. The plot of reformed Discipline not liking hereof so well taketh order that every former assembly before it break up should itself appoint both the time and place of their after meeting again. But because I find not anything on that side particularly alleged against us herein a longer disputation about so plain a cause shall not need.

Of their power in making ecclesiastical laws.

6. The case is not like when such assemblies are gathered together [6.1; κ6.4] by supreme authority concerning other affairs of the *Church* and when they meet about the making of *Ecclesiastical* laws or statutes. For in the one they are only to advise, in the other they are to decree. The persons which are of the one the *King* doth voluntarily assemble as being in respect of gravity fit to consult withal. Them which are of the other he calleth by prescript of law as having right to be thereunto called. Finally the one are but themselves and their sentence hath but the weight of their own judgement, the other represent the whole clergy and their voices are as much as if all did give personal verdict. Now the question is whether the Clergy alone so assembled ought to have the whole power of making Ecclesiastical laws or else consent of the Laity may thereunto be made necessary and the *King's* assent so necessary, that his sole denial may be of force to stay them from being laws.

. . . .

The natural subject of power civil all men confess to be the body [κ6.1] of the Commonwealth. The good or evil estate whereof dependeth so much upon the power of making laws that in all well settled States yea though they be *Monarchies* yet diligent care is evermore had that the *Commonwealth* do not clean resign up herself and make over this power wholly into the hands of any one. For this cause *William* whom we call the *Conqueror* making war against England in right of his title to the crown and knowing that as Inheritor thereof he could not lawfully change the laws of the land by himself for that the English Commonwealth had not invested her *Kings* before with the fulness of so great power, therefore he took the style and title of a Conqueror. Wherefore as they themselves cannot choose but grant that the natural subject of power to make laws civil is the *Commonwealth:* so we affirm that in like congruity the true original subject of power also to make church laws is the whole entire body of that church for which they are made. Equals cannot impose laws and statutes upon their equals. Therefore neither may any one man indifferently impose *Canons Ecclesiastical* upon another nor yet one

Church upon another. If they go about at any time to do it they must either show some Commission sufficient for their warrant or else be justly condemned of presumption in the sight both of God and men. But nature itself doth abundantly authorize the *Church* to make laws and orders for her Children that are within her. For every whole thing being naturally of greater power than is any part thereof that which a whole *Church* will apoint may be with reason exacted indifferently of any within the compass of the same *Church* and so bind all unto strict obedience.

[6.2]   The greatest agents of the *Bishop* of *Rome's* inordinate Sovereignty strive against no one point with such earnestness as against this that *Jurisdiction* (and in the name of jurisdiction they also comprehend the power of dominion spiritual) should be thought originally to be the right of the whole *Church* and that no person hath or can have the same otherwise than derived from the body of the *Church*.

The reason wherefore they can in no wise brook this opinion is as *Friar Soto* confesseth because they which make *Councils* above *Popes* do all build upon this ground and therefore even with teeth and all they that favour the *Papal* throne must hold the contrary. Which thing they do. For as many as draw the Chariot of the Pope's preeminence the first conclusion which they contend for is, *ˣThe power of jurisdiction Ecclesiastical doth not rest derived from Christ immediately into the whole body of the Church but into the Prelacy.* Unto the Prelacy alone it belongeth as ours also do imagine. Unto the Governors of the *Church* alone it was first given and doth appertain even of very divine right in every *Church* established to make such laws concerning orders and ceremonies as occasion doth require.

[6.3] Wherein they err for want of observing as they should in what manner the power whereof we speak was instituted. One thing it is to ordain a power and another thing to bestow the same being ordained, or to appoint the special subject of it or the person in whom it shall rest. Nature hath appointed that there should be in a civil Society power to make laws, but the consent of the people (which are that society) hath instituted the Prince's person to be the subject wherein supremacy of that power shall reside. The act of instituting such power may and sometimes doth go in time before

---

ˣ Cajetan in his Opuscule *On the Comparison of Pope and Council.* Joannes de Turrecremata, *Summa on the Church*, Bk 2, ch. 71. Domingo de Soto, *Commentaries on the Fourth Book of Sentences of Peter Lombard*, distinction 20, question 1, article 4.

the act of conferring or bestowing it. And for bestowing it there may be order two ways taken, namely either by appointing thereunto some certain person one or many, or else without any personal determination and with appointment only of some determinate condition touching the quality of their persons (whosoever they be that shall receive the same) and for the form or manner of taking it.

Now God himself preventeth sometimes these communities, himself nominateth and appointeth sometimes the subject wherein their power shall rest and by whom either in whole or in part it shall be exercised, which thing he did often in the *Commonwealth* of *Israel*. Even so *Christ* having given unto his *Church* the power whereof we speak, what he doth by her appointed agents that duty though they discharge yet is it not theirs peculiarly, but hers, her power it is which they do exercise. But *Christ* hath sometimes prevented his *Church* conferring that power and appointing it unto certain persons himself, which otherwise the *Church* might have done. Those persons excepted which *Christ* himself did immediately bestow such power upon, the rest succeeding have not received power as they did, *Christ* bestowing it upon their persons, but the power which *Christ* did institute in the *Church*, they from the *Church* do receive according to such laws and Canons as *Christ* hath prescribed and the light of nature or scripture taught men to institute.

But in truth the whole body of the *Church* being the first original subject of all mandatory and coercive power within itself in case a Monarch of the world together with his whole kingdom under him receive *Christianity*, the question is whether the *Monarch* of that *Commonwealth* may without offense or breach of the law of God have and exercise power of dominion Ecclesiastical within the compass of his own territories in such ample sort as the *Kings* of this land may do by the laws thereof.

· · · ·

What laws may be made for the affairs of the Church and to whom the power of making them appertaineth.

If they with whom we dispute were uniform strong and constant [6.4; κ6.5] in that which they say, we should not need to trouble ourselves about their persons to whom the power of making laws for the *Church* belongeth. For they are sometimes very vehement in contention that from the greatest thing unto the least about the *Church* all must needs be immediately from God. And to this they apply the pattern of the ancient *Tabernacle* which *God* delivered unto *Moses* and was therein so exact that there was not left so much as the least pin for the wit of man to devise in the framing of it. To this they also apply that strict and severe charge which God so often gave concerning his own law. *ʸWhatsoever I command you take heed you do it. Thou shalt put nothing thereunto, thou shalt take nothing from it.* Nothing whether it be great or small. Yet sometime bethinking themselves better they speak as acknowledging that it doth suffice to have received in such sort the principal things from God, and that for other matters the *Church* hath sufficient authority to make laws, whereupon they now have made it a question, what persons they are whose right it is to take order for the *Church's* affairs when the institution of any new thing therein is requisite. Laws may be requisite to be made either concerning things that are only to be known and believed in or else touching that which is to be done by the *Church* of *God*.

*ᶻThe law of nature and the law of God are sufficient for declaration in both, what belongeth unto each man separately as his soul is the spouse of *Christ*, yea so sufficient that they plainly and fully show whatsoever God doth require by way of necessary introduction unto the state of everlasting bliss. But as a man liveth joined with others in common society and belongeth unto the outward politic body of the *Church* albeit the said law of nature and of scripture have in this respect also made manifest the things that are of greatest necessity, nevertheless by reason of new occasions still arising which the *Church* having care of souls must needs take order for as need requireth, hereby it cometh to pass, that there is and ever will be great use even of human laws and ordinances deducted by way of discourse as conclusions from the former divine and natural, serving for principles thereunto. No man doubteth but that for matters of action and practice in the affairs of God, for the manner of divine service, for order in Ecclesiastical proceedings about the regiment of the *Church* there may be oftentimes cause very urgent

ʸ Deut. 12:32, 4:2. Joshua 1:7.
ᶻ Thomas Aquinas, *Summa Theologiae*, 1a2ae, q. 108, art. 2.

to have laws made. But the reason is not so plain wherefore human laws should appoint men what to believe. Wherefore in this we must note two things. First, that in matter of opinion the law doth not make that to be truth which before was not, as in matter of action it causeth that to be duty which was not before, but it manifesteth only and giveth men notice of that to be truth, the contrary whereunto they ought not before to have believed. Secondly, that as opinions do cleave to the understanding and are in heart assented unto it is not in the power of any human law to command them, because to prescribe what men shall think belongeth only unto God. [a]*Corde creditur ore fit confessio,* saith the *Apostle.* As opinions are either fit or inconvenient to be professed, so man's law hath to determine of them. It may for public unity's sake require men's professed assent or prohibit contradiction to special articles, wherein as there happily hath been controversy what is true, so the same were like to continue still not without grievous detriment to a number of souls except law to remedy that evil should set down a certainty which no man is to gainsay. Wherefore as in regard of divine laws which the *Church* receiveth from God, we may unto every man of wisdom apply those words of *Solomon.* [b]*Conserva fili mi præcepta Patris tui. My Son keep thou thy Father's precepts.* Even so concerning the statutes and ordinances which the *Church* itself maketh we may add thereunto the words that follow. *Et ne dimittas legem Matris tuæ. And forsake not thou thy Mother's law.* It is undoubtedly a thing [6.5; κ6.6] even natural that all free and independent societies should themselves make their own laws, and that this power should belong to the whole not to any certain part of a politic body though happily some one part may have greater sway in that action than the rest. Which thing being generally fit and expedient in the making of all laws we see no cause why to think otherwise in laws concerning the service of God, which in all well ordered States and Commonwealths is [c]the first thing that law hath care to provide for. When we speak of the right which naturally belongeth to a Commonwealth we speak of that which needs must belong to the *Church of God.*

[a] Rom. 10:10.   [b] Prov. 6:20.

[c] Archytas, *On Law and Justice. It behoveth the Law first to establish or settle those things which belong to the Gods, and divine powers, and to our parents, and universally those things which be virtuous and honourable. And in the second place those things that be convenient or profitable: for it is fit that matters of the less weight should come after the greater* [ed. 1822, p. 14; ed. 1958, 2:86].

For if the Commonwealth be *Christian*, if the people which are of it do publicly embrace the true religion, this very thing doth make it the *Church*, as hath been showed. So that unless the verity and purity of religion do take from them which embrace it that power wherewith otherwise they are possessed, look what authority as touching laws for religion a commonwealth hath simply; it must of necessity being *Christian* have the same as touching laws for *Christian* religion.

[6.6; κ6.7]   It will be therefore perhaps alleged that a part of the verity of *Christian* religion is to hold the power of making Ecclesiastical laws a thing appropriated unto the Clergy in their *Synods* and that whatsoever is by their only voices agreed upon it needeth no further approbation to give unto it the strength of a law, as may plainly appear by the *Canons* of that first most venerable Assembly where those things which the *Apostles* and *James* had concluded were afterward ^d published and imposed upon the *Churches* of the *Gentiles* abroad as laws, the records thereof remaining still in the *Book* of God for a testimony that the power of making Ecclesiastical laws belongeth to the Successors of the Apostles, the Bishops and Prelates of the *Church* of God.

To this we answer that the *Council* of *Jerusalem* is no argument for the power of the Clergy alone to make laws. For first there hath not been since any *Council* of like authority to that in *Jerusalem*. Secondly, the cause why that was of such authority came by a special accident. Thirdly, the reason why other *Councils* being not like unto that in nature the Clergy in them should have no power to make laws by themselves alone is in truth so forcible that except some commandment of God to the contrary can be showed, it ought notwithstanding the aforesaid example to prevail.

The Decrees of the *Council* of *Jerusalem* were not as the *Canons* of other *Ecclesiastical* assemblies human, but very divine ordinances. For which cause the *Churches* were far and wide ^e commanded everywhere to see them kept, no otherwise than if Christ himself had personally on earth been the author of them. The cause why that *Council* was of so great authority and credit above all others which have been since is expressed in those words of principal observation, ^f *Unto the Holy Ghost and to us it hath seemed good*, which form of

---

^d Acts 15:7, 13, 23.   ^e Acts 16:4.   ^f Acts 15:28.

speech though other *Councils* have likewise used, yet neither could they themselves mean nor may we so understand them as if both were in equal sort assisted with the power of the *Holy Ghost*, but the later had the favour of that general assistance and presence which *Christ* doth promise unto all his ^gaccording to the quality of their several estates and callings, the former that grace of special miraculous rare and extraordinary illumination in relation where- unto the *Apostle* comparing the old *Testament* and the new together ^htermeth the one a *Testament* of the letter for that God delivered it written in stone, the other a *Testament* of the Spirit because God imprinted it in the hearts and declared it by the tongues of his chosen Apostles through the power of the *Holy Ghost* framing both their conceipts and speeches in more divine and incomprehensible manner. Wherefore inasmuch as the *Council of Jerusalem* did chance to consist of men so enlightened it had authority greater than were meet for any other *Council* besides to challenge, wherein no such kind of persons are. As now the state of the *Church* doth stand, [6.7; κ6.8] *Kings* being not then that which now they are and the Clergy not now that which then they were, till it be proved that some special law of *Christ* hath forever annexed unto the Clergy alone the power to make Ecclesiastical laws, we are to hold it a thing most consonant with equity and reason that no *Ecclesiastical* law be made in a *Christian Commonwealth* without consent as well of the laity as of the Clergy but least of all without consent of the highest power.

For of this thing no man doubteth, ⁱnamely that in all societies companies and corporations what severally each shall be bound unto it must be with all their assents ratified. Against all equity it were that a man should suffer detriment at the hands of men for not observing that which he never did either by himself or by others mediately or immediately agree unto. Much more that a king should constrain all others unto the strict observation of any such human ordinance as passeth without his own approbation. In this case there- fore especially that vulgar axiom is of force. ^j*Quod omnes tangit ab omnibus tractari et approbari debet.* Whereupon *Pope Nicholas*, although otherwise not admitting lay persons, no not Emperors themselves

---

^g Matt. 16 at the end.   ^h 2 Cor. 3:6.
ⁱ Gregory IX, *Decretals*, 5.31.14. Justinian, *Digest*, 8.3.11 and *Institutes*, 2.1.9.
^j [*What touches all ought to be treated and approved by all.*] *Glossa ordinaria* to Gratian, *Decretum*, 1.96.4.

to be present at *Synods*, doth notwithstanding seem to allow of their presence when matters of faith are determined whereunto all men must stand bound. *[k]Ubinam legistis Imperatores Antecessores vestros Synodalibus Conventibus interfuisse, nisi forsitan in quibus de fide tractatum est quæ universalis est quæ omnibus communis est quæ non solum ad Clericos verum etiam ad Laicos et omnes pertinet Christianos?* A law be it civil or Ecclesiastical is as a public obligation wherein seeing that the whole standeth charged, no reason it should pass without his privity and will whom principally the whole doth depend upon. *[l]Sicut Laici Jurisdictionem Clericorum perturbare ita Clerici Jurisdictionem Laicorum non debent imminuere*, saith *Innocent*. As the laity should not hinder the Clergy's jurisdiction, so neither is it reason that the laity's right should be abridged by the Clergy, saith *Innocent*. But were it so that the Clergy alone might give laws unto all the rest, forasmuch as every estate doth desire to enlarge the bounds of their own liberties, is it not easy to see how injurious this might prove unto men of other condition? Peace and justice are maintained by preserving unto every order their rights and by keeping all estates as it were in an even balance. Which thing is no way better done than if the *King* their common parent whose care is presumed to extend most indifferently over all, do bear the chiefest sway in the making of laws which all must be ordered by.

[6.8; κ6.9]   Wherefore of them which in this point attribute most to the Clergy I would demand what Evidence there is which way it may clearly be showed that in ancient kingdoms *Christian* any *Canon* devised by the Clergy alone in their *Synods* whether provincial, national or general hath by mere force of their agreement taken place as a law making all men constrainable to be obedient thereunto without any other approbation from the King before or afterwards required in that behalf. But what speak we of ancient kingdoms, when at this day even in the *Papacy* itself the very *Tridentine Council* hath not everywhere as yet obtained to have in all points the strength of *Ecclesiastical* law? Did not Philip King of Spain *[m]*publishing that *Council* in the low Countries add thereunto an express clause of

---

[k] [*Where do you read that your predecessors as emperor were present at synodal gatherings except perhaps at those where a matter of faith was treated, which is universal, which is common to all, which pertains indeed not only to clerics but also to laymen and to all Christians?*] Gratian, *Decretum*, 1.96.4.

[l] Gregory IX, *Decretales*, 2.1.13.

[m] Boethius Epo, *Six Books of Heroic and Ecclesiastical Questions*, Bk 1, sect. 284.

special provision that the same should in no wise prejudice hurt or diminish any kind of privilege which the *King* or his Vassals aforetime had enjoyed, either touching possessory judgements of Ecclesiastical livings or concerning nominations thereunto or belonging to whatsoever rights they had else in such affairs? If therefore the *King's* exception taken against some part of the *Canons* contained in that *Council* were a sufficient bar to make them of none effect within his *Territories*, it followeth that the like exception against any other part had been also of like efficacy and so consequently that no part thereof had obtained the strength of a law if he which excepted against a part had so done against the whole. As what reason was there but that the same authority which limited might quite and clean have refused that *Council?* Whoso alloweth the said act of the *Catholic King* for good and lawful must grant that the *Canons* even of general *Councils* have but the force of wise men's opinions concerning that whereof they treat till they be publicly assented unto where they are to take place as laws and that in giving such public assent as maketh a *Christian* Kingdom subject unto those laws the *King's* authority is the chiefest. That which an university of men, a company or corporation doth without consent of their *Rector* is as nothing. Except therefore we make the *King's* authority over the Clergy less in the greatest things than the power of the meanest governor is in all things over the College or *Society* which is under him, how should we think it a matter decent that the Clergy should impose laws, the supreme governor's assent not asked?

. . . .

Yea that which is more, the laws thus made God himself doth [6.9; κApp. 1] in such sort authorize that to despise them is to despise in them him. It is a loose and licentious opinion which the *Anabaptists* have embraced, holding that a *Christian* man's liberty is lost and the soul which *Christ* hath redeemed unto himself injuriously drawn into servitude under the yoke of human power if any law be now imposed besides the gospel of *Christ* in obedience whereunto the Spirit of God and not the constraint of men is to lead us according to that of the blessed Apostle, *"Such as are led by the Spirit of God they are the Sons of God* and not such as live in thraldom unto men.

" Rom. 8:14.

187

Their judgement is therefore that the *Church* of *Christ* should admit no lawmakers but the *Evangelists*, no courts but *Presbyteries*, no punishments but *Ecclesiastical Censures*. As against this sort we are to maintain the use of human laws and the continual necessity of making them from time to time as long as this present world doth last: so likewise the authority of laws so made doth need much more by us to be strengthened against another sort who although they do not utterly condemn the making of laws in the *Church*, yet make they a great deal less account of them than they should do. There are which think simply of human laws that they can in no sort touch the conscience, that to break and transgress them cannot make men in the sight of God culpable as sin doth; only when we violate such laws we do thereby make ourselves obnoxious unto external punishment in this world so that the Magistrate may in regard of such offense committed justly correct the Offender and cause him without injury to endure such pain as the law doth appoint, but further it reacheth not. For first the *Conscience* is the proper court of God, the guiltiness thereof is sin and the punishment eternal death. Men are not able to make any law that shall command the heart, it is not in them to make the inward conceipt a crime or to appoint for any crime other punishment than corporal. Their laws therefore can have no power over the Soul, neither can the heart of man be polluted by transgressing them. *St. Augustine* rightly defineth sin to be that which is spoken done or desired not against any law, but against the law of the living God. The law of God is proposed unto men as a glass wherein to behold the stains and spots of their sinful souls. By it they are to judge themselves and when they find themselves to have transgressed against it then to bewail their offences with *David, ᵒAgainst thee only O Lord have I sinned and done wickedly in thy sight*, that so our present tears may extinguish the flames which otherwise we are to feel and which *God* in that day shall condemn the wicked unto when they shall render account of the evil which they have done, not by violating *Statute* laws and *Canons*, but by disobedience unto his law and word.

For our better instruction therefore in this point. First we must note that the law of God himself doth require at our hands subjection, *ᵖBe ye Subject*, saith *St. Peter*. And *St. Paul, Let every Soul be*

ᵒ Ps. 51:4.   ᵖ 1 Pet. 2:13. Rom. 13:1.

subject, subject all unto such powers as are set over us. [q]For if such as are not set over us require our subjection we by denying it are not disobedient to the law of God, or undutiful unto higher powers, because though they be such in regard of them over whom they have lawful dominion, yet having not so over us, unto us they are not such. Subjection therefore we owe, and that by the law of God we are in conscience bound to yield it even unto every of them that hold the seats of authority and power in relation unto us, howbeit not all kind of subjection unto every such kind of power. Concerning *Scribes* and *Pharisees* our Saviour's precept was [r]*What-soever they shall tell you, do it,* was it his meaning that if they should at any time enjoin the people to levy an army or to sell their lands and goods for the furtherance of so great an enterprise and in a word that whatsoever simply it were which they did command, they ought without any exception forthwith to be obeyed? No, but what-soever they shall tell you must be understood *in pertinentibus ad cathedram,* it must be construed with limitation and restrained unto things of that kind which did belong to their place and power. For they had not power general absolutely given them to command in all things. The reason why we are bound in conscience to be subject unto all such powers is because [s]*All powers are of God.* They are of God either instituting or permitting them. Power is then of divine institution when either God himself doth deliver or men by light of nature find out the kind thereof. So that the power of parents over children and of husbands over their wives, the power of all sorts of superiors made by consent of commonwealths within them-selves or grown from agreement amongst nations, such power is of God's own institution in respect of the kind thereof. Again if respect be had unto those particular persons to whom the same is derived, if they either receive it immediately from God as *Moses* and *Aaron* did or from nature as *Parents* do or from men by a natural and orderly course as every Governor appointed in any Common-wealth by the orders thereof doth, then is not the kind of their

[q] *The true and proper difference of citizen from stranger is, therefore, that one is obligated to the commanding authority and civil power, the other can reject the orders of an alien ruler. The ruler is bound to protect the former from injuries by both enemies and citizens, but not the latter, unless he is asked and is moved by the duties of humanity,* saith Bodin, *The Six Books of a Commonwealth,* Bk 1, ch. 6, not far from the end. P. 61B in the Lyons folio edition, 1586.
[r] Matt. 23:3.   [s] Rom. 13:1.

power only of God's institution, but the derivation thereof also into their persons is from him. He hath placed them in their rooms and doth term them his Ministers. Subjection therefore is due unto all such powers inasmuch as they are of God's own institution even then when they are of man's creation, *Omni humanæ creaturæ* which thing the *Heathens* themselves do acknowledge: ʹΣκηπτοῦχος βασιλεὺς, ᾧ τε Ζεὺς κῦδος ἔδωκεν. As for them that exercise power altogether against order, although the kind of power which they have may be of God, yet is their exercise thereof against God, and therefore not of God otherwise than by permission as all injustice is.

Touching such Acts as are done by that power which is according to his institution that God in like sort doth authorize them and account them to be his though it were not confessed it might be proved undeniable. For if that be accounted our deed which others do whom we have appointed to be our agents how should God but approve those deeds even as his own, which are done by virtue of that Commission and power which he hath given? *"Take heed* (saith *Jehosaphat* unto his *Judges*), *be careful and circumspect what ye do; ye do not execute the Judgements of men but of the Lord.* The authority of *Cæsar* over the Jews from whence was it? Had it any other ground than the law of nations which maketh Kingdoms subdued by just war to be subject unto their Conquerors? By this power *Cæsar* exacting tribute our *Saviour* confesseth it to be his right, a right which could not be withheld without injury; yea disobedience herein to him had been rebellion against God.

Usurpers of power, whereby we do not mean them that by violence have aspired unto places of highest authority but them that use more authority than they did ever receive in form and manner before mentioned, for so they may do whose title unto the rooms of authority which they possess no man can deny to be just and lawful, even as contrariwise some men's proceedings in government have been very orderly, who notwithstanding did not attain to be made governors without great violence and disorder, such usurpers therefore as in the exercise of their power do more than they have been authorized to do cannot in conscience bind any man to obedience.

That subjection which we owe unto lawful powers doth not only

---

ᵗ *A Scepter-swaying King to whom even Jupiter himself hath given honour or command.* Homer, *Iliad*, Bk I [line 279].   ᵘ 2 Chron. 19:6.

import that we should be under them, by order of our *State*, but that we show all submission towards them both by honour and obedience. *He that resisteth them resisteth God.* And resisted they are if either the authority itself which they exercise be denied, as by *Anabaptists* all secular jurisdiction is: or if resistance be made but only so far forth as doth touch their persons which are invested with power, for they which said *Nolumus hunc regnare* did not utterly exclude regiment, nor did they wish all kind of government clean removed which would not at the first have *David* govern; or if that which they do by virtue of their power, namely their laws edicts sentences or other acts of jurisdiction be not suffered to take effect contrary to the blessed Apostle's most holy precept, *ᵛObey them that have the oversight of you.* Or if they do take effect yet is not the will of God thereby satisfied neither as long as that which we do is contemptuously or repiningly done because we can do no otherwise; in such sort the *Israelites* in the desert obeyed *Moses* and were notwithstanding deservedly plagued for disobedience. The Apostle's precept therefore is, *Be subject even for God's cause; be subject not for fear, but for mere conscience knowing that he which resisteth them purchaseth unto himself condemnation.* Disobedience therefore unto laws which are made by men is not a thing of so small account as some would make it. Howbeit too rigorous it were that the breach of every human law should be held a deadly sin. A mean there is between these extremities, if so be we can find it out.

. . . .

Of the authority of making Laws.

There are which wonder that we should count any *Statute* a law [6.10] which the high *Court* of *Parliament* in *England* hath established about the matter of *Church* regiment, the *Prince* and *Court* of *Parliament* having as they suppose no more lawful means to give order to the *Church* and *Clergy* in these things, than they have to make laws for the *Hierarchies of Angels in Heaven*, that the *Parliament* being a mere temporal *Court* can neither by the law of nature, nor of *God* have competent power to define of such matters: that supremacy of power in this kind cannot belong unto *Kings* as *Kings* because

---

ᵛ Heb. 13:17.

Pagan Emperors whose *Princely* power was notwithstanding true Sovereignty never challenged thus much over the *Church*: that power in this kind cannot be the right of any earthly crown, *Prince* or *State* in that they be *Christian*, forasmuch as if they be *Christians* they all owe subjection unto the *Pastors* of their souls: that the *Prince* therefore not having it himself cannot communicate it unto the *Parliament* and consequently cannot make laws, hear or determine of the Church's regiment by himself, *Parliament* or any other *Court* in such sort subjected unto him.

[6.11]   The *Parliament* of *England* together with the *Convocation* annexed thereunto is that whereupon the very essence of all government within this kingdom doth depend. It is even the body of the whole Realm, it consisteth of the *King* and of all that within the *Land* are subject unto him for they all are there present either in person, or by such as they voluntarily have derived their very personal right unto. The *Parliament* is a *Court* not so merely temporal as if it might meddle with nothing but only leather and wool. Those days of *Queen Mary* are not yet forgotten wherein the *Realm* did submit itself unto the *Legate* of *Pope Julius*. At which time had they been persuaded as this man seemeth now to be, had they thought that there is no more force in laws made by *Parliament* concerning the *Church's* affairs than if men should take upon them to make orders for the Hierarchies of Angels in heaven, they might have taken all former *Statutes* in that kind as cancelled and by reason of nullity abrogated in themselves. What need was there that they should bargain with the *Cardinal* and purchase their pardon by promise made beforehand that what laws they had made assented unto or executed against the *Bishop* of *Rome's* supremacy the same they would in that present *Parliament* effectually abrogate and repeal? Had they power to repeal laws made, and none to make laws concerning the regiment of the *Church*? Again when they had by suit obtained his confirmation for such foundations of *Bishoprics, Cathedral Churches, Hospitals, Colleges* and *Schools*, for such marriages before made for such institutions unto Livings Ecclesiastical, and for all such judicial processes as having been ordered according to laws before in force, but contrary to the *Canons* and orders of the *Church* of *Rome*, were in that respect thought defective. Although the Cardinal in his letters of dispensation did give validity unto those Acts even *Apostolicæ firmitatis robur* the very strength of Apostolical solidity, what had all this been without those grand authentical words, *"Be it enacted by the authority of this present Parliament, that all and singular articles and clauses contained in the said Dispensation shall remain and be reputed and taken to all intents and constructions in the laws of this Realm lawful good and effectual to be alleged and pleaded in all Courts Ecclesiastical and temporal for good and sufficient matter either for the plaintiff or defendant without any allegation or objection to be made against the validity of them by pretence of any general Council Canon or Decree to the Contrary* Somewhat belike they thought there was in this mere temporal *Court* without which the *Pope's* own mere *Ecclesiastical* Legate's dispensation had taken small effect in the *Church of England*. Neither did they or the *Cardinal* himself as then imagine anything committed against the law of nature or of God, because they took order for the Church's affairs and that even in the *Court* of *Parliament*. The most natural and religious course in making of laws is that the matter of them be taken from the judgement of the wisest in those things which they are to concern. In matters of God, to set down a form of public prayer, a solemn confession of the Articles of *Christian* faith, rites and ceremonies meet for the exercise of religion, it were unnatural not to think the *Pastors* and *Bishops* of our souls a great deal more fit than men of secular trades and callings. Howbeit when all which the wisdom of all sorts can do is done for devising of laws in the *Church* it is the general consent of all that giveth them the form and vigor of laws without which they could be no more unto us than the *Counsels* of *Physicians* to the sick, well might they seem as wholesome admonitions and instructions but laws could they never be without consent of the whole *Church*; which is the only thing that bindeth each member of the *Church* to be guided by them, whereunto both nature and the practice of the *Church* of God set down in Scripture is found every way so fully consonant that God himself would not impose no not his own laws upon his people ˣby the hand of *Moses* without their free and open consent. Wherefore to define and determine even of the *Church's* affairs by way of assent and approbation as laws are defined of in that right of power which doth give them the force of laws; thus to define of our own *Church's* regiment, the *Parliament* of *England* hath competent authority.

ᵂ Years 1 and 2 of Philip and Mary, ch. 8 [*SR*, 4.1:246–254].   ˣ Exod. 19[:5–8].

Touching the supremacy of power which our *Kings* have in this case of making laws it resteth principally in the strength of a negative voice, which not to give them were to deny them that, without which they were but *Kings* by mere title and not in exercise of dominion. Be it in states of regiment popular aristocratical or regal, principality resteth in that person or those persons unto whom is given the right of excluding any kind of law whatsoever it be before establishment. This doth belong unto *Kings* as *Kings*. Pagan Emperors even *Nero* himself had not less, but much more than this in the laws in his own *Empire*. That he challenged not any interest in giving voice in the laws of the *Church* I hope no man will so construe as if the cause were conscience and fear to encroach upon the Apostles' right. If then it be demanded by what right from *Constantine* downward the *Christian* Emperors did so far intermeddle with the *Church's* affairs either we must herein condemn them utterly as being over-presumptuously bold or else judge that by a law which is termed *Regia* that is to say *Royal,*[y] the people having derived into the Emperor their whole power for making of laws and by that mean his Edicts being made laws, what matter soever they did concern as imperial dignity endowed them with competent authority and power to make laws for religion so they were taught by Christianity to use their power, being Christians unto the benefit of the *Church* of *Christ*. Was there any Christian Bishop in the world which did then judge this repugnant unto the dutiful subjection which *Christians* do owe to the *Pastors* of their souls? To whom in respect of their sacred order it is not by us neither may be denied that *Kings* and *Princes* are as much as the very meanest that liveth under them bound in conscience to show themselves gladly and willingly obedient receiving the Seals of salvation the blessed *Sacraments* at their hands as at the hands of our *Lord Jesus Christ* with all reverence, not disdaining to be taught and admonished by them nor withholding from them as much as the least part of their due and decent honour. All which for anything that hath been alleged may stand very well without resignation of supremacy of power in making laws, even laws concerning the most spiritual affairs of the *Church*. Which laws being made amongst us are not by any of us so taken or interpreted as

---

[y] *What has pleased the prince has the force of law, since by the royal law, which was enacted about his authority to command, the people have conceded to him all their power and authority to command.* Justinian, *Institutes*, 1.2.6.

if they did receive their force from power which the *Prince* doth communicate unto the *Parliament* or to any other *Court* under him, but from power which the whole body of this *Realm* being naturally possessed with hath by free and deliberate assent derived unto him that ruleth over them so far forth as hath been declared. So that our laws made concerning religion do take originally their essence from the power of the whole *Realm* and *Church* of England than which nothing can be more consonant unto the law of nature and the will of our *Lord Jesus Christ.*

To let these go and to return to our own men. [z]*Ecclesiastical* [6.12] *governors* (they say) *may not meddle with the making of civil laws and of laws for the Commonwealth, nor the Civil Magistrate high or low with making of orders for the Church.* It seemeth unto me very strange that those men which are in no cause more vehement and fierce than where they plead that *Ecclesiastical* persons may not κυριεύειν should hold that the power of making *Ecclesiastical* laws which thing is of all other most proper unto dominion, belongeth to none but persons *Ecclesiastical* only. Their oversight groweth herein for want of exact observation what it is to make a law. *Tully* speaking of the law of nature saith [a]"that thereof *God* himself was *Inventor Disceptator Lator*, the deviser the discusser the deliverer. Wherein he plainly alludeth unto the chiefest parts which then did appertain to this public action. For when laws were made the first thing was to have them devised, the second to sift them with as much exactness of judgement as any way might be used, the next by solemn voice of sovereign authority to pass them and give them the force of laws. It cannot in any reason seem otherwise than most fit that unto *Ecclesiastical* persons the care of devising *Ecclesiastical* laws be committed even as the care of *Civil* unto them which are in those affairs most skilful. This taketh not away from *Ecclesiastical* persons all right of giving voice with others, when Civil laws are proposed for regiment of that Commonwealth whereof themselves howsoever now the world would have them annihilated are notwithstanding as yet a part. Much less doth it cut off that part of the power of *Princes* whereby as they claim so we know no reasonable cause wherefore we may not grant them without offence to Almighty God so much authority in making of all manner of laws within their own dominions

[z] T.C., Bk 1, p. 192 [*W*, 3:295–296].
[a] Cicero, *On the Republic*, Bk 3, in Lactantius, *Divine Institutes*, Bk 6, ch. 8.

that neither civil nor Ecclesiastical do pass without their royal assent. In devising and discussing of laws wisdom is specially required, but that which establisheth and maketh them is power, even power of dominion the Chiefty whereof amongst us resteth in the person of the *King.* Is there any law of *Christ's* which forbiddeth *Kings* and rulers of the earth to have such sovereign and supreme power in the making of laws either civil or Ecclesiastical? If there be, our [6.13] Controversy hath an end. Christ in his *Church* hath not appointed any such law concerning temporal power as God did of old deliver unto the *Commonwealth* of *Israel,* but leaving that to be at the world's free choice his chiefest care was that the spiritual law of the gospel might be published far and wide. They that received the law of *Christ* were for a long time people scattered in sundry kingdoms, *Christianity* not exempting them from the laws which they had been subject unto, saving only in such cases as those laws did enjoin that which the religion of *Christ* forbade. Hereupon grew their manifold persecutions throughout all places where they lived. As often as it thus came to pass there was no possibility that the Emperors and *Kings* under whom they lived should meddle any whit at all with making laws for the *Church.* From *Christ* therefore having received power who doubteth but as they did, so they might bind themselves to such orders, as seemed fittest for the maintenance of their religion without the leave of high or low in the *Commonwealth,* forasmuch as in religion it was divided utterly from them and they from it. But when the mightiest began to like of the *Christian* faith, by their means whole free states and *Kingdoms* became obedient unto *Christ.*

Now the question is whether *Kings* by embracing *Christianity* do therein receive any such law, as taketh from them the weightiest part of that sovereignty which they had even when they were Heathens: whether being Infidels they might do more in causes of religion than now they can, by the law of God being true believers. For whereas in *Regal States* the *King* or supreme *Head of* the *Commonwealth* had before *Christianity* a supreme stroke in the making of laws for religion, he must by embracing *Christian* religion utterly thereof deprive himself and in such causes become a subject to his own subjects, having even within his own Dominions them whose Commandment he must obey unless this power be placed in the hand of some foreign spiritual potentate, so that either a foreign or domestical Commander on earth he must needs admit more now than before he had and that in the chiefest things whereupon Commonwealths do stand. But apparent it is unto all men which are not strangers in the doctrine of *Jesus Christ*, that no *State* in the world receiving *Christianity* is by any law therein contained bound to resign the power which they lawfully held before, but over what persons and in what causes soever the same hath been in force it may so remain and continue still. That which as *Kings* they might do in matter of religion and did in matters of false religion being Idolaters or superstitious *Kings*, the same they are now even in every respect as fully authorized to do in all affairs pertinent unto the state of true and *Christian* religion.

.   .   .   .

Power to make laws.

And concerning their supreme power for making laws for all persons [6.14] in all causes to be guided by, it is not to be let pass that the head enemies of this *Headship* are constrained [b]to acknowledge the *King* endowed even with this very power so that he may and ought to exercise the same, taking order for the *Church* and her affairs of what nature or kind soever in case of necessity as when there is no lawful ministry which they interpret then to be (and this surely is a point very remarkable) whensoever the ministry is wicked. A wicked ministry no lawful ministry? and in such sort no lawful ministry that what doth belong to them as ministers by right of their calling the same to be annihilated in respect of their bad quality? Their wickedness in itself a deprivation of right to deal in the affairs of the *Church*, and a warrant for others to deal in them which are held to be of a clean other society the members whereof have been before so peremptorily forever excluded from power of dealing with the affairs of the *Church*? They which have once thoroughly learned this lesson will quickly be capable perhaps of another equivalent unto it. For if the wickedness of the ministry transfer their right unto the *King*, in case the *King* be as wicked as they to whom shall the right descend? There is no remedy, all must come by devolution at the length even as the family of *Brown* will have it unto the godly

[b] T.C., Bk 3, p. 159.

amongst the people; for confusion to the wise and to the great the poor and the simple, some Knipperdoling with his retinue must take the work of the *Lord* in hand and the making of *Church* laws must prove to be their right in the end. If not for love of the truth yet for very shame of so gross absurdities let these contentions and shifting fancies be abandoned.

The cause which moved them for a time to hold a wicked ministry no lawful ministry and in this defect of a lawful ministry authorized *Kings* to make laws and orders for the affairs of the *Church* till the *Church* be well established is surely this. First they see that whereas the continual dealing of the *Kings* of *Israel* in the affairs of the *Church* doth make now very strongly against them, the burden thereof they shall in time well enough shake off, if it may be obtained that it is for *Kings* lawful indeed to follow those holy examples, howbeit no longer than during the aforesaid case of necessity, while the wickedness and in respect thereof the unlawfulness of the ministry doth continue. Secondly they perceive right well that unless they should yield authority unto *Kings* in case of such supposed necessity the discipline they urge were clean excluded as long as the Clergy of *England* doth thereunto remain opposite. To open therefore a door for her entrance there is no remedy but the *Tenet* must be this. That now when the ministry of *England* is universally wicked and in that respect hath lost all authority and is become no lawful ministry, no such ministry as hath the right which other-wise should belong unto them if they were virtuous and godly as their Adversaries are, in this necessity the *King* may do somewhat for the *Church*, that which we do imply in the name of *Headship* he may both have and exercise till they be entered which will disbur-den and ease him of it; till they come the *King* is licensed to hold that power which we call *Headship*. But what afterwards? In a *Church* well ordered ᶜthat which the supreme Magistrate hath is to see that the laws of God touching his worship and touching all matters and orders of the *Church* be executed and duly observed, to see that every Ecclesiastical person do that office whereunto he is appointed, to punish those that fail in their office, in a word (that which *Allen* himself acknowledgeth) ᵈunto the earthly power, which God hath given him, it doth belong to defend the laws of the *Church*,

---

ᶜ T.C., Bk 1, p. 192 [*W*, 3:295–301].
ᵈ William Allen, *Apology*, f. 4, p. 2 [*STC* 369, fol. 40ᵛ].

to cause them to be executed and to punish the *Transgressors* of the same. On all sides therefore it is confessed that to the *King* belongeth power of maintaining laws made for the *Church* regiment and of causing them to be observed. But principality of power in making them which is the thing that we attribute unto *Kings*, this both the one sort and the other doth withstand.

[Appendix to Chapter 6]

Wherein it is from the purpose altogether alleged that *Constantine* [κ6.14; ed. 1888, termeth *Church* officers *[e]overseers of things within the Church, himself* *p. 418 n.1*] *of those without the Church*; that *Hilary [f]*beseecheth the *Emperor Constans* to provide that the Governors of his Provinces should not presume to take upon them the judgement of Ecclesiastical causes, unto whom Commonwealth matters only belonged; that *Ambrose [g]*affirmeth *Palaces to belong unto the Emperor but Churches to the Minister*, the Emperor to have authority of the Common walls of the City and not over holy things. For which cause he would never yield to have the causes of the *Church* debated in the *Prince's Consistory* but excused himself to the Emperor *Valentinian* for that being convented to answer concerning *Church* matters in a *Civil Court*, he came not; that *Augustine [h]*witnesseth how the Emperor not daring to judge of the *Bishop's* cause committed it unto the *Bishops* and was to crave pardon of the *Bishops*, for that by the *Donatists'* importunity which made no end of appealing unto him, he was being weary of them drawn to give sentence in a matter of theirs. All which hereupon may be inferred reacheth no further than only unto the *administration of Church affairs or the determination of strifes and controversies* rising about the matter of religion: It proveth that in former ages of the world it hath been judged most convenient for *Church* officers to have the hearing of causes merely Ecclesiastical and not the Emperor himself in person to give sentence of them. No one man can be sufficient for all things.

[e] Eusebius, *Life of Constantine*, Bk 4 [ch. 24].
[f] Hilary of Poitiers, *Book to Constantius Augustus* [CSEL, 65:181–182].
[g] Book 5, epist. 33 [*PL*, 16:999; *FOTC*, 26:371].
[h] Epist. 166 [or 105; *CSEL*, 34:600–601; *FOTC*, 18:201–2]. Epist. 162 [or 43; *CSEL*, 34:87–102, *FOTC*, 12:185–200].

And therefore public affairs are divided each kind in all well ordered States allotted unto such kind of persons as reason presumeth fittest to handle them. Reason cannot presume *Kings* ordinarily so skilful as to be personal Judges meet for the common hearing and determining of *Church Controversies*, but they which are hereunto appointed, and have all their proceedings authorized by such power as may cause them to take effect. The principality of which power in making laws whereupon all these things depend is not by any [K6.14] of these allegations proved incommunicable unto *Kings* although not both in such sort but that still it is granted by the one that albeit Ecclesiastical Councils consisting of *Church Officers* did frame the laws, whereby the *Church* affairs were ordered in ancient times, yet no *Canon* no not of any *Council* had the force of a law in the *Church* unless it were ratified and confirmed by the *Emperor* being *Christian.*

Seeing therefore it is acknowledged 'that it was then the manner of the Emperor to confirm the ordinances which were made by the Ministers, which is as much in effect to say that the Emperor had in *Church* Ordinances a voice negative and that without his confirmation they had not the strength of public ordinances, why are we condemned as giving more unto *Kings* than the *Church* did in those times we giving them no more but that supreme power which the Emperor did then exercise with much larger scope than at this day any *Christian King* either doth or possibly can use it over the *Church?*

Of their power in making ecclesiastical governors.

[7.1] 7. Touching the advancement of *Prelates* unto their rooms by the *King*, whereas it seemeth in the eyes of many a thing very strange that *Prelates* the officers of God's own Sanctuary than which nothing is more sacred should be made by persons secular; there are that will not have kings be altogether of the laity but to participate that sanctified power which God hath endowed his Clergy with and that in such respect they are *Anointed* with oil. A shift vain and needless forasmuch as if we speak properly we cannot say *Kings*

' T.C., Bk I, p. 193 [*W*, 3:303–308].

do make, but that they only do place *Bishops*. For in a *Bishop* there are these three things to be considered, the power whereby he is distinguished from other *Pastors*, the special portion of the Clergy and people over whom he is to exercise that Bishoply power; and the place of his seat or throne together with the profits preeminences honours thereunto belonging. The first every *Bishop* hath by consecration, the second his election investeth him with, the third he receiveth of the *King* alone.

With consecration of the *King* intermeddleth not further than only [7.2] by his letters to present such an elect *Bishop* as shall be consecrated. Seeing therefore that none but *Bishops* do consecrate, it followeth that none but they only do give unto every *Bishop* his being. The manner of uniting *Bishops* as heads unto the flock, and clergy under them, hath often altered. For if some be not deceived this thing was sometime done even without any election at all. *ʲAt the first* (saith he to whom the name of *Ambrose* is given) *the first created in the College of Presbyters was still the Bishop. He dying the next Senior did succeed him. Sed quia cœperunt Sequentes Presbyteri indigni inveniri ad primatus tenendos immutata est ratio prospiciente Concilio ut non ordo sed meritum crearet Episcopum multorum Sacerdotum judicio constitutum ne indignus temere usurparet et esset multis scandalum.* In elections at the beginning the Clergy and the people both had to do, although not both after one sort. The people gave their testimony and showed their affection either of desire or dislike concerning the party which was to be chosen. But the choice was wholly in the sacred College of *Presbyters*. Hereunto it is that those usual speeches of the ancient do commonly allude, as when *Pontius* concerning *St. Cyprian's* election saith he was chosen *ᵏjudicio Dei et populi favore*, by the judgement of God and favour of the people, the one branch alluding to the voices of the Ecclesiastical senate which with religious sincerity chose him, the other to the people's affection, who earnestly desired to have him chosen their *Bishop*. Again *Leo, ˡNulla ratio sinit, ut inter Episcopos habeantur qui nec a Clericis sunt electi nec a plebibus*

ʲ Pseudo-Ambrose on Ephes. 4 [*CSEL*, 81:99–100]. [*But because the following presbyters began to be found unworthy of holding the primacy, this course was changed, and it was provided for by council that not order but merit should make a bishop, decided upon by the judgement of many priests, lest someone unworthy should chance to take office and there be scandal to many.*]

ᵏ Pontius the Deacon, *Life of Cyprian* [*CSEL*, 3(3):xcv; *FOTC*, 15:9].

ˡ Gratian, *Decretum*, 1.62.1.

expetiti. No reason doth grant that they should be reckoned amongst *Bishops* whom neither Clergy hath elected, nor *Laity* coveted. In like sort *Honorius,* *"Let him only be established Bishop in the See of Rome, whom Divine judgement and universal consent hath chosen.*

[7.3]   That difference which is between the form of electing *Bishops* at this day with us and that which was usual in former ages riseth from the ground of that right which the *Kings* of this land do claim in furnishing the place where *Bishops* elected and consecrated are to reside as *Bishops.* For considering the huge charges which the ancient famous Princes of this land have been at as well in erecting *Episcopal Sees,* as also in endowing them with ample possessions sure of their religious magnificence and bounty we cannot think but to have been most deservedly honoured with those royal prerogatives, taking the benefit which groweth out of them in their vacancy and of advancing alone unto such dignities what persons they judge most fit for the same. A thing over and besides even therefore the more reasonable for that as the *King* most justly hath preeminence to make *Lords* temporal which are not such by right of birth, so the like preeminence of bestowing where pleaseth him the honour of spiritual nobility also cannot seem hard, Bishops being Peers of the realm and by law itself so reckoned.

    Now whether we grant so much unto *Kings* in this respect or in the former consideration whereupon *"the laws have annexed it into the Crown it must of necessity being granted both make void whatsoever interest the people aforetime hath had towards the choice of their own *Bishop* and also restrain the very act of canonical election usually made by the *Dean* and *Chapter* as with us in such sort it doth that they *"neither can proceed unto any election till leave be granted, *"nor elect any person but that is named unto them. If they might do the one it would be in them to defeat the *King* of his profits: if the other then were the *King's* preeminences of granting those dignities nothing. And therefore were it not for certain *"Canons* requiring canonical election to be before consecration I see no cause but that the *King's* letters patent alone might suffice well enough to that purpose as by law they do in case those *Electors* should happen not to satisfy the *King's* pleasure. Their election is now but a matter

m Epistle of the Emperor Honorius to Boniface I, *Councils* [Venice, 1585], Tome 1[:813].
n 25 Edward III [*SR*, 1:316–318].   *o* 25 Edward III [*SR*, 1:318].
p 25 Henry VIII, ch. 20 [*SR*, 3:463].   *q* Gratian, *Decretum*, 1.62.3.

of form. It is the *King's* mere grant which placeth and the *Bishops'* consecration which maketh *Bishops*. Neither do the *Kings* of this [7.4] Land use herein any other than such prerogatives as foreign nations have been accustomed unto.

About the year of our *Lord* 425, 'Pope Boniface solicited most earnestly the Emperor *Honorius* to take some order that the *Bishops* of *Rome* might be created without ambitious seeking of the place. A needless petition if so be the Emperor had no right at all in the placing of *Bishops* there. But from the days of *Justinian* the Emperor about the year 553, *'Onuphrius* himself doth grant that no man was *Bishop* in the *See* of *Rome* whom first the Emperor by his letters patent did not license to be consecrated till in *Benedict's* time it pleased the Emperor to forgo that right which afterwards was restored to *Charles* with augmentation and continued in his Successors till such time as *Hildebrand* took it from *Henry IV*, and ever since the *Cardinals* have held it as at this day.

Had not the right of giving them belonged to the Emperors of *Rome* within the compass of their dominions what needed Pope *Leo IV* to trouble *Lotharius* and *Lodowick* with those his letters whereby having done them to understand that the *Church* called *Reatina* was without a *Bishop*, he maketh suit that one *Colonus* might have the room, or if that were otherwise disposed of his next request was, *'Tusculanam Ecclesiam quæ viduata existit illi vestra Serenitas dignetur concedere ut consecratus a nostro presulatu Deo omnipotenti, vestroque imperio grates peragere valeat.* May it please your Clemencies to grant unto him the *Church* of *Tusculum* now likewise void that by our Episcopal authority he being after consecrated may be to Almighty God and your *Highness* therefore thankful.

Touching other Bishoprics extant, there is a very short but a [7.5] plain "Discourse written almost 500 years since by occasion of that miserable contention raised between the Emperor *Henry IV* and *Pope Hildebrand* named otherwise *Gregory VII*, not as *Platina* would bear men in hand for that the *Bishop* of *Rome* would not brook the Emperor's simoniacal dealings, but because the right which *Christian Kings* and Emperors had to invest *Bishops* hindered so

′ Tome I, *Councils* [Venice, 1585; pp. 812, 813].

ˢ Onuphrius Panvinius on Bartolomeo Platina's *Life* of Pelagius II.

ᵗ Gratian, *Decretum*, 1.63.16.

ᵘ Walthramus of Naumburg, *On the Investiture of Bishops to be Done by Emperors.*

much his ambitious designments that nothing could detain him from attempting to wrest it violently out of their hands. This treatise I mention for that it shortly comprehendeth not only the forealleged right of the Emperor of *Rome* acknowledged by six several Popes even with bitter execration against whomsoever of their successors that should by word or deed, at any time go about to infringe the same but also further these other specialties appertaining thereunto. First, that the Bishops likewise of *Spain, England, Scotland, Hungary* had by ancient institution always been invested by their *Kings* without opposition or disturbance. Secondly, that such was their royal interest partly for that they were founders of *Bishoprics*, partly because they undertook the defence of them against all ravenous oppressions and wrongs, partly inasmuch that it was not safe, that rooms of so great power and consequence in their estate should without their appointment be held by any under them. And therefore that Bishops even then did homage and took their oaths of fealty unto the *Kings* which invested them. Thirdly, that what solemnity or ceremony *Kings* do use in this action it skilleth not, as namely whether they do it by word or by precept, set down in writing or by delivery of a staff and a ring, or by any other means whatsoever, only that use and custom would to avoid all offence be kept. Some base *Canonists* there are which contend that neither *Kings* nor Emperors had ever any right hereunto saving only by the *Pope's* either grant or toleration. Whereupon not to spend any further labour we leave their folly to be controlled by men of more ingenuity and judgement even amongst themselves: *Duarenus, Papon, Choppinus, Ægidius, Magister, Arnulphus Ruzæus, Costlius, Philippus Probus*, and the rest, by whom the right of *Christian Kings* and *Princes* herein is maintained to be such as the Bishop of Rome cannot lawfully either withdraw or abridge or hinder. But of this thing there is with us no question although with them there be; the laws and customs of the Realm approving such regalities in case no reason thereof did appear, yet are they hereby abundantly warranted unto us, except some law of God or nature to the contrary could be showed.

How much more when they have been everywhere thought so reasonable that *Christian Kings* throughout the world use and exercise if not altogether yet surely with very little odds the same; so far ^vthat *Gregory X* forbidding such regalities to be newly begun

^v Boniface VIII, *The Sixth Book*, 1.6.13.

where they were not in former times, if any do claim those rights from the first foundation of *Churches* or by ancient custom of them he only requireth that neither they nor their agents damnify the *Church* of God by using the said prerogatives. Now as there is no doubt but the *Church* of *England* by this means is much eased of some inconveniences, so likewise a special care there is requisite to be had that other evils no less dangerous may not grow. By the history of former times it doth appear that when the freedom of elections was most large men's dealings and proceedings therein were not the least faulty. [7.6]

Of the people *St. Jerome* complaineth [w]that their judgements many times went much awry and that in allowing of their Bishops every man favoured his own quality, every one's desire was not so much to be under the regiment of good and virtuous men as of them which were like himself. What man is there whom it doth not exceedingly grieve to read the tumults tragedies and schisms which were raised by occasion of the *Clergy* at such time as diverse of them standing for some one place, there was not any kind of practice though never so unhonest or vile left unessayed whereby men might supplant their competitors and the one side foil the other. *Sidonius* speaking of a *Bishopric* void in his time, [x]*The decease of the former Bishop* (saith he) *was an Alarm to such as would labour for the room: Whereupon the people forthwith betaking themselves unto parts, storm on each side; few there are that make suit for the advancement of any other man; many who not only offer, but enforce themselves. All things light variable counterfeit. What should I say? I see not anything plain and open but impudence only.*

In the *Church* of *Constantinople* about [y]the election of *St. Chrysostom* by reason that some strove mightily for him and some for *Nectarius*, the troubles growing had not been small but that *Arcadius* the Emperor interposed himself; even as at *Rome* the Emperor *Valentinian*, [z]whose forces were hardly able to establish *Damasus Bishop* and to compose the strife between him and his competitor *Ursicinus*

---

[w] *Against Jovinian*, Bk 1 [ch. 34; *PL*, 23:258].

[x] Bk 7, Epist. 5 [*PL*, 58:568].

[y] Theodoret, *Ecclesiastical History*, Bk 5, ch. 27. Sozomen, *Ecclesiastical History*, Bk 8, ch. 2.

[z] Ammianus Marcellinus, *Rerum Gestarum*, Bk 15 [Bk 27, ch. 3; *L*, 3:18–21]. Socrates, *Ecclesiastical History*, Bk 2, ch. 27; Bk 4, ch. 29. Theodoret, *Ecclesiastical History*, Bk 2, chs. 15–17. Sozomen, *Ecclesiastical History*, Bk 4, ch. 11 and Bk 6, ch. 23.

about whose election the blood of a 137 was already shed. Where things did not break out into so manifest and open flames yet between them which obtained the place and such as before withstood their promotion, that secret heart-burning often grew which could not afterwards be easily slaked; insomuch that *ªPontius* doth note it as a rare point of virtue in *Cyprian*, that whereas some were against his election, he notwithstanding dealt ever after in most friendly manner with them, all men wondering that so good a memory was [7.7] so easily able to forget. These and other the like hurts accustomed to grow from ancient elections we do not feel. Howbeit lest the *Church* in more hidden sort should sustain even as grievous detriment by that order which is now of force we are most humbly to crave at the hands of our Sovereign *Kings* and *Governors*, the highest *Patrons* which this *Church* of *Christ* hath on earth that it would please them to be advertised thus much.

Albeit these things which have been sometimes done by any sort may afterwards appertain unto others and so the kind of agents vary as occasions daily growing shall require, yet sundry unremovable and unchangeable burdens of duty there are annexed unto every kind of public action, which burdens in this case *Princes* must know themselves to stand now charged with in God's sight no less than the people and the Clergy, when the power of electing their *Prelates* did rest fully and wholly in them.

A fault it had been if they should in choice have preferred *ᵇ*any whom desert of most holy life and the gift of divine wisdom did not commend, *ᶜ*a fault if they had permitted long the rooms of the principal *Pastors* of God to continue void, not to preserve the *Church* patrimony as good to each successor as any predecessor did enjoy the same, had been in them a most odious and grievous fault. Simply, good and evil do not lose their nature. That which was is the one or the other whatsoever the subject of either be. The faults mentioned are in *Kings* by so much greater for that in what *Churches* they exercise those regalities whereof we do now entreat the same churches they have received into their special care and custody, with no less effectual obligation of conscience than the *Tutor* standeth bound in for the person and state of that pupil

---

ª Life of Cyprian [*CSEL*, 3(3):xcvi; *FOTC*, 15:10; *ANF*, 5:269].
ᵇ Gratian, *Decretum*, 1.63.4.
ᶜ Gratian, *Decretum*, 1.63. 18.

whom he hath solemnly taken upon him to protect and keep. All power is given unto edification, none to the overthrow and destruction of the *Church*. Concerning therefore the fourth branch of spiritual dominion, thus much may suffice, seeing that they with whom we contend do not directly oppose themselves against Regalities but only so far forth as generally they hold that no *Church-dignity* should be granted without consent of the Common People, and that there ought not to be in the *Church* of *Christ* any Episcopal rooms for Princes to use their regalities in. Of both which questions we have sufficiently spoken before.

.   .   .   .

One man. Then could not any of them be under another's auth- [App.4] ority so far as thereby to be either licensed or hindered in those things which he doth by the said power but God alone should himself on earth authorize and disauthorize all that bore rule in the *Church*. Wherefore to set down briefly that which we hold for truth. Power Ecclesiastical itself is originally God's ordinance he hath appointed it to be, and therefore in that respect on him only they all which have it are most rightly said to depend. The derivation of that power into the several persons which have it is the proper deed of the *Church* and of those high *Ministers* which are in that case appointed to ordain and consecrate such as from time to time shall exercise and use the same. Furthermore since when they have that power, it resteth nevertheless unexercised except some part of the people of God be permitted them to work upon, they must of necessity for the peaceable and quiet practice of their authority upon the persons of men where all are subject to a *Christian King* depend in that respect on him also.

By holding therefore this dependency whereof we speak it is not meant that either the *King* did first institute or that he doth confer and give the grace of *Ecclesiastical* presidency but only add unto it exercise by the furtherance of his supereminent authority and power without the predominant concurrency whereof spiritual jurisdiction could take no effect, men's persons could not in open and orderly sort be subject thereunto. A Bishop whose calling is authorized wholly from God and received by imposition of sacred hands can execute safely no act of *Episcopal* authority on any one of the

King's liege people, otherwise than under him who hath sovereignty over them all.

· · · ·

Of their power in judgement ecclesiastical.

[8.1] 8. Touching the *King's* supereminent authority in commanding and in the judging of causes *Ecclesiastical,* first to explain therein our meaning, it hath been taken as if we did hold that *Kings* may prescribe what themselves think good to be done in the service of God, how the word shall be taught, how Sacraments administered; that *Kings* may personally sit in the *Consistory* where *Bishops* do, hearing and determining what causes soever do appertain unto the *Courts*; that *Kings* and *Queens* in their own proper persons are by judicial sentence to decide the questions which rise about matter of faith and *Christian* religion; that *Kings* may excommunicate; finally that Kings may do whatsoever is incident unto the office and duty of an Ecclesiastical judge. Which opinion because we count as absurd as they who have fathered the same upon us, we do them to wit that thus our meaning is and no otherwise. There is not within this realm any Ecclesiastical officer that may by the authority of his own place command universally throughout the *King's* dominions, but they of his people, whom one may command are to another's commandment unsubject. Only the *King's* royal power is of so large compass that no man commanded by him according to order of law can plead himself to be without the bounds and limits of that authority, I say according to order of law, because with us the highest have thereunto so tied themselves that otherwise than so they take not
[8.2] upon them to command any. And that *Kings* should be in such sort supreme commanders over all men we hold it requisite as well for the ordering of spiritual as of civil affairs inasmuch as without universal authority in this kind they should not be able when need serves to do as virtuous kings have done. *Joash* purposing to renew the house of the *Lord* assembled the *Priests* and *Levites* and when they were together gave them their charge saying *[d]Go out unto the Cities of* Judah, *and gather of all* Israel *money to repair the house of*

[d] 2 Chron. 24:5–9, 30:6.

208

your God, *from year to year and haste the thing. But the* Levites *hasted not. Therefore the king called* Jehoiada *the chief and said unto him, why hast thou not required of the* Levites, *to bring in out of* Judah *and* Jerusalem *the tax of* Moses *the servant of the* Lord, *and of the Congregation of* Israel *for the Tabernacle of the Testimony? For wicked* Athalia *and her children broke up the house of* God, *and all the things that were dedicated for the house of the* Lord *did they bestow upon* Balaam. *Therefore the King comanded and they made a chest, and set it at the gate of the house of the* Lord *without, and they made a Proclamation through* Judah *and* Jersualem, *to bring unto the* Lord *the tax of* Moses, *the servant of* God, *laid upon* Israel *in the wilderness.* Could either he have done this or after him *Hezekiah* the like concerning the celebration of the Passover but that all sorts of men in all things did owe unto those their Sovereign Rulers the same obedience which sometime *Joshua* had them by solemn vow and promise bound unto? *ᵉWhosoever shall rebel against thy Commandments, and will not obey thy words in all that thou commandest him, let him be put to death, only be strong and of good courage.* Furthermore judgement Ecclesiastical [8.3] we say is necessary for decision of Controversies rising between man and man and for correction of faults committed in the affairs of God, unto the due execution whereof there are three things necessary: *Law judges and a Supreme Governor* of judgements. What *Courts* there shall be and what causes shall belong to each *Court* and what judges shall determine of every cause and what order in all judgements shall be kept; of these things the laws have sufficiently disposed, so that his duty which sitteth in every such *Court* is to judge not of but after the said laws. *ᶠImprimis illud observare debet Judex, ne aliter judicet quam Legibus aut constitutionibus aut moribus proditum est.* Which laws (for we mean the positive laws of our own Realm concerning Ecclesiastical affairs) if they otherwise dispose of any such thing than according to the law of reason and of God; we must both acknowledge them to be amiss and endeavour to have them reformed. But touching that point what may be objected shall after appear.

Our Judges in causes Ecclesiastical are either Ordinary or Commissionary. Ordinary those, whom we term Ordinaries, and such by the laws of the land, are none but *Prelates* only, whose power

---

ᵉ Joshua 1:18.   ᶠ Justinian, *Institutes*, 4.17, pref.

to do that which they do is in themselves, and belongeth unto the nature of their *Ecclesiastical* calling. In spiritual causes a lay person may be no Ordinary; a Commissionary Judge there is no let but that he may be. And that our laws do evermore reserve the Ordinary judgement of spiritual causes unto *Spiritual* Persons such as are termed *Ordinaries* no man which knoweth any thing in the practice of this Realm can easily be ignorant.

[8.4]   Now besides them which are authorized to judge in several territories is required an universal power, which reacheth over all importing supreme authority of government over all Courts all Judges all Causes, the operation of which power is as well to strengthen maintain and uphold particular jurisdictions, which happily might else be of small effect, as also to remedy that which they are not able to help and to redress that wherein they at any time do otherwise than they ought to do. This power being sometime in the *Bishop* of *Rome*, who by sinister practices had drawn it into his hands, was for just considerations by public consent annexed unto the *King's* royal seat and crown. From thence the *Authors* of reformation would translate it into their *National* assemblies and Synods, which Synods are the only help that they think lawful to use against such evils in the *Church* as particular jurisdictions are not sufficient to redress. In which case our laws have provided ᵍthat the *King's* supereminent authority and power shall serve, as namely when the whole Ecclesiastical state or the principal persons therein do need visitation and reformation; when in any part of the *Church* errors, heresies, schisms, abuses, offences, contempts, enormities are grown which men in their several jurisdictions either do not or cannot help. Whatsoever any spiritual authority or power (such as *Legates* from the *See* of *Rome* did sometimes exercise) hath done or might heretofore have done for the remedy of those evils in lawful sort, that is to say without violation of the law of God or nature in the deed done as much in every degree our laws have fully granted that the *King* forever may do not only by setting *Ecclesiastical Synods* on work, that the thing may be their act and the *King* their motioner unto it (for so much perhaps the Masters of reformation will grant) but by Commissionaries few or many who having the *King's* letters Patent may in the virtue thereof execute the premises* as agents in the

---

ᵍ 1 Elizabeth, ch. 1 [*SR*, 4.1:352].

---

* *F:* promises

right not of their own peculiar and ordinary but of his supereminent power.

When men are wronged by inferior *Judges* or have any just cause [8.5] to take exception against them, their way for redress is to make their appeal. An appeal is a present delivery of him which maketh it, out of the hands of their power and jurisdiction from whence it is made. *Pope Alexander* having sometime the *King* of *England* at the advantage caused him amongst other things to agree, that as many of his subjects as would might appeal to the *Court of Rome.* *[h]And thus* (saith one) *that whereunto a mean person at this day would scorn to submit himself, so great a* King *was content to be subject. Notwithstanding even when the* Pope (saith he) *had so great authority amongst* Princes *which were far off, the* Romans *he could not frame to obedience, nor was able to obtain that himself might abide at* Rome, *though promising not to meddle with other than* Ecclesiastical *affairs.* So much are things that terrify more feared by such as behold them a loof of, than at hand. Reformers I doubt not in some cases will admit *Appeals* made unto their *Synods* even as the *Church* of *Rome* doth allow of them so they be made to the *Bishop* of *Rome.*

As for that kind of *[i]Appeal* which the *English* laws do approve from the Judge of any particular *Court,* unto the *King* as the only supreme Governor on earth who by his *Delegates* may give a final definitive sentence from which no further appeal can be made, will their platform allow of this? Surely forasmuch as in that estate which they all dream of the whole *Church* must be divided into *Parishes* of which none can have greater or less authority and power than another. Again, the *King* himself must be but as a common member in the body of his own parish and the causes of that only parish must be by the officers thereof determinable. In case the *King* had so much preferment as to be made one of those Officers (for otherwise by their positions he were not to meddle any more than the meanest amongst his subjects with the judgement of any *Ecclesiastical* cause) how is it possible they should allow of *Appeals* to be made from any other abroad to the *King?* To receive appeals from all [8.6] other *Judges* belongeth unto the highest in power over all, and to be in power over all as touching the judgement of *Ecclesiastical* causes, this as they think belongeth only unto *Synods.* Whereas therefore

---

[h] Machiavelli, *History of Florence*, Bk 1.   [i] 25 Henry VIII, ch. 19 [*SR*, 3:461].

with us *Kings* do exercise over all kinds of persons and causes power, both of voluntary and litigious jurisdiction so that according to the one they visit reform and command, according to the other they judge universally doing both in far other sort than such as have ordinary spiritual power; oppugned herein we are, by some colourable show of argument, as if to grant thus much unto any secular person it were unreasonable. *[j]For since it is* (say they) *apparent out of the* Chronicles *that judgement in Church matters pertaineth unto God; seeing likewise it is evident out of the Apostle that the high* Priest *is set over those matters in God's behalf, it must needs follow that the principality or direction of the judgement of them is by God's ordinance appertaining unto the high* Priest *and consequently to the ministry of the* Church, *and if it be by God's ordinance appertaining unto them how can it be translated from them unto the Civil Magistrate?* Which argument briefly drawn into form lieth thus. That which belongeth unto God may not be translated unto any other than whom he hath appointed to have it in his behalf. But principality of judgement in *Church matters* appertaineth unto God, which hath appointed the *High Priest* and consequently the Ministry of the *Church* alone to have it in this behalf. Therefore it may not from them be translated to the *Civil Magistrate.* The first of which three propositions we grant, as also in the second, that branch which ascribeth unto God *Principality* in the *Church matters.* But that either he did appoint none but only the high *Priest* to exercise the said principality for him, or that the Ministry of the *Church* may in reason from thence be concluded to have alone the same principality by his appointment, these two points we deny utterly.

For concerning the high Priest there is first no such ordinance of God to be found. *[k]Every high Priest* (saith the Apostle) *is taken from among men and is ordained for men in things pertaining to God.* Whereupon it may well be gathered that the *Priest* was indeed ordained of *God* to have power in things pertaining unto God, for the Apostle doth there mention the power of offering gifts and sacrifices for sins, which kind of power was not only given of God unto Priests but restrained unto *Priests* only. The power of jurisdiction and ruling authority this also God gave them but not them alone. For it is held as all men know that others of the *Laity* were herein

---

[j] T.C., Bk 3, p. 154. 2 Chron. 19:8. Heb. 5:1.   *[k]* Heb. 5:1.

joined by the law with them. But concerning principality in *Church* affairs (for of this our question is and of no other) the *Priests* neither had it alone nor at all but (as hath been already showed) principality in spiritual affairs was the royal prerogative of *Kings*.

Again though it were so that *God* had appointed the high *Priest* to have the said principality of government in those matters, yet how can they who allege this enforce thereby that consequently the Ministry of the *Church* and no other ought to have the same, when they are so far off from allowing as much to the Ministry of the Gospel as the priesthood of the law had by God's appointment; that we but collecting thereout a difference in authority and jurisdiction amongst the Clergy to be for the polity of the *Church* not inconvenient, they forthwith think to close up our mouths by answering that the Jewish high Priests had authority above the rest, only in that they prefigured the sovereignty of *Jesus Christ*. As for the Ministers of the *Gospel* it is (they say) altogether unlawful to give them as much as the least title any syllable that any way may sound towards principality, and of the regency which may be granted; they hold others even of the *Laity* no less capable than Pastors themselves. How shall these things cleave together? The truth is that they have [8.7] some reason to think it not all of the fittest for *Kings* to sit as ordinary Judges in matters of faith and religion. An Ordinary Judge must be of that quality which in a supreme judge is not necessary because the person of the one is charged with that which the other's authority dischargeth without employing personally himself therein.

It is an error to think that the *King's* authority can have no force or power in the doing of that which himself may not personally do. For first impossible it is, that at one and the same time the *King* in person should order so many and so different affairs as by his power everywhere present are wont to be ordered both in peace and at war at home and abroad. Again the *King* in regard of his nonage or minority may be unable to perform that thing wherein years of discretion are requisite for personal action, and yet his authority even then be of force. For which cause we say that the *King's* authority dieth not but is and worketh always alike. Sundry considerations there may be effectual to withhold the *King's* person from being a doer of that, which his power must notwithstanding give force unto. Even in civil affairs, where nothing doth either more concern the duty or better beseem the *Majesty* of *Kings*, than personally to administer justice unto their people as most famous Princes have done, yet if it be in case of felony or treason the learned of the laws of this *Realm* do plainly affirm *'*that well may the *King* commit his authority unto another to judge between him and the offender but the *King* being himself here a party he cannot personally sit to give judgement. As therefore the person of the *King* may for just consideration even where the cause is civil be notwithstanding withdrawn from occupying the seat of judgement and others under his authority be fit, he unfit himself to judge: so the considerations for which it were happily not convenient for *Kings* to sit and give sentence in spiritual *Courts*, where causes Ecclesiastical are usually debated can be no bar to that force and efficacy which their sovereign power hath over those very *Consistories* and for which we hold without any exception that all *Courts* are the *King's*. All men are not for all things sufficient. And therefore public affairs being divided, such persons must be authorized Judges in each kind as common reason may presume to be most fit. Which cannot of *Kings* and *Princes* ordinarily be presumed in causes merely Ecclesiastical, so that even *Common* sense doth rather adjudge this burden unto other men. We see it hereby a thing necessary to put a difference as well between that ordinary jurisdiction, which belongeth to the Clergy alone and that Commissionary wherein others are for just consideration appointed to join with them as also between both these *Jurisdictions* and a third whereby the *King* hath a transcendent authority and that in all causes over both. Why this may not lawfully be granted [8.8] unto him there is no reason. A time there was when *Kings* were not capable of any such power as namely while they professed themselves open adversaries unto *Christ* and *Christianity*. A time there followed when they being capable took sometimes more sometimes less to themselves as seemed best in their own eyes because no certainty touching their right was as yet determined. The Bishops who alone were before accustomed to have the ordering of such affairs saw very just cause of grief when the highest favoring heresy withstood by the strength of sovereign authority religious proceedings, whereupon they oftentimes against this new unresistable power pleaded that use and custom which had been to the contrary, namely that the affairs of the *Church* should be dealt in by

---

¹ Staundford, *Pleas of the Crown*, Bk 2, ch. 3.

the *Clergy* and by no other. Unto which purpose the sentences that then were uttered in defence of unabolished orders and laws, against such as did of their own heads contrary thereunto are now altogether impertinently brought in opposition against them who use but the power which laws have given them, unless men can show that there is in those laws some manifest iniquity or injustice. Whereas therefore against the force judicial and imperial which supreme authority hath *[m]*it is alleged how *[n]Constantine* termeth *Church officers* overseers of things within the *Church*, himself of those without the *Church*; how *[o]Augustine* witnesseth that the *Emperor* not daring to judge of the *Bishop's* cause committed it unto the *Bishops* and was to crave pardon of the *Bishops* for that by the *Donatists'* importunity, which made no end of appealing unto him he was (being weary of them) drawn to give sentence in a matter of theirs; how *[p]Hilary* beseecheth the *Emperor Constans* to provide that the Governors of his provinces should not presume to take upon them the judgement of *Ecclesiastical* causes to whom *Commonwealth* matters only belonged; how *[q]Ambrose* affirmeth that Palaces belong unto the Emperor, Churches to the minister; that the Emperor hath authority over the Common walls of the City and not in holy things, for which cause he never would yield to have the causes of the *Church* debated in the *Prince's Consistory* but excused himself to the Emperor *Valentinian* for that being convented to answer concerning *Church Matters* in a *Civil* court he came not. Besides these testimonies of antiquity which *Mr. Cartwright* bringeth forth, *Dr. Stapleton* who likewise *[r]*citeth them one by one to the same purpose hath augmented the number of them by adding other of the like nature, namely how *Hosius* the *Bishop* of *Cordova* answered the Emperor saying, *[s]God hath committed to thee Empire; with those things that belong to the Church he hath put us in trust;* how *Leontius Bishop* of *Tripolis* also told the selfsame Emperor as much, *[t]I wonder how thou which*

[m] T.C., Bk 3, p. 155.

[n] Eusebius, *Life of Constantine*, Bk 4 [ch. 24].

[o] Epist. 166 [*CSEL*, 34:600–601; *FOTC*, 18:201–202]. Epist. 162 [*CSEL*, 34:87–102; *FOTC*, 12:185–200].

[p] Hilary of Poitiers, *Book to Constantius Augustus* [*CSEL*, 65:181–182].

[q] Book 5, epist. 33 [*PL*, 16:999; *FOTC*, 26:371].

[r] Stapleton, Bk 5, controversy 2, ch. 18.

[s] In Athanasius' *Epistle to those Leading the Monastic Life* [*PG*, 25:745].

[t] Suidas on the word Leontius.

*art called unto one thing takest upon thee to deal in another. For being
placed in military and politic affairs in things that belong unto Bishops
alone thou wilt bear rule.* We may by these testimonies drawn from
antiquity if we list to consider them discern how requisite it is that
authority should always follow received laws in the manner of proceeding. For inasmuch as there was at the first no certain law determining what force the principal civil Magistrate's authority should
be of, how far it should reach and what order it should observe
but *Christian* Emperors from time to time did what themselves
thought most reasonable in those affairs. By this means it cometh
to pass that they in their practice vary and are not uniform.

Virtuous Emperors, such as *Constantine* the Great was, made conscience to swerve unnecessarily from the customs which had been
used in the *Church* even when it lived under Infidels. *Constantine*
of reverence to *Bishops* and their spiritual authority rather abstained
from that which himself might lawfully do than was willing to claim
a power not fit or decent for him to exercise. The order which
had been before he ratified exhorting *Bishops* to look to the *Church*
and promising that he would do the office of a *Bishop* over the
Commonwealth. Which very *Constantine* notwithstanding did not
thereby so renounce all authority in judging of spiritual causes but
that sometime he took "as *St. Augustine* witnesseth even personal
cognition of them. Howbeit whether as purposing to give therein
judicially any sentence I stand in doubt. For if the other of whom
St. Augustine elsewhere speaketh did in such sort judge, surely there
was cause why he should excuse it as a thing not usually done.
Otherwise there is no let but that any such great person may hear
those causes to and fro debated and deliver in the end his own
opinion of them, declaring on which side himself doth judge that
the truth is. But this kind of sentence bindeth no side to stand
thereunto, it is a sentence of private persuasion and not of solemn
jurisdiction albeit a *King* or an Emperor pronounce it. Again on
the contrary part when governors infected with heresy were possessed of the highest power they thought they might use it as pleased
themselves to further by all means therewith that opinion which
they desired should prevail. They not respecting at all what was
meet presumed to command and judge all men in all causes without

---

" Epist. 68 [or 88; *CSEL*, 34:411; *FOTC*, 18:27].

either care of orderly proceeding or regard to such laws and customs as the *Church* had been wont to observe. So that the one sort feared to do even that which they might, and that which the other ought not they boldly presumed upon. The one sort modestly excused themselves where they scarce needed the other though doing that which was inexcusable bore it out with main power not enduring to be told by any man how far they roved beyond their bounds. So great odds between them, whom before we mentioned and such as the younger *Valentinian* by whom *St. Ambrose* being commanded to yield up one of the *Churches* under him unto the *Arians*, whereas they which were sent on the message alleged that the Emperor did but use his own right forasmuch as all things were in his power, the answer which the holy *Bishop* gave them was *^vThat the* Church *is the house of God and that those things which be God's are not to be yielded up and disposed of at the Emperor's will and pleasure; his Palaces he might grant unto whomsoever, but God's own habitations not so.* A cause why many times Emperors did more by their absolute authority than could very well stand with reason, was the over-great importunity of wicked *Heretics* who being enemies to peace and quietness cannot otherwise than by violent means be supported. In this respect therefore we must needs think the state of our own [8.9] *Church* much better settled than theirs was because our laws have with far more certainty prescribed bounds unto each kind of power. All decisions of things doubtful and corrections of things amiss are proceeded in by order of law, what person soever he be unto whom the administration of judgement belongeth. It is neither permitted unto Prelates nor Prince to judge or determine at their own discretion, but law hath prescribed what both shall do. What power the *King* hath he hath it by law, the bounds and limits of it are known. The entire community giveth general order by law how all things publicly are to be done and the *King* as the head thereof the highest in authority over all causeth according to the same law every particular to be framed and ordered thereby. The whole body politic maketh laws which laws give power unto the *King* and the *King* having bound himself to use according unto law that power, it so falleth out that the execution of the one is accomplished by the other in most religious and peaceable sort. There is no cause

---

^v Epist. 20.16 [*PL*, 16:999; *FOTC*, 26:371].

given unto any to make supplication as *Hilary* did that *Civil Governors* to whom *Commonwealth matters* only belong might not presume to take upon them the judgement of *Ecclesiastical* causes. If the cause be spiritual, secular Courts do not meddle with it; we need not excuse ourselves with *Ambrose* but boldly and lawfully we may refuse to answer before any Civil judge in a matter which is not Civil: so that we do not mistake the nature either of the cause or of the *Court* as we easily may do both without some better direction than can be had by the rules of this new-found Discipline. But of this most certain we are that our laws do neither suffer *"*a spiritual Court to entertain those causes which by law are civil, nor yet if the matter be indeed spiritual, a mere civil Court to give judgement of it. Touching supreme power therefore to command all men, and in all manner of causes of judgement to be highest, let thus much suffice as well for declaration of our own meaning as for defence of the truth therein.

Of their exemption from judicial kinds of punishment by the clergy

[9.1] 9. The last thing of all which concerns the *King's* Supremacy is whether thereby he may be exempted from being subject to that judicial power which *Ecclesiastical* consistories have over men. It seemeth first in most men's judgements to be requisite that on earth there should not be any alive altogether without standing in awe of some by whom they may be controlled and bridled.

The good estate of a *Commonwealth* within itself is thought on nothing to depend more than upon these two special affections fear

---

" See the statutes of Edward I [*SR*, 1:147] and Edward II [*SR*, 1:171–172] and *The New Nature of Briefs* [*STC* 10962, fol. 39ᵛ] touching prohibition. See also in Bracton these Sentences, Bk 5, ch. 2 [ed. 1968–77, 4:248–251]. *There is one jurisdiction, ordinary or delegated, which pertains to the Priesthood and the Ecclesiastical forum, as in spiritual causes and those annexed to a spirituality. There is also another Jurisdiction, ordinary or delegated, which pertains to the Crown and dignity of the King and to the Realm, in causes and pleas touching temporal things in the secular forum. Again, Since there are different Jurisdictions and different Judges and different causes, every judge ought first to decide whether the jurisdiction is his, lest he seem to put his sickle into another's harvest. Again, It is not for the King or the secular Judge to enjoin penances, nor do they have cognizance of things annexed to spiritualities, as tithes and other profits of the Church. Again, A Layman is not to be brought before an Ecclesiastical Judge about anything that could and should be determined in the secular forum.*

and love: fear in the highest Governor himself and love in the subjects that live under him. The Subjects' love for the most part continueth as long as the righteousness of *Kings* doth last in whom virtue decayeth not as long as they fear to do that which may alienate the loving hearts of their Subjects from them. Fear to do evil groweth from the harm which evil-doers are to suffer. If therefore private men which know the danger they are subject unto, being malefactors do notwithstanding so boldly adventure upon heinous crimes, only because they know it is possible for some Transgressor sometimes to escape the danger of law, in* the mighty upon earth (which are not always so virtuous and holy that their own good minds will bridle them) what may we look for considering the frailty of man's nature if the world do once hold it for a *Maxim* that *Kings* ought to live in no subjection that how grievous disorders soever they fall into, none may have coercive power over them? Yet so it is that this we must necessarily admit as a number of right well learned men are persuaded. Let us therefore set down first what there is [9.2] which may induce men so to think, and then consider their several inventions or ways, who judge it a thing necessary even for *Kings* themselves to be punishable and that by men. The question itself we will not determine. The reasons of each opinion being opened it shall be best for the wise to judge which of them is likeliest to be true. Our purpose being not to oppugn any save only that which *Reformers* hold and of the rest rather to enquire than to give sentence. Inducements leading men to think the highest Magistrate should not be judged of any saving God alone are specially these.

First, as there could be in natural bodies no motion of any thing unless there were some which moveth all things and continueth unmovable, even so in politic societies there must be some unpunishable or else no man shall suffer punishment. For since punishments proceed always from Superiors to whom the administration of justice belongeth, which administration must have necessarily a fountain that deriveth it to all others, and receiveth it not from any because otherwise the course of justice should go infinitely in a Circle, every Superior having his Superior without end, which cannot be; therefore a wellspring it followeth there is and a supreme head of justice whereunto all are subject, but itself in subjection to none. Which

---

* F: law. In

kind of preeminence if some ought to have in a kingdom, who but the *King* should have it? *Kings* therefore no man can have lawfully power and authority to judge. If private men offend there is the *Magistrate* over them which judgeth, if *Magistrates* they have their *Prince*, if *Princes* there is heaven, a *Tribunal* before which they shall appear, on earth they are not accountable to any. Which thing likewise the very original of kingdoms doth show.

. . . . .

His second point whereby he would make us odious is that we think [9.3] the Prince may be subject to excommunication, that is, *that he is a Brother,* *that He is not without but within the Church.* If this be dangerous why is it printed and allowed in the famous writings of *Bishop Jewel?* *In that the High priest doth his office when he excommunicates and cuts off a dead member from the body so far forth the Prince, be he never so mighty is inferior to him. Yea not only to a Bishop but to a simple Priest?* Why is it suffered which *Mr. Nowell* hath written, *The Prince ought patiently to abide excommunication at the Bishop's hands?* Why are not the worthy examples of Emperors erased out of the *Histories* seeing they have been subject to his *Censure?*

The Jews were forbidden to choose an alien *King* over them inasmuch as there is not anything more natural, than that the head and the body subject thereunto should always if it were possible be linked in that bond of nearness also which birth and breeding as it were in the bowels of one common mother usually causeth, which being true did not greatly need to be alleged for proof that *Kings* are in the *Church* of God of the same spiritual fraternity with their subjects, a thing not denied nor doubted of. Indeed the *King* is a Brother, but such a brother as unto whom all the rest of the brethren are subject. He is a sheaf of the *Lord's* field as the rest are, howbeit *a sheaf which is so far raised up above the rest that they all owe reverence unto it. The *King* is a brother which hath dominion over all his breathren. A strange conclusion to gather

---

x Deut. 17:15. Matt. 18:15.   *y* 1 Cor. 5:12–13.
z *Defence of the Apology* [STC 14601], part 6, p. 720.
a Tome 2 [STC 18742], fol. 53 [51ᵛ].
b Eusebius, *Ecclesiastical History*, Bk 6, ch. 14 [34; N2, 1:278]. Theodoret, *Ecclesiastical History*, Bk 5, ch. 18 [or 17; N2, 3:143].
c *Counter-Poison* [STC 10770], p. 174 [the source of the entire paragraph].   *d* Gen. 37:7.

hereby that therefore some of his brethren ought to have the authority of correcting him. We read that God did say unto *David, If Solomon thy Son forget my laws I will punish his transgressions with a rod.* But that he gave Commission unto any of *Solomon's* Brethren to chastise *Solomon* we do not read. It is a thing very much alleged that the Church of the Jews had the sword of excommunication. Is any man able to allege where the same was ever drawn forth against the *King?* Yet how many of their *Kings* how notoriously spotted? Our Saviour's words are, *If thy Brother offend thee:* And St. Paul's, *Do ye not judge them that are within?* Both which speeches are but indefinite. So that neither the one nor the other is any let but some brother there may be whose person is exempt from being subject to any such kind of proceeding. Some within, yet not therefore under the jurisdiction of any other. Sentences indefinitely uttered must sometimes universally be understood, but not where the subject or matter spoken of doth in particulars admit that difference which may in reason seclude any part from society with the residue of that whole, whereunto one common thing is attributed. As in this case it clearly fareth where the difference between *Kings* and others of the *Church* is a reason sufficient to separate the one from the other in that which is spoken of brethren, albeit the name of brethren itself do agree to both. Neither doth our Saviour nor the Apostle speak in more general sort of Ecclesiastical punishments than *Moses* in his law doth of civil, *'If there be found men or the man amongst you that hath served other Gods.* Again, *The man that committeth adultery.* The punishment of both which transgressions being death what man soever did offend therein? Why was not *Manasses* for the one, for the other, why not *David* accordingly executed? *Rex judicat non judicatur* sayth one. The *King* is appointed a judge of all men that live under him but not any of them his judge.

· · · ·

ᶠThe King is not subject into laws, that is to say the punishment which breach of laws doth bring upon inferiors taketh not hold on the *King's* person although the general laws which all mankind is bound unto do tie no less the *King* than others, but rather more.

ᵉ Deut. 17:2–5.

ᶠ Harmenopoulos, *Promptuarium Juris*, Bk 1, title 1, sects. 48 andf 39 [ed. 1851, pp. 32 and 30 as sects. 39 and 32].

For the grievousness of sin is aggravated by the greatness of him that committeth it, for which cause it also maketh him by so much the more obnoxious unto divine revenge by how much the less he [9.4] feareth human. Touching *Bishop Jewel's* opinion hereof, there is not in the place alleged any one word or syllable against the *King's* prerogative royal to be free from the coercive power of all spiritual both persons and Courts within the compass of his own dominions. *ᵍIn that* (saith he) *the Priest doeth his office in that he openeth God's word or declareth his threats or rebuketh sin or excommunicateth and cutteth off a dead member from the body so far forth the Prince be he never so mighty is inferior unto him. But in this respect the Prince is inferior not only to the Pope or Bishop but also to any other simple Priest.* He disputeth earnestly against that *Supremacy* which the *Bishop* of *Rome* did challenge over his Sovereign *Lord* the *Emperor* and by many allegations he laboureth to show that *Popes* have been always subject unto his supreme dominion not he to theirs, he supreme judge over them, not they over him.

Now whereas it was objected that within the *Church* when the *Priest* doth execute his office the very *Prince* is inferior to him, so much being granted by *Mr. Jewel* he addeth that this doth no more prove the *Pope* than the simplest Priest in the *Church* to be *Lord* and *Head* over *Kings*. For although it doth hereby appear that in those things which belong to his Priestly office the *Pope* may do that which *Kings* are not licensed to meddle with, in which respect it cannot be denied but that the *Emperor* himself hath not only less power than the chiefest *Bishop* but even less than the meanest Priest within his *Empire* and is consequently every Priest's inferior that way. Nevertheless since this appertaineth nothing at all to judicial authority and power how doth this prove *Kings* and *Emperors* to be by way of subjection inferior to the *Pope* as to their Ecclesiastical judge? Impertinently therefore is the answer which to such effect that admirable Prelate maketh, brought by way of evidence to show that in his opinion the *King* may not be exempted from the coercive authority and power of his own Clergy but ought for his faults to be as punishable in their Courts as any other subject under him.

[9.5] The excommunication which good *Mr. Nowell* thinketh that *Princes* ought patiently to suffer at the *Bishop's* hands is no other than that which we also grant may be exercised on such occasions and in

---

ᵍ *Defence of the Apology* [STC 14601], part 6, p. 720.

such manner as those two alleged examples out of antiquity do enforce. [h]*It is reported (saith Eusebius) that one of the* Philips *which succeeded* Gordian *came being a Christian to join with the rest of the people in prayer the last festival day of Easter. At which time he which governed the Church there whither the Emperor did resort would in no case admit him unless he first made confession and were contented afterwards to stay his time in the place appointed for penitents* (according to the manner of *Church* discipline in those days whereof we have spoken in the sixth book sufficiently) *because he was known to be many ways faulty. To this he readily condescended making manifest by his deeds his true and religious affection to Godwards.* Another example there is of the Emperor *Theodosius* who understanding that violence in the city of *Thessalonica* had been offered unto certain Magistrates sent in great rage a band of men and without any examination had to know where the fault was slew melpell both guilty and innocent to the number of 7000. It chanced afterwards that the Emperor coming to *Milan* and intending to go to the Church as his accustomed manner was, *St. Ambrose* the *Bishop* of that city who before had heard of the Emperor's so cruel and bloody an act met him before the gate of the *Church* and in this wise forbade him to enter. [i]*Emperor, it seemeth that how great the slaughter is which thyself hast made thou weighest not, nor as I think, when wrath was settled did reason ever call to account what thou hadst committed. Peradventure thine imperial royalty hindereth the acknowledgment of thy Sin and thy power is a let to reason. Notwithstanding know thou shouldst what our nature is, how frail a thing and how fading and that the first original from whence we have all sprung was the very dust whereunto we must slide again. Neither is it meet that being inveigled with the show of thy glistering robes thou shouldst forget the imbecility of that flesh which is covered therewith. Thy subjects (O Emperor) are in nature thy Colleagues yea even in service thou art also joined as a fellow with them. For there is one Lord and Emperor the maker of this whole assembly of all things. With what eyes therefore wilt thou look upon the habitation of that Common Lord? With what feet wilt thou tread upon that sacred floor? How wilt thou stretch forth those hands from which the blood as yet of unrighteous slaughter doth distill? The body of our Lord all holy how wilt thou take into such hands? How wilt thou put his honourable blood unto that mouth the wrathful*

[h] Eusebius, *Ecclesiastical History*, Bk 6, ch. 33 [or 34; *N2*, 1:278].
[i] Sozomen [properly Theodoret], *Ecclesiastical History*, Bk 5, ch. 18 [or 17; *N2*, 3:143].

word whereof hath caused against all order of law the pouring out of so much blood? Depart therefore and go not about by after-deeds to add to thy former iniquity; receive that bond wherewith from heaven the Lord of all doth give consent that thou shouldest be tied a bond which is medicinable and procureth health. Hereunto the *King* submitted himself (for being brought up in religion he knew very well what belonged unto Priests, what unto *Kings*) and with sobbing tears returned to the *Court* again. Some eight months after came the feast of our Saviour's nativity, but yet the *King* sat still at home mourning and emptying the lake of tears, which when *Rufinus* beheld being at that time commander over the *King's* house and by reason of usual access the bolder to speak he came and asked the cause of those tears. To whom the *King* with bitter grief and tears more abundantly gushing out answered, *Thou O Ruffin dalliest, for mine evils thou feelest not, I mourn and bewail mine own wretchedness considering that Servants and beggars go freely to the house of God and there present themselves before their Lord whereas both from thence and from heaven also I am excluded. For in my mind I carry that voice of our Lord which saith with express terms,* Whomsoever ye shall bind on earth, he in Heaven shall be bound also. The rest of the history which concerneth the manner of the Emperor's admission after so earnest repentance needeth not to be here set down.

It now remaineth to be examined whether these alleged examples prove that which they should do yea or no. The thing which they ought to confirm is that no less *Christian Kings* than other persons under them ought to be subject to the selfsame coercive authority of *Church Governors* and for the same kinds of transgressions to receive at their hands the same spiritual censure of excommunication judicially inflicted by way of punishment. But in the aforesaid examples whether we consider the offence itself of the Excommunicate or the persons excommunicating or the manner of their proceeding which three comprehend the whole substance of that which was done, it doth not by any of these appear that *Kings* in suchwise should be subject. For concerning the offences of men there is no breach of *Christian Charity* whether it be by deed or by word; no excess, no lightness of speech or behavior, no fault for which a man in the course of his life is openly noted as blameable but the same being unamended through admonition ought (as they say) with the spiritual Censure of excommunication to be punished.

Wherefore unless they can show that in some such ordinary transgression *Kings* and *Princes* upon contempt of the *Church's* more mild censure have been like other men in ancient times excommunicated; what should hinder any man to think but that the rare and unwonted crimes of those two Emperors did cause their *Bishops* to try, what unusual remedy would work in so desperate diseases? Which opinion is also made more probable inasmuch as the very histories which have recorded them propose them for strange and admirable patterns, the *Bishops* of boldness, the Emperors of meekness and humility. They wonder at the one for adventuring to do it unto Emperors, at the other for taking it in so good part at the hands of *Bishops*. What greater argument that all which was herein done proceeded from extraordinary zeal on both sides, and not from a settled judicial authority, which the one was known to have over the other by a common received order in the *Church*. For at such things who would wonder?

Furthermore if ye consider their persons, whose acts these excommunications were, he which is said to have excommunicated *Philip* Emperor of *Rome* was *Babylas* the Bishop of *Antioch*, and he which *Theodosius* Emperor of *Constantinople*, *Ambrose* the Bishop of *Milan*. Neither of which two *Bishops* (as I suppose) was ordinary unto either of the two Emperors and therefore they both were incompetent Judges and such as had no authority to punish whom they excommunicated except we will grant the Emperor to have been so much the more subject than his subjects that whereas the meanest of them was under but some one *Diocesan*, any that would might be judge over him. But the manner of proceeding doth as yet more plainly evict that these examples make less than nothing for proof, that *Ecclesiastical Governors* had at that time judicial authority to excommunicate *Emperors* and *Kings*. For what form of judgement was there observed when neither judges nor parties judged did once dream of any such matter till the one by chance repaired unto the place where the others were and at that very instant suffered a sudden repulse not only besides their own expectation but also without any purpose beforehand in them who gave it? Judicial punishment hath at the leastwise sentence going always before execution. Whereas all which we read of here is that the guilty being met in the way were presently turned back and not admitted to be partakers of those holy things whereof they were famously known unworthy.

[9.6]   I therefore conclude, that these excommunications have neither the nature of judicial punishments nor the force of sufficient arguments to prove that *Ecclesiastical* judges should have authority to call their own Sovereign to appear before them into their *Consistories* there to examine, to judge, and by excommunication to punish them if so be they be found culpable. But concerning excommunication such as is only a dutiful religious and holy refusal to admit Notorious transgressors in so extreme degree unto the blessed communion of Saints especially the mysteries of the body and blood of Christ till their humbled penitent minds be made manifest, this we grant every king bound to abide at the hands of any Minister of God wheresoever through the world. As for judicial authority to punish malefactors, if the *King* be as the *Kings* of *Israel* were and as every of ours is a supreme *Lord* than whom none under God is by way of ruling authority and power higher where he reigneth, how should any man there have the high place of a judge over him? He must be more than thine equal that hath a chastising power over thee. So far is it off that any under thee should be thy judge. Wherefore since the *Kings* of *England* are within their own dominions the most high and can have no peer how is it possible that any either civil or Ecclesiastical person under them should have over them coercive power when such power would make that person so far forth his Superior's superior ruler and judge? It cannot therefore stand with the nature of such Sovereign regiment that any Subject should have power to exercise on kings so highly authorized the greatest censure of excommunication according to the platform of reformed discipline, but if this ought to take place the other is necessarily to give place. For which cause till better reason be brought to prove that *Kings* cannot lawfully be exempted from subjection unto Ecclesiastical Courts we must and do affirm their said exemption lawful.

A guide to Hooker's sources
and to the Elizabethan debate about religion and society

An asterisk indicates that there is also
a separate entry under this name.

ALCINOUS. Apparently a misnomer for Albinus, a Platonist active in the mid-second century AD. For the passages cited at 1.7.6, see the edition of the *Epitome* (of Alcinous) by Pierre Louis (Paris, 1945), pp. 150–153.

ALLEN, WILLIAM (1532–94). Chief organizer of the Roman Catholic mission to England during the reign of Elizabeth, founder of colleges for this work at Douai, Rome, and Valladolid, created a cardinal in 1587. Hooker's discussion at VIII.6.11 of parliament's role in the reconciliation of England with the papacy under Philip and Mary is directly responsive to Allen's contention that prince and parliament, "have no more lawful means to give order to the Church and Clergy in these things, than they have to make laws for the hierarchies of angels in heaven." Hooker cites Allen's *An Apology and True Declaration. . . of the two English Colleges* (Mounts in Henault [i.e. Rheims], 1581; *STC* 369; reprinted 1970).

AMBROSE, ST. (339?–397). Bishop of Milan; one of the four traditional doctors of the Latin church (with Augustine, whom he greatly influenced, Jerome, and Gregory the Great). Before his ordination, Ambrose had had a distinguished career in the Roman imperial government. Afterwards, he opposed the vestiges of traditional paganism (in *Against Symmachus*), resolutely defended catholic possession of churches against imperially mandated concessions to Arians (the issue in the passage cited in VIII.6.14 and 8.8), and successfully imposed the discipline of excommunication on the emperor Theodosius the Great (the incident discussed in VIII.9.5, a dramatic precedent for Puritan claims that the Christian ministry was autonomous or even had jurisdictional supremacy in relation to secular authority).

AMMIANUS MARCELLINUS (330?–395). The last great Roman historian, a pagan, but tolerant of Christianity. The surviving portions of his *Rerum gestarum libri* cover the period 353–378.

ANABAPTISTS. The "rebaptizers," so called because they refused to recognize the validity of infant baptism. The principal groups to emerge from this sixteenth-century movement – the Mennonites and Hutterites – have remained signally faithful to the principle of nonviolence. Hooker was by no means alone, however, in seeing the violence of Thomas Münzer and his followers as a natural outcome of their repudiation of the traditional conception of a Christian society sacramental from cradle to grave. Excerpts from Guy de *Brès, the source for chapter 8 of Hooker's preface and for his reference to Knipperdoling at VIII.6.14, were published in Cambridge, Massachusetts in 1668 to counter "the reviving of this Root of Bitterness in the Quaker, after its being dead above an hundred years."

AQUINAS. *See* Thomas Aquinas.

ARCHYTAS. *See* Pythagorean political thinkers.

ARISTOTLE (384–322 BC). Hooker's major non-Biblical source. For "Aristotelical demonstration" – reasoning productive of scientific knowledge of necessary connections – see Book I of the *Posterior Analytics*. The *Rhetoric to Alexander* cited as Aristotelian at *Laws*, I.10.5 is generally considered spurious.

ARNOBIUS (d. *c.* 330). Christian apologist. Hooker's edition of Arnobius' *Against the Nations* included the dialogue *Octavius* of Minucius Felix (second or third century).

ATHANASIUS, ST. (296?–373). Bishop of Alexandria, proponent against the Arians, sometimes "against the world," of the divinity of the Son or Word as the second person of the Christian Trinity.

AUGUSTINE, ST. (354–430). The most influential father of the western church. Before his conversion in 386, he was a professor of rhetoric and a seeker of wisdom in many religious and philosophical positions, including those of Cicero, the Manichaeans, and the Neoplatonist Plotinus. He became bishop of Hippo in north Africa in 396. His eventual acceptance of coercion by the secular power as a legitimate resource for the church to call upon grew from his struggle with the Donatists, who had themselves appealed to the emperor Constantine for judgement against their opponents. Augustine's last work, the *Retractations*, was an attempt to acknowledge and correct errors in his own writings.

BANCROFT, RICHARD (1544–1610). From the 1580s, the most active foe of English Puritanism, first as investigator for the ecclesiastical court of High Commission under *Whitgift, then as Bishop of London (1597–1604) and Archbishop of Canterbury. The *Brief Discovery of the Untruths... in a Sermon... by Dr. Bancroft* (STC 19603) cited at *Laws*, Preface, 8.1, n. *u* has been attributed to John Penry, who was hanged for separatism in 1593.

BARROWIST. *See* Nonconformists.

BELLARMINE, ST. ROBERT (1542–1621). Jesuit professor of theology at Louvain and at the Collegium Romanum in Rome, a learned but vigorous opponent of "the heretics of these times." Hooker takes issue with Bellarmine's theology of penance in *Laws*, VI.6.

BEZA, THEODORE (1519–1605). Calvin's biographer, the editor of his letters, and his successor as chief pastor at Geneva, as well as a distinguished Biblical scholar and theologian in his own right. Beza was the chief living continental authority for the presbyterian polity which Hooker's reformist opponents considered a mark of the true church. His *Tractatus pius et moderatus de vera Excommunicatione, et christiano Presbyterio*, written against *Erastus, was first published in England (STC 2048). Five English editions of Beza's *Confessio Christianae fidei*, first published in French in 1559 and in Latin in 1560, appeared between 1563 and 1589.

BODIN, JEAN (1529?–96). The most important theorist of the conception of state sovereignty which in one form or another was to dominate early modern political theory. Bodin visited England in 1581–82, when he had the pleasure of seeing his work taught at Cambridge. Hooker's care in giving the precise location of the one passage in Bodin's *République* that he cites in the *Laws* (VIII.6.9; K App. 1) suggests an awareness of its atypicality and hence a conscious attempt to turn the course of constitutional thought towards a more diffused conception of supreme authority – towards power-sharing, as we would say today.

BOETHIUS (480?–524?). Philosopher and statesman, whose classic *Consolation of Philosophy* was written in prison, where the appearance of confusion and disorder in this world was especially vivid.

BONIFACE VIII (1234?–1303). Promulgator in 1298 of the *Liber Sextus*, the sixth book of papal decretals, consisting largely of his own edicts as pope from 1294.

BRACTON, HENRY DE (d. 1268). The classic exponent of the English common law. Hooker's use in VIII.2.3 and VIII.3.3 (K VIII.2.13) of Bractonian "axioms" on the supremacy of law and his citation of Bracton on the distinct jurisdictions of secular and ecclesiastical courts in VIII.8.9 and the Dublin notes are part of a subtle but broad and far-reaching effort to regularize the ecclesiastical side of Tudor government. The statement ascribed to Bracton at VIII.3.1.⁵ (K 2.6) is not a direct quotation, but similar views are expressed in the second of the two passages Hooker cites for the rule of law at VIII.3.3 (Bracton, ed. 1968–77, 2:33 and 2:305). *Bracton de Legibus et Consuetudinibus Angliae: Bracton on the Laws and Customs of England*, ed. George E. Woodbine, trans. with revisions and notes by Samuel E. Thorne, 4 vols. (Cambridge, Mass. and London, England, 1968–77).

BRÈS, GUY DE (1522–67). A Belgian Reformed pastor martyred in Valenciennes by troops of the Regent Margaret of Parma. As author of the Belgic Confession of 1561, which included "discipline" as an essential mark of the church, Brès was an ideal source for Hooker's account of the *Anabaptists in Preface, 8.6–12. His *La Racine, Source et Fondement des Anabaptistes* was published in 1565, perhaps at Geneva.

BROWN, FAMILY OF. *See* Nonconformists.

CAJETAN (Tomasso de Vio, 1469–1534). Italian Dominican theologian, author of detailed commentaries on Thomas Aquinas' *Summa Theologiae*, participant in important practical affairs of his day, a cardinal from 1517. In his *De comparatione authoritatis Papae et Concilii*, occasioned by the schismatic Council of Pisa against Julius II (1511), Cajetan sought to refute the so-called Gallican theses affirming the freedom of the French church from papal authority. The tract was included in collections of his *opuscula* often published with the works of Aquinas.

CALVIN, JOHN (1509–64). The leading theologian and model for practical organizing in the Reformed – in contrast to the Lutheran – branch of continental Protestantism. Hooker's account of Calvin's acquisition of theological knowledge ("not by hearing or reading so much, as by teaching others," Pref., 2.1) is misleading, since Calvin had studied divinity in Paris for five years before turning to legal studies in a period of doubt about his vocation. Calvin's international reputation was based on his *Institutes of the Christian Religion*, first published in 1536 and constantly revised. Although Hooker's professed intention in Pref., 2 is to reduce Calvin's authority with respect to church polity alone, he was later accused of serious deviations from Calvinist orthodoxy on the matter of predestination as well. His notes for a reply to this attack may be the last thing he wrote (Folger ed., vol. 4). See William J. Bouwsma's *John Calvin: A Sixteenth Century Portrait* (New

York and Oxford: Oxford University Press, 1988) for a balanced account of Calvin's life and work.

CARTWRIGHT, THOMAS. *See* T. C.

CHOPPIN, RENÉ (1537–1606). French jurist. In his working notes for Book VIII Hooker used the *De Sacra Politia Forensi* as a source of citations from other authors documenting the long tradition of imperial and royal involvement in church affairs.

CICERO, MARCUS TULLIUS (hence "Tully," 106–43 BC). Roman orator, philosopher, and statesman. He made a triumphant return to Rome from banishment in 57 BC.

CLEMENT OF ALEXANDRIA, ST. (150?–215?). The first great theologian in the tradition which seeks to integrate Christianity with the ideas of Greek philosophy.

COUNTER-POISON. *See* Fenner.

COURIN (*or* Cousin), G. *See* More, St. Thomas.

CUSANUS (Nicholas of Cusa, 1401–64). German philosopher and cardinal, a reconciler in both speculative and practical matters.

CYPRIAN, ST. (d. 258). Martyred bishop of Carthage, a pivotal source in the controversy about episcopal authority which occupied Hooker in *Laws* VII. Cyprian's emphasis on Christ as unique head of the church was part of an attack on separatists in his time.

A DEFENCE AGAINST TYRANTS. The most substantial statement of the French Hugeonot theory of revolution, designed to justify resistance to the forceful imposition of Roman Catholicism, published in 1579, attributed to Philippe Du Plessis Mornay (1549–1623).

DIONYSIUS THE AREOPAGITE (First century). Converted by Paul at Athens (Acts 17:34), the subject of a legend in which he is said to have observed an eclipse in Egypt at the time of the crucifixion of Christ (1.3.4), and the supposed author of important Christian–Neoplatonic theological works which were actually composed in the fifth or sixth century.

DIONYSIUS OF HALICARNASSUS (b. 62–55 BC). Historian and teacher of rhetoric who wrote enthusiastically about things Roman for his fellow Greeks.

DUARENUS, PAPON, CHOPPINUS, AEGIDIUS, MAGISTER, ARNUL-
PHUS RUZÆUS, COSTLIUS, PHILIPPUS PROBUS. Except for Aegidius
Romanus (Giles of Rome, 1243?–1316, theologian, adviser by turns to Boni-
face VIII and Philip the Fair of France), the authors cited in this list at
VIII.7.5 were sixteenth-century French Roman Catholic legal writers.

ECPHANTUS. *See* Pythagorean political thinkers.

EGESIPPUS (Hegesippus, second century). A Christian converted from
Judaism, whose writings are quoted by *Eusebius.

EPO, BOETHIUS. Professor of canon law at Douai, 1578.

ERASTUS, THOMAS (1524–83). Professor of medicine at Heidelberg. In
opposing the introduction of the Genevan polity at Heidelberg in 1568,
Erastus argued that all coercive jurisdiction belongs to the civil ruler. This
central thesis of Erastianism was to be maintained in more extreme form
by others, for example, Hobbes, than by Erastus himself. Both Erastus'
and *Beza's parts of the controversy about excommunication were first published in England (*STC* 2048 and 10511).

EUSEBIUS OF CAESAREA (260?–340?). The father of church history, biographer of the emperor Constantine the Great and his adviser at the Council
of Nicaea and afterwards.

EVAGRIUS ("Scholasticus," 536?–600). Lawyer and church historian. His
Ecclesiastica Historia covers the period 431–594.

FENNER, DUDLEY (1558?–87). Author of *A Counter-Poison... to make
answer to... the answerer* (*STC* 10770), written in reply to Richard Cosin's
Answer (*STC* 5815) to the Puritan contention that English law supported
their Discipline as against Archbishop *Whitgift's 1584 campaign to enforce
clerical conformity to officially prescribed practices. Fenner's *Defence of the
godly ministers* (1587, *STC* 10771) upheld the Puritan side against "the
slanders... contained" in John Bridges' *A defence of the government established*
(*STC* 3734).

FICINO, MARSIGLIO (1433–99). Italian humanist and philosopher, head
of the Platonic Academy founded at Florence by Cosimo de'Medici.

GALEN (130?–200?). Prolific and influential Greek physician and philosopher employed by Roman emperors, including Marcus Aurelius. His works
were widely published in the late fifteenth and sixteenth centuries. *Opera*,
ed. C. G. Kühn (Leipzig, 1821–33; repr. 1965).

GRATIAN (twelfth century). Compiler of the *Decretum*, a large collection of patristic texts, conciliar decrees, and papal pronouncements which became the first and largest part of the late medieval church's canon law (the *Corpus juris canonici*). The standard commentary (*glossa ordinaria*) on the *Decretum*, by Joannes Teutonicus (d. 1246), is to be found in the margins of most early printed editions of Gratian.

GREGORY IX (1148?–1241). Papal sponsor of the collection of *Decretals* making up the second main part of the canon law.

GREGORY NAZIANZEN, ST. (329–89), "the Theologian." One of the Cappadocian fathers, Gregory was a major influence in the promulgation of the Nicene doctrine of the Trinity at the Council of Constantinople in 381. He was chosen bishop of Constantinople during the council but resigned the see shortly afterwards.

GUALTER, RUDOLPH (1519–86). An associate of Johann Heinrich Bullinger and his successor as chief minister of the church in Zurich.

HARDING, THOMAS (1516–72). Bishop *Jewel's Roman Catholic antagonist in the controversies about the religious settlement at the beginning of Elizabeth's reign.

HARMENOPOULOS (d. 1380?). Byzantine imperial legal adviser. *Promptuarium Juris*, ed. G. E. Heimbeck (Leipzig, 1851).

HILARY OF POITIERS, ST. (315?–367). The *Athanasius of the west, Hilary opposed the interference in church affairs of the Arian emperor Constantius.

HIPPOCRATES (460?–357? BC). The *Oracle* cited at 1.3.4 was attributed by some ancient writers to the great physician, but its authorship is uncertain.

HOSIUS (257?–357). Bishop of Cordova, adviser of the emperor Constantine, champion (except for a brief period, under great pressure) of the divinity of the Son as propounded by *Athanasius.

JEROME, ST. (342?–420). Translator of most of the Bible from the original tongues into Latin (the Vulgate) and energetic participant in the theological controversies of his day. His *Contra Ruffinum* was written against certain doctrines of Origen espoused by Ruffinus of Aquileia. Like *Cyprian, Jerome was a pivotal authority in the controversy over episcopacy handled in *Laws*, VII.

JEWEL, JOHN (1522–71). Bishop of Salisbury, chief early defender of the Elizabethan religious settlement, and an early patron of Hooker, whom he helped attend Oxford.

JOSEPHUS (37?–100?). Jewish historian and apologist, a priest of aristocratic descent who recorded and vigorously defended the traditional religion of his people but favored political accommodation with Rome.

JUSTINIAN (483–565). Roman emperor in the East from 527. He sponsored the collections of legal opinions and enactments making up the Roman civil law, the *Corpus juris civilis*. The maxims Hooker gives at 1.8.7.^{y} and 1.9.1.^{m} are summaries of the passages cited.

KNIPPERDOLING. One of the consuls set up, with a senate, when the citizens of Münster abandoned the town to the *Anabaptists.

LACTANTIUS (240?–320?). Christian apologist, whose attempt to commend Christianity to well-educated contemporaries led him to include in his *Divine Institutes* passages from pagan writers which are now otherwise lost.

LEONTIUS (fourth century). Bishop of Tripolis, ally of Athanasius in the struggle against Arianism.

LIVY (Titus Livius, 59 BC–17 AD or 64 BC–12 AD). Roman historian. In the story from Livy alluded to at VIII.4.4, Tarquin the Proud cut off the heads of the tallest poppies to indicate to his son that he should consolidate his power at Gabii by ridding himself of the leading men of the city.

MACABEUS (Macbeth, eleventh century). Scottish king. The law Hooker cites at VIII.3.5 (K 3.4) was one of several laid down by this ruler to strengthen ecclesiastical authority.

MACHIAVELLI, NICCOLO (1469–1527). Hooker takes issue at *Laws*, V.2.4 with a politic use of religion practised by "wise malignants" (with a reference to Machiavelli's *Discourses*), from which he distinguished the "true" politic use of religion exemplified in his own work. His citation of Machiavelli's history of Florence at VIII.8.5. is unusual for an Elizabethan religious controversialist.

MAGDEBURG CENTURIES. A church history "by centuries" published at Basle from 1562–74, chiefly edited by the Lutheran Matthias Flacius Illyricus.

MARTIN MARPRELATE. Pseudonymous author (probably Job Throckmorton) of a series of bitterly satirical anti-episcopal tracts published illegally in 1588–89.

MASTER OF SENTENCES. *See* Peter Lombard.

MERCURIUS TRISMEGISTUS (Hermes the Thrice-great). Supposed author of a group of second- and third-century, mainly Neoplatonic, moral and theological treatises which were highly regarded during the Renaissance, when they were thought to have been written in ancient Egypt. Franciscus Patrizi recommended these works to the papacy as an ecumenically promising alternative to the prevailing scholastic Aristotelianism. *Hermetica*, ed. Walter Scott (Oxford, 1924).

MINUCIUS FELIX. *See* Arnobius.

MONTECATINI, ANTONIO (1568–97). Professor of civil law at Ferrara. His commentary on Aristotle's *Politics* was published there in 1587.

MORE, ST. THOMAS (1478–1535). Lord Chancellor of England under Henry VIII, until he was imprisoned, tried, and executed for refusing to acknowledge the king's headship of the English church. The statement quoted by Hooker at VIII.4.12 (K 4.8) is from the beginning of the speech given by More immediately after his conviction. The letter about More's death and that of Bishop Fisher is from G. Courin (or Cousin, a canon of Nozeroy in the Jura) to Philip Montanus and was published in *Thomae Mori, Angliae Ornamenti Eximii, Lucubrationes* (Basle, 1563).

THE NEW NATURE OF BRIEFS. A legal manual compiled by Sir Anthony Fitzherbert (1470–1538), first published in 1534 and reprinted many times in the sixteenth century both in Latin and in English.

NICEPHORUS CALLISTUS (1256?–1335?). Byzantine historian. His *Ecclesiastical History* covers the period from the birth of Christ to the death of the Emperor Phocas in 610.

NONCONFORMISTS. The long reproach in quotation marks in Preface, 8.1 seems to have been composed by Hooker himself, but it reflects the views of such separatists as Robert Browne (1550?–1633), Robert Harrison (d. 1585?), Henry Barrow (1550?–93), and John Greenwood (d. 1593), some of whose writings have been published in A. Peel and L. Carlson, eds., *Elizabethan Nonconformist Texts* (London, 1953–66). Especially relevant passages are to be found in Peel and Carlson at 2:153, 154, 169, 208–209, 217, 407–408, 411–412, and 462; 3:60 and 500–501; and 4:34–35.

NOWELL, ALEXANDER (1507?–1602). Dean of St. Paul's, deeply sympathetic with reformist demands for effective moral discipline in the church and author of three catechisms and a defence of the English Royal Supremacy against Roman Catholic objections, *The Reproof of Mr. Dorman* (enlarged edn., *STC* 18742).

ONUPHRIUS PANVINIUS (1529–68). Papal and ancient historian, continued Bartolomeo *Platina's *Lives of the Popes*.

ORPHEUS. Perhaps purely mythical, perhaps the real founder of the mystery religion Orphism (as early as the seventh century BC). The verses attributed to Orpheus at 1.4.1 and 1.15.4 are from a collection written by Neoplatonists in the second century AD.

PETER LOMBARD (1100?–60). His *Four Books of Sentences*, or opinions (based on numerous passages collected from the church fathers), was the standard theological textbook of the later middle ages.

PHILO OF ALEXANDRIA (20 BC?–50 AD?). Jewish speculative theologian and exegete, one of the most important figures in western religious thought due to his use of allegorical interpretation of Scripture to assimilate Greek philosophical ideas.

PIGHIUS, ALBERTUS (1490?–1542). Dutch Roman Catholic defender of tradition and hierarchy as principles of religious authority. His *Hierarchiae Ecclesiasticae Assertio* was published at Cologne in 1538.

PLATINA, BARTOLOMEO (1421–81). Humanist and papal historian, Vatican librarian under Sixtus IV. The English translation of his *Historia... de Vitis Pontificum Romanorum* published in 1685 was edited by W. Benham in 1888.

POLYBIUS (d. after 118 BC). Greek historian of the rise of Rome.

PONTIUS (third century). Deacon and biographer of St. *Cyprian.

PSEUDO-AMBROSE (Ambrosiaster, fourth century?). Author of Latin commentaries on the epistles of Paul. The ascription to Ambrose was first questioned by Erasmus.

PYTHAGORAS (sixth century BC). Philosopher, mathematician, mystic, founder of a religious community in southern Italy.

PYTHAGOREAN POLITICAL THINKERS: Archytas, Ecphantus, Stheni-das. With the possible exception of the treatise *On Law and Justice* ascribed by *Stobaeus to Archytas (early fourth century BC mathematician, philoso-pher, and statesman, a friend of Plato), the Pythagorean political writings quoted in *Laws* VIII.3.1 (K 2.5), 3.3 (K 2.12), and 6.5 (K 6.6), and in Hooker's working notes for Book VIII were composed from Hellenistic times to the second century AD. They were used in this period to support a more absolutist theory of kingship than Hooker's. Ed. 1822 = Thomas Taylor, *Political Fragments of Archytas, Charondas, Zaleucus, and other Ancient Pythagoreans, preserved by Stobaeus* (Chiswick). Ed. 1958 = C. Wachsmuth and O. Hense, *Joannis Stobaei Anthologium* (Berlin, 1884–1912, repr. 1958).

RAMISTRY. The pedagogically and practically oriented transformation of logic, rhetoric, and the rest of the traditional curriculum by the French humanist Peter Ramus (1515–72). Its influence is evident in several Eliza-bethan Puritan authors.

SALLUST (probably 86–35 BC). Roman historian (after his withdrawal from public life) whose indictment of aristocratic avarice, ambition, and luxury was a model for later accounts of the political and moral decline of Rome.

SCOTUS, JOHN DUNS (1265?–1308). Franciscan professor of theology at Oxford and Paris, the Subtle Doctor (or the Marian Doctor, for his decisive contribution to the theology of the Immaculate Conception).

SIDONIUS APOLLINARIS (423?–480?). Statesman and bishop of Clermont.

SOCRATES ("Scholasticus," *c.* 380–450). Continued Eusebius' church his-tory, covering the years from 305 to 439.

SOPHOCLES (496?–406 BC). The lines cited at I.8.9, in which Antigone challenges the ultimate validity of directives laid down by those in power in the state, secured a lasting place in philosophical discussions of law when Aristotle quoted them in his *Rhetoric* (373b), just after the passage from the *Rhetoric* cited by Hooker at I.10.1.

SOTO, DOMINGO DE (1494–1560). Spanish Dominican theologian, appointed by Charles V as imperial theologian at the Council of Trent.

SOZOMEN (early fifth century). Church historian whose work covers the period from 323 to 425.

STAPLETON, THOMAS (1513–98). Leading English Roman Catholic con-troversialist of the later sixteenth century. His comprehensive *Principiorum*

Fidei Doctrinalium Demonstratio Methodica was printed four times (in two editions) between 1578 and 1581 but is now very rare. Stapleton and, on the Puritan side, Thomas Cartwright (*T. C.) were Hooker's chief antagonists regarding the Royal Supremacy, often citing the same patristic texts against the English establishment. In his working notes for Book VIII Hooker made heavy use of Stapleton's collection of *Protestant* views on the authority of lay magistrates in religious affairs.

STAUNDFORD (*or* Stamford), SIR WILLIAM (1509–58). Judge of the Common Pleas from 1554. His *Les Plees Del Coron*, a digest of criminal law, first appeared in 1557.

STHENIDAS. *See* Pythagorean political thinkers.

STOBAEUS (late fourth–early fifth century). Excerpted poets and prose writers from Homer to the fourth century; the only source for the *Pythagorean political thinkers cited by Hooker in *Laws* VIII and in his working notes. C. Wachsmuth and O. Hense, *Joannis Stobaei Anthologium* (Berlin, 1884–1912, repr. 1958).

STRABO (64 BC?–21 AD or later). Greek historian and geographer, partly Asiatic in descent.

SUIDAS. Supposed author of an encyclopedic Byzantine *Lexicon* compiled around the year 1000. Critical edn. Stuttgart, 1967.

T. C. THOMAS CARTWRIGHT (1535–1603). Hooker's principal presbyterian opponent, cited as follows:

> T. C., Bk 1 = *A reply to An answer made of Master doctor Whitgift Against the Admonition*, 2nd. edn. ([Hemel Hempstead?, 1573]; *STC* 4712). Whitgift quoted the first edition of the *Reply* (*STC* 4711) in full in his *Defense of the Answer to the Admonition* (1574). In the present volume Hooker's references to the *Reply* are supplemented by references to Whitgift's quotations in the Parker Society edition of his *Works* (*W*).
> T. C., Bk 2 = *The second reply of Thomas Cartwright: against master Whitgift's second answer* ([Heidelberg], 1575; *STC* 4714).
> T. C., Bk 3 = *The rest of the second reply against master Whitgift's second answer* ([Basle], 1577; *STC* 4715).

TELESIO, BERNARDINO (1509–88). Italian humanist and critic of Aristotelian natural philosophy.

TERTULLIAN (160?–225?). African church father, arguably the father of
Latin theology, who eventually joined the apocalyptic, ascetic, "spirit-filled"
Montanist sect. In pleading for toleration for Christians, Tertullian argued
that they were good citizens of the empire (although he did not allow that
they could do military service). He particularly emphasized their wholesome
morality and mutual, communal concern. Tertullian was an important source
for both Hooker and his opponents.

THEODORET (393?–466?). A native of Antioch, bishop of Cyrrhus. His
Cure for the Affections of the Greeks sets Christian and pagan answers to
fundamental religious questions side by side. His *Ecclesiastical History* continues that of Eusebius down to 428.

THEOPHRASTUS (d. 287 BC?). Student and successor of Aristotle as head
of the Lyceum. *Metaphysics*, ed. W. D. Ross and F. H. Forbes (Oxford,
1929).

THOMAS AQUINAS, ST. (1225?–74). Greatest of the Christian Aristotelian
theologians and philosophers of the later middle ages, Thomas was deeply
respected by some among the English Puritans. The conclusion of Hooker's
note at the end of *Laws*, I.3.1 is a summary paraphrase of the passage from
Thomas at the beginning of the note. The commentary on 1 Peter cited
at VIII.3.5 (K 3.6) is no longer attributed to St. Thomas.

TRIDENTINE COUNCIL. The Council of Trent, which met intermittently
from 1545 to 1563, was the chief official embodiment of Roman Catholic
impulses to clarification of doctrine and reform of discipline in the period
of the Reformation.

TULLY. *See* Cicero.

TURRECREMATA (Torquemada), JOANNES DE (1388–1468). Spanish
Dominican, attended the Council of Constance, papal theologian at the
Council of Basle, cardinal from 1439, and uncle of the grand inquisitor
Tomaso de Torquemada. Joannes de Turrecremata's *Summa de Ecclesia*
(published in 1489) is a massive defense of the pope's infallibility and pleni-
tude of spiritual power.

WALTHRAMUS (Waleran), BISHOP OF NAUMBURG (early twelfth cen-
tury). The tract *De investitura episcoporum per imperatores facienda* cited by
Hooker at VIII.7.5 was included by Simon Schardius in his collection *De
Jurisdictione, Autoritate, et Praeeminentia Imperiali, ac Potestate Ecclesiasticae*
(Basle, 1566), pp. 711–717.

WHITAKER, WILLIAM (1548–95). Master of St. John's College and Regius professor of divinity at Cambridge, a strict and learned Calvinist. Whitaker believed that the pope was the anti-Christ and attacked the writings of Edmund Campion, Thomas *Stapleton, and Robert *Bellarmine. Hooker's reference at 1.14.5 is to Whitaker's *Disputatio de sacra scriptura contra R. Bellarminum et T. Stapletonum* (Cambridge, 1588; *STC* 25366), p. 384; *A Disputation on Holy Scripture* (Cambridge, 1949), p. 513.

WHITGIFT, JOHN (1530?–1604). Hooker's most direct predecessor in controversy with the Disciplinarians, especially with Thomas Cartwright, whom he opposed both at Cambridge and in polemical exchanges stemming from the *Admonition to Parliament* of 1572 (*see* T. C.). During Archbishop Grindal's suspension and later, during his own tenure as archbishop of Canterbury, Whitgift directed measures to enforce conformity to official ceremonial and disciplinary rules. Hooker dedicated Book V of the *Laws* to him in gratitude for "the long continued and more than ordinary favour" Whitgift had been pleased to show him.

WILLIAM THE CONQUEROR (1028?–87). The mistaken belief, expressed at VIII.6.1, that William assumed the title of conqueror and claimed the right of conquerors to make their own laws was common among Hooker's contemporaries.

ZONARAS, JOHANNES (twelfth century). Byzantine historian and commentator on Greek canon law, beginning with the so-called Apostolic Canons, actually composed in the late fourth century.

Index of scriptural citations

242

Index of persons

For Biblical authors, see also the Index of scriptural citations.

An asterisk indicates that there is an entry under this name in the Guide to Hooker's Sources beginning on page 227.

Aaron, 176, 189
Abraham, 89
Adam, 88, 97, 105
Aegidius Romanus [Giles of Rome], 204
*Alcinous, 73
Alexander III, Pope, 211
*Allen, William, 131, 133–4, 198
*Ambrose, St., 104, 150, 177, 199, 201, 215, 217, 218, 223, 225
*Ammianus Marcellinus, 205
Anaxagoras, 55
Arcadius, Emperor, 205
*Archytas, 147, 183
*Aristotle, 69; *Magna Moralia*, 75; *Metaphysics*, 15, 64, 79, 101; *Nicomachean Ethics*, 76, 80, 95, 101, 122, 125; *On the Heavens*, 67; *On the Soul*, 67, 75; *Physics*, 121; *Politics*, 75, 79, 90, 94, 97, 132, 146; *Rhetoric*, 61, 76, 87; attributed, *Rhetoric to Alexander*, 91
*Arnobius, 22
Asa, 128, 176
Athalia, 209
*Athanasius, 215
*Augustine, St., 12, 50, 109, 188, 216; *Against the Letter of Petilian*, 174; *Confessions*, 59; Epistles, 19, 134, 199, 215, 216; *On Christian Teaching*, 82–3, 104; *On the Agreement of the*

Evangelists, 110; *On the City of God*, 59, 82; *On the Trinity*, 102; attributed, *Questions on the Old and New Testaments*, 108

Babylas, 225
Benedict II, Pope, 203
Bertelier, citizen of Geneva, 7
*Beza, Theodore, 9, 11, 31, 160
*Bodin, Jean, 189
*Boethius, 57
Boniface I, Pope, 202–3
*Boniface VIII, Pope, 204
*Bracton, Henry de, 141, 218
*Brès, Guy de, 41–7
*Brown [Browne], Robert, 197

*Cajetan [Tomasso de Vio], 180
*Calvin, John, 3–11, 13, 25, 175, 176
*Cartwright, Thomas, see T.C.
Charles [Charlemagne], Emperor, 203
*Choppin, René, 147, 204
Chrysostom, St. John, 22, 205
*Cicero, Marcus Tullius, 5, 86, 91, 97, 144, 149, 195
*Clement of Alexandria, St., 21, 64
Colonus, 203
Constans [error for Constantius], Emperor, 199, 215

243

Subject index